DEAR

G. JIM

MERRY

CHRISTMAS '09!

Love,

Eli Hardie Haves, and Latte

Suomalaisen Kirjallisuuden Seuran Toimituksia 819

Jyrki Siukonen

Uplifted Spirits, Earthbound Machines

Studies on Artists and the Dream of Flight, 1900–1935

Suomalaisen Kirjallisuuden Seura ▪ Helsinki 2001

To the memory of my father.

Cover pictures: Artist Vladimir Tatlin demonstrating his ornithopter, early 1930s. (Zhadova 1988.)

Description of body position during flight, drawing by V. Tatlin. (Zhadova 1988.)

ISSN 0355-1768

ISBN 951-746-280-8

www.finlit.fi

Hakapaino Oy

Helsinki 2001

■ Contents

■ Acknowledgements

I first began to think about this study during my time as Gregory Fellow at the University of Leeds in 1994–1995. I want to thank the Henry Moore Foundation for the opportunity to work in Leeds and my colleagues at the Fine Art Department for their support. The actual work was done as part of the Doctoral Programme at the Academy of Fine Arts in Helsinki 1997–2001. I am especially grateful to Satu Kiljunen, the head of the programme, for making remarkable things happen. Over the years in Helsinki I have greatly benefitted from the numerous inspiring discussions with my colleagues Eija-Liisa Ahtila, Jan Kaila, Teemu Mäki, Tarja Pitkänen, and Jan-Kenneth Weckman. I also want to express my gratitude to the Academy of Finland and to the Arts Council of Finland for their generous financial support.

Along my way I have received ample specialist help from special friends and colleagues. Penelope Curtis (Henry Moore Institute, Leeds) has seen this work grow from the leisurely hours in the Leeds studio into a manuscript. Her friendship and criticism has helped me to solve many difficult questions and encouraged me to leave even more unsolved. Hannu Valtonen (Finnish Air Force Museum, Tikkakoski) knows aeroplanes in and out. No matter how trivial my questions, he has always provided me with more than an answer. Besides, his museum now houses the P-39 *Airacobra* which I saw in pieces on a happy summer day when I was twelve years old. Lauri Anttila (Academy of Fine Arts, Helsinki) and Heikki Mikkeli (Renvall Institute, University of Helsinki) have always shared their knowledge and enthusiasm regarding all matters of art, natural philosophy, historical technology and *varia*. Their critical comments on my work were encouraging and helpful. Christina Lodder (University of St Andrews) once wrote that her desire to learn about Russian Constructivism was awakened by seeing a reconstruction of the *Letatlin*. It is with gratitude that I now recall that moment. Her generosity in sharing her erudition and her warm and supportive criticism have made the last phases of this work especially happy. The art of Juhana Blomstedt has played a special role in my life; the same boy who once saw the *Airacobra* also stood in front of his painting *Illuminated Configuration*. It is now my pleasure to thank him for his support in the final stages of this process.

I am much indebted to people who have helped me during the years by offering testgrounds for my more or less levitating ideas: Jaakko Lintinen (*Taide* Art Magazine), Aija Jaatinen (Kuopio Art Museum), Bengt von Bonsdorff (Amos Anderson Art Museum, Helsinki), Ullamaria Pallasmaa (Oulu Art Museum), Paula Toppila (FRAME), and Maaretta Jaukkuri (Kiasma, Museum of Contemporary Art, Helsinki).

I would like to thank Kimmo Sarje, who read my manuscript as a scholar and as an artist and made some valuable comments. I am also grateful to Ilkka Karttunen who provided me with translations from Russian, and Andrij Stasevskij who did the same with Ukrainian. Anna-Kaisa Laine's help with the illustrations was crucial. Erik Ahonen accompanied me in Moscow, and Richard Wrigley took care of my well-being on both sides of the English Channel. Towards the end of my work I had the pleasure of discussing many niceties of meaning with Virginia Mattila, who corrected my language. Any mistakes, either linguistic or factual, which may remain are my own responsibility. As a one-time library worker I have greatly enjoyed the hospitality of the following institutions: The British Library, the Brotherton Library (Leeds), Cambridge University Library, Helsinki University Library, the Henry Moore Institute (Leeds), the Museum of Finnish Architecture (Helsinki), the Finnish Aviation Museum (Vantaa), the Royal Aeronautical Society (London), Tampere City Library, Tampere University of Technology Library, and Tampere University Library.

Finally, I would like to thank the Finnish Literature Society for accepting this work for their publication series and editor Rauno Endén in particular for his enthusiasm and help.

My mother Terttu Kervinen has seen me building model aeroplanes, observing birds, drawing pictures, and using the livingroom sofa as a drumkit, among other things. She has never questioned the meaning behind these activities but has always encouraged me. Päivi Mehtonen has flown with me in the clouds and shared the thermals and turbulences of everyday life, and our daughter Meeri has continuously reminded me of the importance of imagination. Their love and company is what has really made this work a happy flight.

Tampere, 18 March 2001

Jyrki Siukonen

A note on transliteration

Russian proper names appear in the text in the English form where the soft sign ' is dropped and the final –ii and –yi are rendered as y (e.g. Mayakovsky rather than Maiakovskii; Pavilonov rather than Pavil'onov).

■ Introduction

Classical psychoanalysis lacks the requisite curiosity in at least two respects: it does not account for the aesthetic character of the dream flight; it does not account for the efforts toward rationalization which shape and deform this fundamental dream.[1]

Gaston Bachelard

All that can be said is that a really efficient machine is more intriguing than one that is a failure, and a polished pebble more than a mere scrap of stone. For certain forms are pleasant, others painful, and everything the intellect produces must be of interest to us. But starting from this point, to place the machine on the pedestal of great sculpture, seems to me blindness, silly snobbishness, and ridiculous also.[2]

Amédée Ozenfant

Machines can clearly evoke powerful emotions and sensual delight for men.[3]

Judy Wajcman

From the beginning of aeronautics flying has been called beautiful. Reporting on an early balloon ascent in January 1784 the *Journal de Bruxelles* wrote: "It is impossible to describe that moment: the women in tears, the common people raising their hands toward the sky in deep silence; the passengers, leaning out of the gallery, waving and crying out in joy. . . you follow them with your eyes, you call to them as if they could hear, and the feeling of fright gives way to one of wonder. No one said anything but, 'Great God, how beautiful!' "[4]

Similar feelings were expressed in almost the same tone in August 1908, when Wilbur Wright made his first flights in Europe. Franz Reichel, reporter for the Paris newspaper *Le Figaro* wrote: "Nothing can give an idea of the emotion

. . . .

1   Gaston Bachelard, *L'Air et les Songes*. Paris: Librairie José Corti 1943. Translation from *On Poetic Imagination and Reverie*, selections from Gaston Bachelard, transl. by Colette Gaudin. Dallas: Spring Publications 1987, p. 65.
2   Ozenfant 1952, p. 155.
3   Wajcman 1991, p. 145.
4   A quotation in Robert Darnton's book *Mesmerism and the End of the Enlightenment in France*. Cambridge, Mass. – London: Harvard University Press 1968, p. 20, with the original French on p. 193.

experienced and the impression felt, at this last flight, a flight of masterly assurance and incomparable elegance." In 1908, however, Reichel was receptive not only to the miracle of flying but to the flying machine as well; he let his eyes rest upon the simple construction of the *Wright A*, and wrote: "How beautiful it is!"[5]

Start Ups

The spark for this work came from observations such as Franz Reichel's. I was fascinated by that short moment of amazement which seemed to reveal something of the essence of the flying machine, and my first intention was to study how the concept of beauty was used in describing new technical innovations, especially aeroplanes.[6] I was not alone in my feelings. Robert Wohl has pointed out in the beginning of his book *A Passion for Wings*, how the invention of the aeroplane was at first perceived by many as an aesthetic event.[7] The idea still finds occasional support; it has even been suggested, using the making of the classic *Wright Flyer* of 1903 as an example, that technology in general could be read by the method developed in aesthetic criticism for literary texts.[8] But as I proceeded from feelings to work, everything did not go as aesthetically as the crow flies. I had an idea about the direction but I often met turbulence *en route*, and more than once saw the whole textual apparatus glide over a strange territory. I soon found myself writing on an unexpected variety of things, and started to feel like the famous aviation reporter Harry Harper, whom "duty frequently took down the lunatic byways of aeronautics."[9] Therefore, let me begin by drawing a few lines of demarcation.

First of all, this is a study on flying but not on practical aviation; the emphasis rests on the machines which were merely *meant* to fly. Secondly, I am in the line of beauty, yet the subject of the present work is not aesthetics proper. Academic definitions notwithstanding, I feel quite content with Ozenfant's maxim: "There are beautiful objects (not to be too difficult over the significance of the word 'beauty')."[10] Throughout this work the word is taken as people use it in common language; when Wilbur Wright called a Rolls-Royce car beautiful he probably meant it, and was not saying something else. The same goes for technology; if I use the word it appears in the concrete meaning of "devices." More philosophical definitions of technology, such as "practical implementation of intelligence," given by Frederick Ferré, are problematic simply because many of the

. . . .

5   As quoted in Wohl 1994, p. 7. The article by Franz Reichel was published on 11 August 1908. Later Reichel experienced the beauty of flying from another angle, flying with Wilbur Wright on 3 October 1908. See Peyrey 1909, p. 183.
6   The essence of the flying machine is of course not one and the same thing for everyone. See for example the articles in *The Wright Flyer. An Engineering Perspective* 1987. The writers describe the *Wright Flyer* in great detail but none of them uses the word "beautiful."
7   Wohl 1994, p. 1.
8   Choe 1989, p. 2; on the *Wright Flyer*, pp. 29–37.
9   Wallace 1958, p. 66.
10   Ozenfant 1952, p. 155.

machines discussed in this work did not appear practical at all.[11] Yet it is not only beautiful devices, such as attempts at flying machines, but also people's thoughts and feelings about these machines that I am interested in. Flying, actual, potential, and dreamlike, has always implied more than a mechanism for overcoming gravity.[12] Consequently, the Pocus is not on the development of machines. On the following pages I will not write a history of technology but propose to read some of the ideas behind the flying machine in a wider context of visual culture. In his inspiring book *Super Constellation – Flugzeug und Raumrevolution* Christoph Asendorf has shown how rich in material are the twentieth-century intersections of art, architecture, and aviation. All three areas meet in this work, too, but whereas Asendorf set out to decide on the effect of aviation on modern art and culture, my starting point remains much more limited.[13] In the course of this work I will be asking questions such as: What was it like to see a new technical invention for the first time? What were the conventions and contexts for displaying machines? And how did artists see the new machines? While looking for answers to these questions (and more) I will mostly study two kinds of things. On the one hand, my focus is on aeroplanes and proposals for flying apparatuses as they were shown in different kinds of European exhibitions between the years 1900 and 1935. On the other, I am interested in the personalities and thoughts of the inventors and artists who, during that time, worked with these machines or used them in expanding their view of the world. But there is a third aspect as well: the ambiguity of the thing under scrutiny. Why contemplate the history of machines which did not work?

In the evolution of technology the machines I have chosen to study have no great historical importance as such, but they illustrate approaches to construction – intrinsic rather than extrinsic – that interest me as an artist. It is clear that some of the apparatus builders discussed in this work were stubbornly following a vision rather than using large measures of conventional logic. In art this is acceptable, in technology usually not. One good thing about art is that it does not need to be progressive in the same way as science and technology are. Favouring vision, the inventor/artist enters a domain where art and technology overlap, where the quest to overcome a technical problem and the passion for beauty genuinely meet, and the latter usually wins. The resulting constructions – they often are the only ones of their kind – such as the "flying machines" by the French engineer Clément Ader or the Soviet artist Vladimir Tatlin, both of whom we will meet in the course of this study, did not further practical aviation, but they certainly contributed to the beautiful history of the age-old longing for flying.

. . . .

11 Frederick Ferré, *Philosophy of Technology*. Athens, Ga. – London: The University of Georgia Press 1995, p. 26. In Ferré's definition, "practical" requires that they not be wholly ends in themselves.
12 Joseph J. Corn has rightly remarked that because the aviation books have usually been written within the tradition of aviation enthusiasm, the authors have not documented or analyzed the feelings, attitudes, and behaviour which characterize the phenomena (Corn 1983, vii–viii).
13 "[…] die Wirkung der Luftfahrt auf Kunst und Kultur der Moderne zu bestimmen […]." Asendorf 1997, vi.

Structure

On the following pages, flying itself plays a minor part, and it remains an underlying fact that most of the machines to be discussed never left the ground. And yet it is important to note that those feeble constructions were often exhibited alongside planes that were successful, planes that made history. One could say that the failed machines I am writing about were nothing but beautiful daydreams.[14] But even dreams follow a structure, and I have tried my best to do the same. Instead of first laying out the main points and then expanding on them, I have chosen a form that might be best described as a long takeoff. There are two reasons for doing this. The first is to acknowledge that cultural approaches to writing may, and should, vary even if texts are written using a *lingua franca*. The second emanates from the variety of the material itself. The present work is divided into three parts, the second of which has four independent chapters.

BEGINNING. The first third of the study concentrates mainly on pre-aeroplane developments in Britain and France and on the emergence of what is here called the beautiful machine. This means also taking a look at the underlying biological metaphors of the concept. It will also be suggested that the new kind of "mechanic" buildings and the early flying machines have some things in common. To begin with, I will circumscribe two important constructions of the era, the *Crystal Palace* and the *Palais des Machines*, and discuss contemporary notions of their dreamlike beauty, part of which radiates to the later chapters as well. On the way from the Great Exhibition of 1851 to the days of the first Futurist Manifesto I will map out some points of departure for the case studies in the succeeding chapters.

MIDDLE. The second third of the study builds on the themes introduced above and consists of four independent case-studies. Chapter One will introduce the French inventor Clément Ader and the prize-winning display of his *Avion III* at the *Exposition Universelle* in Paris in 1900. The case of Ader throws light on the contemporary uses of a rather stunning but altogether useless machine. Since his aeroplane never flew, it could imply flying only figuratively. As an exhibit at the *Musée des Arts et Métiers* in Paris the *Avion III* stands (or rather hangs) out as an exception. Its only function was, and still is, to represent an imaginative but non-functional machine. Chapter Two opens with a look at the public reactions to Louis Blériot's Channel crossing aeroplane and moves then to the first major aeronautical exhibition in Paris in October 1909, and finally to the story of three artists – Constantin Brancusi, Marcel Duchamp, and Fernand Léger – visiting it. The focus is on the ways these artists perceived the

. . . .

14   When talking about the main subject of this study I will use the word *aeroplane,* although it is not a proper expression for flapping-wing machines. The word (*aéroplane*) was coined by a little known French sculptor Joseph Pline in 1855 and later in English in 1866 by F. W. Wenham, member of the Aeronautical Society of Great Britain. See Stubelius 1958, pp. 226–232. The history of the English names for all kinds of aircraft is well documented in the thorough studies of Stubelius 1958 and 1960.

P-39 Airacobra in Tampere in the early 1970s. (Suomen Siivet 1/1971, p. 18.)

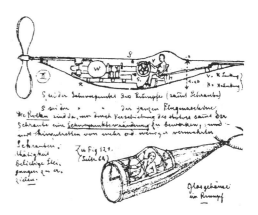

Artist Carl Steiger's 1891 plan for an aeroplane. (Gibbs-Smith 1968, p. 107.)

exhibits not as functional machines but as aesthetic objects. Since the visit is well-known but poorly documented in art history literature, and its timing is open to controversy, I will discuss its factual background in a separate appendix.

The early aeronautical exhibitions were very popular occasions and contributed greatly to ideas about machine beauty. Chapter Three concentrates on one of the smallest of such exhibitions. The protagonist is the sculptor Adolf Aarno, the first person in Finland to buy an aeroplane. Aarno had no knowledge of flying but he displayed the machine on a pedestal in the small town of Tampere in April 1911. The reactions of his contemporaries, when facing for the first time the *Demoiselle* aeroplane, the miracle of the twentieth century, illustrate the difficulties of understanding the visual appearance of the machine without first knowing the principles of its function. Chapter Four, the only one on actual flying, begins with the first aviation experience of another Finn, the architect Alvar Aalto, who in February 1921 circled over Helsinki. Aalto's playful yet purely modernistic comments on flying and city planning will be compared to those of his colleague Le Corbusier. The effect of flying upon architecture had been anticipated, for instance in the fantasies of the Russian poet Velimir Khlebnikov, but in the 1920s the flying architect's feeling of omnipotence throws a dark shadow over the old cities. The new architectural ideas for a better future have brutal stipulations written into them.

END. In the last third of the work many of the themes introduced in the preceding parts come together in the case of one individual. The focus is on the work of Vladimir Tatlin, the famous Russian artist, who in the 1920s and 1930s spent several years building a flapping-wing flying machine, the *Letatlin*. On the one hand, Tatlin's project will be studied in the context of the modern history of man-powered flying (for there really is such a history); on the other, the *Letatlin* will be discussed with reference to the wider social utopias of the time, especially those expressed in the works of the Soviet architects Ivan Leonidov and Konstantin Melnikov. *Letatlin's* role as an exhibition piece links it to the earlier examples like Ader's *Avion III* or Aarno's *Demoiselle*, while the poetic architectural dimension in its background is in stark contrast with the Corbusian visions of a future city. As the architectural theme reappears, the study loops back to the dreamlike constructions introduced in the first part. Towards the end of the work I will discuss dreams lost and dreams regained. It seems that the apparent impossibility at the heart of Tatlin's work does not require a logical explanation but a leap of faith.

Technology and Art

When reading Otto Lilienthal's classic work *Der Vogelflug als Grundlage der Fliegekunst* I was struck how, amid all diagrams and calculations, he suddenly desides to write a poem about the happiness of storks who fly in the blue and sunny sky.[15] The German engineer did not hesitate to deviate from his logical course for a moment or two. In a similar, though less poetic way my reader will meet digressions, by-plots and by-talk: things jump out from the horizon on various scales. Rather than methodology, this is a matter of personal philosophy: this is how I see things in general. Somewhere underneath these clustering contingencies the reader can imagine the chronological history of modern aviation – the span of this work extends from the time preceding the invention of the aeroplane to the early days of regular long-distance air travel; the London – Capetown route opened in 1932 and the Berlin – Buenos Aires service started in 1934. Although the first part pushes the timeline back to the mid-nineteenth century, it seemed logical that the opening of this work should be the year 1900. As I will explain, an unsuccessful aeroplane was then for the first time shown to the public as an exhibition piece of some aesthetic value. Where to end was more unclear. There are, however, two good reasons for bringing this work to a close soon after the mid-1930s. First of all, it was then that Vladimir Tatlin was

. . . .
15   Lilienthal 1889, pp. 148–149.

forced to give up his dream of building a man-powered flying machine for every man. Secondly, the mid-1930s was the time when the concept of machine beauty became part of the mainstream and was no longer considered controversial. In 1934, the Museum of Modern Art in New York mounted its influential exhibition *Machine Art* and only a year later the Coldspot refrigerator designed by Raymond Loewy was advertised to millions with phrases like "Study its beauty."[16] A period of aestheticizing the flying machine finally culminated with Le Corbusier's book *Aircraft* in 1935, two years before the bombing of Guernica.[17]

Flying can be related to many things. According to historians like Clive Hart, images of ascension permeate the whole of Western culture.[18] This I consider in passing. Although I began with a quote from Bachelard, flying will not be discussed here in psychoanalytical terms. In all it seems that my study falls somewhere between the history of technology and the history of art – but perhaps there is no exact name for this topic. Historians of art and historians of technology rarely mix, and Melvin Kranzberg has even suggested which half should be blamed: "Perhaps most guilty of neglecting technology are those concerned with the history of the arts and with the entire panoply of humanistic concerns. Indeed, in many cases they are disdainful of technology, regarding it as somehow opposed to the humanities. This might be because they regard technology solely in terms of mechanical devices and do not even begin to comprehend the complex nature of technological developments and their direct influences on the arts, to say nothing of their direct influence on mankind's humanistic endéavors."[19] Kranzberg's colleague, Cyril Stanley Smith, goes further: "Humanists have shown a widespread disregard for technology's role in human affairs [...]."[20]

If the situation really is that bad, then this work will not change things in the least. I have already joined the guilty ones by reading technology as "devices."[21] I do agree with scholars like Kranzberg and Smith that a lot of work remains to be done in this field; I feel that artists at least have always been much readier to

. . . .

16 Raymond Loewy, *Industrial Design*. London: Lawrence King 2000, p. 99. Before *Machine Art* there was of course the seminal *Machine Age* exhibition in 1927, exploring a wide spectrum of modern phenomena. The difference is that *Machine Art* concentrated fully on industrial products and philosophized about their beauty.

17 Needless to say, the material I have chosen for this work is only a fragment of all the interaction between art and aeroplanes in the course of the first thirty-five years of heavier-than-air aviation. Many interesting cases from Kazimir Malevich to the Italian Aeropainters have been omitted.

18 See his book *Images of Flight*. Berkeley – Los Angeles– London: University of California Press 1988.

19 *In Context. History and the History of Technology* 1989, p. 252. The problem is apparent even in terms of mechanical devices, as one writer complained: "It is rare to find in fine-art magazines serious coverage of technological products." (Durgnat 1972, p. 130.)

20 Smith 1981, p. 191.

21 In my mind this does not eliminate the possibility of talking about aesthetics, as has been suggested for example by Wolhee Choe: "Too often, technological artefacts are regarded merely as instruments rather than as objects that communicate meaning. This attitude toward technological objects undermines the possibility of aesthetic criticism and evaluation. 'Do the objects inspire intelligence, thought, creativity?' is replaced with simply 'Are they efficient?'" (Choe 1989, p. 7.)

use technology than technicians have been ready to use art. As if to support this point of view, Smith has uttered some comforting words: "The artist, if not every art historian, has always known that technology is a basically important human activity."[22]

History and Dreams

When Vladimir Tatlin had to find a way of explaining his inert flying machine in 1932, he said: "I have made it as an artist."[23] It is not always easy to reach the original goal, even a more modest one than Tatlin's, and sometimes it is difficult even to know what the real goal was. As the art historian Ivan Matsa wrote in the 1970s, constructive ideas do not become "constructivist" by miracles and sensations, but are rather the posing of yet unanswered questions. According to Matsa, they are explorations, or experiments, in which the final aim is often not quite clear even to the artist himself.[24] Indeed, what does the need to build a flying machine indicate? What can be learned from the history of this dream? Writing on the history of technology, Ulrich Wengenroth points out that as a branch of knowledge (*Wissenschaft*) history is ideographic, that is descriptive (*"ideographisch", d.h. beschreibend*), and that in descriptive narratives events follow each other without a predictable order: "[...] they are open to the un-explained and alien, to the contingent. Lately no regulating laws are found, whereby we could know the conclusion of a history, whether in the singular or in the plural, from its beginning."[25] I have felt that the lack of regulating laws holds true, if not with Tatlin's project, at least with the present work, the original plan of which implied neither the end, nor the beginning. But as Wengenroth later remarks: "Our need to write history, however, is often greater than our ability to do it following scientific norms; the value of history is not only in its verifiability [...] The motive for taking an interest in history is the search for an indivisible identity."[26]

Seen in that light, much of this work – rather a study on gravity than on levitation – is about personal dreams. The three quotations chosen for the opening above illustrate my interests from different angles. The aesthetic character of the dream flight, mentioned by Bachelard, has always been my

. . . .

22 Smith 1981, p. 217 and pp. 232–233.
23 Zelinsky 1968, p. 78.
24 I. Matsa, "Constructivism: an historical and artistic appraisal," *Studio International*, April 1972, p. 142.
25 "[...] blieb dabei jedoch immer offen für Unerklärbares und Fremdes, für Kontingenz. Es konnte letztlich keine Regel gefunden werden, wonach das Ende einer Geschichte, ob im Singular oder im Plural, aus deren Anfang ableitbar gewesen wäre." Wengenroth 1998, p. 2.
26 "Unser Bedürfnis nach Geschichte und Geschichten ist allemal grösser als unsere Fähigkeit zur wissenschaftlichen Durchdringung der Vergangenheit; und die faktische Überprüf-barkeit einer Geschichte ist nicht das einzige Kriterium ihres Wertes. [...] Zumal die Motiva-tion für das Betreiben von Geschichte die Suche nach unteilbarer Identität ist." *Ibid.* As he says this Wengenroth also underlines that in the writing of history both academic writing and fictional writing are legitimate as long as they are not confused with each other. Whether this is possible is not my concern here.

starting point, and I fully agree with Wacjman about the powerful emotions and the sensual delight evoked by the rationalized results of that dream, the machines themselves. The question of the aesthetic value of these machines, as put forward by Ozenfant, is important too, since it implies another, larger question about "great sculpture," that is, about art, its values, and its place in the society. The emblematic *Letatlin*, in which all the themes of this work eventually meet, is still a good test for all three approaches. Is it a failed machine or a piece of great sculpture, a mere aesthetic dream or a telling symbol of the condition of man? I do not propose to give a full answer but to tell a story. It aims to be, above all, a story true to the dream of flight.

1.
Beginning

■ Rise of the Mechanic Building

This monument not only states its purpose clearly, but reveals the intention of the builder, offering to the gaze, in their infinite variety, the uses of modern science at the service of the builder. The aim appears fully achieved. Examine the ways chosen to achieve it, the lightness of the structure, the bold soaring of the gracious curve of the arches, which cleave space like the wings of a bird spread in flight.[1]

R. Marx

The collection on machinery excites far deeper interest than anything else exhibited.[2]

The Yorkshire Visitors' Guide to the Great Exhibition

In 1850, Prince Albert gave a speech in London in support of an industrial exhibition, declaring: "Nobody who has paid any attention to the peculiar features of the present era, will doubt for a moment that we are living at a period of most wonderful transition [...]."[3] He was rather optimistic about the realization of the unity of mankind, but something did happen. A year later in sunny Hyde Park stood a big glasshouse full of goods, and people all over the world came to see it.[4] This is the place where the story begins; a story about dreams, written in the intertwinings of three sort of things: buildings, machines, and beauty. Some matters in this story are small, some are middle-sized, but the glasshouse certainly belongs to those which are grand.[5]

. . . .

1 From a description of the *Palais des Machines*, printed in *L'Architecture* 1890, p. 382. From an English quotation in Benevolo 1971, p. 109.
2 Robert Arskill, *The Yorkshire Visitors' Guide to the Great Exhibition.* Leeds: Joseph Buckton 1851. Quoted in Auerbach 1999, p. 104.
3 Quoted in Pevsner 1951, p. 16.
4 The expression "sunny" here refers to the contemporary illustrations, always showing the *Crystal Palace* in fine weather. The real London weather was, as always, a different matter. For example, in July 1851 the monthly precipitation was 106.7 mm. (*World Weather Records.* Smithsonian Miscellaneous Collections, Vol. 79. City of Washington: The Smithsonian Institution 1944, pp. 470–472.)
5 In the following my focus will be on the descriptions of the exhibition building, not on the social changes in Victorian England. The subject is, however, so imbued with the glorious history of the Empire that writing simply about the building is often hard work. John McKean, for example, begins his book on the subject saying: "Perhaps we already all know all there is to know about Crystal Palace," (McKean 1994, p. 4.) without wondering at all who are "we all" he is referring to.

In the history of the aesthetization of mechanical things the Great Exhibition of London in 1851 with its six million visitors is difficult to miss. It was a moment when the new machine-driven world was introduced to the public at large in positive terms. And not only introduced but also sold; the exhibition was such a success that 1851 came to be described as a singularly happy year of peace, plenty, good feeling, innocent pleasure, and national glory.[6] Amidst these sentiments a feeling also started to grow for the beauty of the machine. We could say that seeds of the ideas which would later challenge the old pre-industrial concepts of beauty were in the air. The happy context and the imaginative surroundings helped to transform unpleasant and dubious things into something exciting and astounding. A public who would have never entered the dirty and noisy factories were amused to look at the same machinery – now clean and polished – working inside a giant glasshouse.[7] Even Queen Victoria herself was said to have referred to the "beautiful machinery."[8] But most of all, it was the dreamlike exhibition building in the lovely park that played the leading role in shaping people's ideas about future, so much so that they did not want to demolish it even when the exhibition was over. "The fact that the Crystal Palace was re-erected in 1854 at Sydenham near London for a more permanent purpose proves that the new beauty of metal and glass had caught the fancies of progressive Victorians and of the public at large," concluded Nikolaus Pevsner.[9]

The Great Exhibition marked, let us argue, the starting point of machine beauty, yet looking back at the visual culture of the period this may appear somewhat surprising. At times, this surprise has been expressed in a form of an evaluation. As one commentator on Victorian design from the 1970s put it: "Almost without exception design meant decoration rather than function – the decoration of every possible facet and detail, without much thought to the practicalities of such finishes." In the 1950s another writer used a slightly stronger vocabulary and evaluated Victorian design as "[…] a bastardization of taste without parallel in the whole recorded history of aesthetics."[10] But of course, as many historians have later pointed out, the decoration was there for a

- - - - - - - - - -

For the social and political aspects of the Great Exhibition, see Auerbach 1999, with a useful bibliography. For the period, its people, and its material culture in general, see the "Victorian trilogy" by Briggs.

6   Words of Macaulay, quoted by Pevsner 1951, p. 17.
7   For the contemporary glasshouses, see the excellent survey Georg Kohlmaier & Barna von Sartory, *Das Glashaus. Ein Bautypus des 19. Jahrhunderts.* München: Prestel 1981; for the *Crystal Palace* especially, pp. 410–426.
8   According to Auerbach 1999, p. 106.
9   Pevsner 1949, p. 76. Let us not forget, however, that the *Crystal Palace* had also proved to be good business. Moreover, in Sydenham the building was not plain metal and glass but immediately filled with "historical" imitations of Egypt, Greece, Rome, Byzantium, the Alhambra, Middle-Ages, and the Renaissance. See the photographs in Friemert 1984, pp. 100–160.
10   The first comment comes from Allwood 1977, p. 21, the second is from *The Great Exhibition* (1951) by Yvonne ffrench, as quoted in Pevsner 1951, p. 11. For disparaging comments, see also Beaver 1977. The Victorians were of course not unaware of the practical side of things, as can be seen from the report of the 1851 exhibition jury: "Articles of furniture are too often crowded with unnecessary embellishment which interferes with their use, purpose and convenience." Quotation in Briggs 1988, p. 74.

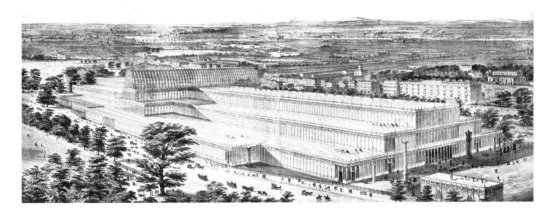

reason: "Although twentieth-century critics may have considered the steam engines' classical ornament absurd, during the nineteenth century the decorative frames were associated with a rich overlay of cultural meanings."[11] That rich overlay, however, is not what I am after. In the following I will presume that in order to be seen beautiful the practical machines of the Victorian era had either to be decorated or, what interests me more, met with fresh eyes and with new concept of beauty. This concept was significant function.

Sculpture and Machines

It is not difficult to find evidence supporting the Victorians' preference for decoration. The Great Exhibition did indeed include machines built in various "historical" styles, such as Egyptian or Gothic.[12] But because the role of the decoration was so clearly separate from the mechanical function, it follows that the essence of those machines (as we now understand it) was not easily understood in the context of contemporary aesthetics. The machines of 1851, no matter how garnished, were not really discussed as works of art. Even the fabulous and much liked building, Joseph Paxton's celebrated *Crystal Palace*, was not taken as a piece of architecture but as an example of pure engineering.[13] With its materials and industrial construction methods – standardized and

. . . .

11 Wosk 1992, p. 183. In defence of Victorian decoration, see for example Julian Barnard, *The Decorative Tradition*. London: The Architectural Press 1973.

12 See for example Pevsner 1951, pp. 24–25. For a discussion on this trend, see the chapter "Classicizing the Machine" in Wosk 1992, pp. 178–210. The trend was by no means a British phenomenon, see for example the Moorish steam-engine in Potsdam in 1848, Kollman 1928, pp. 14–15. Some undecorated and functionalistic machines in the exhibition, such as the ones designed by Joseph Withworth, were not popular. See "History of Machine Art" in *Machine Art* 1994, np.

13 Even some admirers of Paxton's concept had to admit: "[…] hitherto it has usually been treated as a mere matter of engineering, and comparatively little done to bring it within the province of art." (G. G. Scott in 1858 when the *Crystal Palace* was in its new place in Sydenham) Quoted in Pevsner 1949, p. 76.

The Greek Slave. One of the most celebrated exhibits of the 1851 exhibition. (Gibbs-Smith 1981, p. 86.)

prefabricated metal parts, use of specially designed machines, assembly line glazing – the *Crystal Palace* belonged to the same lot as the first iron bridges, that is, a category of inventive construction designed not by architects but by civil engineers.[14] At the same time the work of the professional architect was governed by aesthetic canons that had been evolved before iron had become available.[15]

. . . .

14   For information on the machines and the prefabrication of parts, see Friemert 1984, pp. 17–37. For a wider understanding of the prefabrication, underlining also the importance of the contractors Fox Henderson, see Thorne 1987.

15   McAllister 1996, pp. 143–144. For a discussion of one particular example, the *Forth Bridge* (1889), see Baxandall 1985, pp. 12–40. For the beginnings of iron architecture before the *Crystal Palace*, see for example Giedion 1947, pp. 103–177; Pevsner 1949, pp. 68–75; McAllister 1996, pp. 141–154.

The *Crystal Palace* was assembled rather than built. Before the work started, Paxton said that putting its parts together should work like "a perfect piece of machinery."[16] Because of the possibility to dismantle and reuse it in varied form, the building had more in common with the machines which helped bring it into existence than with buildings of traditional construction.[17] This way both the design and the construction work of the *Crystal Palace* represented a new kind of "mechanical" attitude. Inside the finished building, however, the prevailing attitudes came into their own. The exhibits were organized in six different divisions: *raw materials, machinery, manufactured products (two divisions), miscellaneous* and *fine art*, meaning sculpture or plastic art. This tells something about the age-old status of sculpture as a dirty and mechanical art to be included in the industrial exhibition while painting was not.[18] On view was also the gap between the Victorians' taste in art and their inclination towards engineering. This is not merely a contradiction between decoration and function but a larger question of two different horizons: in the *Crystal Palace* Victorian art was bound to the past while Victorian technology was already promoting the future.[19]

Looking through pictures of the 1851 exhibition I find the contrast between the sculpture and the machines interesting. In one part of the enormous glasshouse was the moving machinery section "where the recently invented mass-production machines of the industrial revolution were hard at work planning, slotting, drilling, boring, riveting, wire-drawing, spinning, coining, and pumping."[20] Not very far away stood the pieces of art, many of them voluptuous statues representing naked or half-naked women.[21] Although similar images are still commonly used in our culture, it was the machine that in the following decades became the more important exhibit.[22] At first things did not seem to go

· · · · · · · ·

16 In a lecture he gave in the winter 1850–1851. *Journal of Design and Manufacturers*, vol. 4, 1850/51. Quoted in Pevsner 1951, p. 15.

17 Thorne 1987, p. 24.

18 On the divisions of the exhibition, see Gibbs-Smith 1981, pp. 16–17. According to Hindle and Lubar: "Exhibits were limited to 'those departments of art which are, in a degree, connected with mechanical processes which are applicable to the arts.' In the nineteenth century, sculpture was considered, in some ways, a mechanical product as well as an artistic one, for it was seldom executed by the artist. He made a model for his assistants to reproduce in stone, mechanically." Hindle & Lubar 1986, pp. 256–257. The idea of the nature of sculpture goes back to Leonardo: "Sculpture is not a science but a very mechanical art." *Paragone*. Oxford: Oxford University Press 1959, p. 94.

19 Both "The pull of the past" and "the lure of the future" (Briggs 1988, plates II a and b.) could be fictional, of course. Think for instance of the simultaneity of the "classical" subjects of Victorian painting (Burne-Jones) and the first science fiction novels (Wells).

20 Allwood 1977, p. 22.

21 For a present day viewer it may be just as difficult to read all the cultural meanings of these statues as it is to read the "classical" decorations of the machines. A good example is the centrepiece of the American exhibit and one of the great hits of the fair, *The Greek Slave*, a much reproduced sculpture by Hiram Powers. "Its popularity came not only from the artistic skill and the uncommon nudity presented, but from the meanings that the Victorian public read into it. The public found in this statue great piety and religious feeling, chastity and spirituality: the spirit of 'true womanhood'." Hindle & Lubar 1986, p. 257. On the artworks, see also Beaver 1977, pp. 56–61.

22 Today the tradition of combining half-naked women with machines lives in a popular form in calenders published by car companies and other machinery producers.

that way: the combination of women and machines was displayed even more explicitly in Paris 1889, where the entrance of the *Palais des Machines* was decorated with two huge allegorical sculptures. One of them was a representation of electricity in the form of two naked ladies eight metres high.[23] But twenty years after this Paris exhibition we find signs of a changing attitude. In 1910 a small but noisy group called the Futurists were suggesting a ten-year ban on the

. . . .
23   Durant 1994, pp. 24–25.

nude in painting and praising instead the beauty of machines.[24] We will meet the Futurists again towards the end of this part, but let us first take a detour and say a few words about the emergence of the new kind of technological beauty.

Dream and Function

In the 1930s, when machine aesthetics was an established fact, Sigfried Giedion crystallized the atmosphere of the 1851 exhibition in the following way: "Industry, after all the blight and disorder it had brought about, now displayed another and a gentler side, aroused feelings that seemed to belong only to the world of dreams."[25] The notion of dreams is splendid and highly useful, but surely the idea of beauty did not change only because new "dreamlike" things were seen. A new inventive logic also made itself known. Lewis Mumford's point, again from the perspective of the 1930s, is worth noticing: "While many of the boasted achievements of industrialism are merely rubbish, and while many of the goods produced by the machine are fraudulent and evanescent, its esthetic, its logic, and its factual technique remain a durable contribution: they are among man's supreme conquests."[26] This brings us to an apparently simple way of thinking about the beauty of the machine: the logic of valuing functionality as such. A beautiful machine would then be something that works as well as possible in the work it is designed for, while an ugly machine would be inefficient, slow, difficult to handle, or perhaps, in our days, overly polluting. H. G. Wells once expressed this machine-centred position: "There is nothing in machinery, there is nothing in embankments and railways and iron bridges and engineering devices to oblige them to be ugly. Ugliness is the measure of imperfection; a thing of human making is for the most part ugly in proportion to the poverty of its constructive thought, to the failure of its producer fully to grasp the purpose of its being."[27] Wells' words suggest that a simple functionalistic machine would be more beautiful than the decorated Egyptian machine of the 1851 exhibition. But Wells also seemed to think that beauty in general would increase hand in hand with good constructive thinking. Since beauty shows when the machine itself gets better, fulfilling its task with less friction, the latest machine is likely to be the most beautiful. Practicality then turns into an aesthetic criterion; *"Etwas Unpraktisches kann nicht schön sein,"* [An unpractical thing cannot be beautiful.] claimed the influential German architect Otto Wagner in 1895.[28]

. . . .
24 "Futurist Painting: Technical Manifesto" (1910), Apollonio 1973, pp. 30–31. See also the discussion about the academic concepts of nude as a limitation to the progress of sculpture, in "Technical Manifesto of Futurist Sculpture" (1912), *ibid.*, pp. 51–52.
25 Giedion 1947, p. 184.
26 Mumford 1963, p. 324.
27 Wells 1994, p. 65.
28 In his *Baukunst unserer Zeit* (1895). Quoted in Kollman 1928, p. 16.

Yet there have always been cases where beauty and impracticality seem to join hands. When twentieth-century engineers, architects, and other constructive thinkers were given a free hand the world did not always turn out more beautiful, practical, or functional. In a later chapter I shall discuss Le Corbusier, whose aeroplane-inspired maxim *la maison est une machine à habiter* (1923) was a brilliant constructive idea in itself. And yet it could easily go wrong in two different ways. Firstly, and I think examples are not difficult to find, a housing block can be very functional and at the same time a rather unpleasant sight. Secondly, the prettier and more private "machines for living in," such as Le Corbusier's famous *Villa Savoye* (1931), did not always function very well. The family who commissioned *Villa Savoye* abandoned the building after a few years, frustrated with the leaking roof and other shortcomings in the construction. The house, an uninhabited machine, is now considered beautiful but *not* because the constructive thinking behind it produced better functional results than in contemporary buildings built with old-fashioned non-leaking roofs.[29] Perhaps it was *form* that always was the most significant function of the *Villa Savoye*.

Ugly as a Bridge

The *Crystal Palace* was, and here critics from all decades seem to agree, a very practical building. But in its own time even plain practicality was not good news for all; many nineteenth century writers and artists saw all technology in a negative light; factories polluted the environment and unreliable machines even killed people.[30] And for some artists and writers technology was more than anything an aesthetic threat. In 1887 there was the famous Artists' Protest against the Eiffel Tower, requesting its demolition, and asking: "Is this city going to continue to be associated with the glories of the baroque, or with the commercial fancies of a builder of machines?"[31] On the other side of the Channel the debate about the ugliness of the new buildings was personified famously in the writings of William Morris and John Ruskin, both fighting with vigor against contemporary technology and its promise of future. Morris, whom a look at the *Crystal Palace* made almost physically ill, was more than convinced: "There never will be an architecture in iron, every improvement in machinery being uglier and uglier, until they reach the supremest specimen of all ugliness – the Forth Bridge," and there was an unmistakeable smell of

. . . .

29 Although the *Villa Savoye* has been discussed in all standard books on Le Corbusier, it is still best understood on site; it is now an excellent machine to visit. William J. R. Curtis sums up the story of the building in a few words: "The Villa Savoye has had a glorious career in history books but a rough time in fact." Curtis 1986, p. 94.
30 For Victorian discussions of the dangers of technology, see for example Klingender 1972 and Wosk 1992.
31 Quoted in Mandell 1967, p. 19.

brimstone in Ruskin's verdict: "The new architecture of glass and metal is eternally separated from all good and great things."[32]

The question of the value of these new "mechanic buildings," as I like to call them, was of course never a purely aesthetic matter but it always implied a question of professional status. In 1889, the year when both the *Forth Bridge* and the *Palais des Machines* were completed, the French architect Anatole de Baudot wrote these often quoted lines: "A long time ago the influence of the architect declined and the engineer, *l'homme moderne par excellence*, is beginning to replace him."[33] The modern man, such as Benjamin Baker, the designer of the *Forth Bridge*, was quick to remind his critics that he had considered his designs from the artistic point of view "from the very first."[34] It is no news that Baker and his antagonists did not share the same idea about art. One side was talking about the form, the other spoke already about the function. What is interesting, however, is that these quarrels did not end with the nineteenth century, and we will actually meet the same discussions again in a later chapter, when we come to the 1920s and the work of Le Corbusier, Konstantin Melnikov, and Vladimir Tatlin. Defending the superiority of his own art, Le Corbusier asked whether the *Garabit Bridge* by Gustave Eiffel would actually remain beautiful. Thus he joined the earlier critics of engineering: "[…] shall we see engineers trying to turn themselves into men of aesthetic sensibility? That would be the real danger: for their equipment would not develop further. An engineer should stay fixed, and remain a calculator, for his particular justification is to work within the confines of mere reason. […] And it is only Architecture which can give all the things which go *beyond* calculation." As a result, says the Russian architect Melnikov, engineering will never produce architecture.[35] Indeed, the nineteenth century concept of *l'homme moderne*, at least when used to describe one profession, may cause us to miss the point. Historically it is true that in many cases – machines, bridges, exhibition halls – the functional form (structure) also became visually important. But what happened when the functional form could not be calculated beforehand? In Baker's case calculating was possible, yet what he came up with was a better bridge rather than the first bridge ever. He improved – in a brilliant way – on an existing idea.

This is worth emphasising here because even a quick look at the early proposals for an aeroplane reveals a more complicated picture. By the end of the nineteenth century men had been erecting functional buildings for ages but they had not yet managed to build a functional aeroplane. Many basic problems with buildings had already been solved (doors, windows, roofs etc.) while the

. . . .

32 Morris according to an unnotated citation in Baxandall 1985, p. 24. Morris' illness according to "History of Machine Art" in *Machine Art* 1994, np. Ruskin quoted in Pevsner 1949, p. 84.
33 Giedion 1947, p. 151.
34 From Baker's answer to Morris' criticism, citation in Baxandall 1985, pp. 24–25.
35 Le Corbusier 1994, pp. 48–50. The English translation here by Frederick Etchells (*The City of To-morrow and its Planning*, 1929). Melnikov in his lecture in 1926, quoted in Cooke 1991, p. 17.

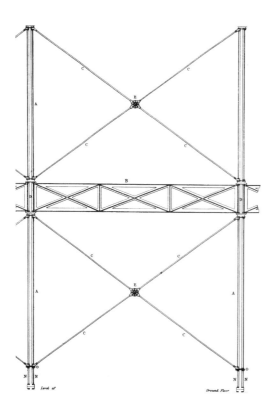

Detail of the standard structures of the Crystal Palace. (McKean 1994, p. 52.)

aeroplane was only in the process of being invented.[36] People were still trying to find out the good constructive forms and their significant functions for making a viable aeroplane. At times calculations were made without knowing exactly what to calculate. I would even say that as the nineteenth century ended no existing design was necessarily better than any other.[37] Clément Ader's *Avion III* from the 1890s was a construction without an elevator and ailerons, and there was no forward visibility from the pilot's seat. Yet the machine was in all its peculiar form a *possible* functional solution.[38] Only after the success of the

. . . .

36 As is well known, Le Corbusier disagreed about the functional aspects of buildings being solved. In his *Vers une architecture* (1923) he wrote the famous line: "Le problème de la maison n'est pas posé." Le Corbusier 1995, p. 83. See below pp. 106–117.

37 I am talking of course about aeroplanes as motor-driven flying machines. I am not denying that there were great differences in the ways people approached the problem of flying. In retrospect it is easy to say that the work of the German engineer Otto Lilienthal was done in a sound scientific manner and therefore was more useful for the development of aviation than, say, the haphazard work of the Belgian shoemaker Vincent de Groof. But if we look at things from another perspective there is a certain similarity in their efforts: both of them died when testing their flying contraptions and neither of them succeeded in inventing an aeroplane. On de Groof, see Gibbs-Smith 1985, pp. 47–48; Dollfus & Bouché 1938, p. 112; Riverain 1970, p. 61.

38 Ader's first plane *Éole* had taken off under its own power in 1890 (before Lilienthal had flown with his glider), so he had all reason to believe that his next machine would do even better. According to Gibbs-Smith, Ader's conception of the aeroplane was romantic and unrealistic, but this, even when it comes from the mouth of a famous aviation historian, is little more than hindsight.

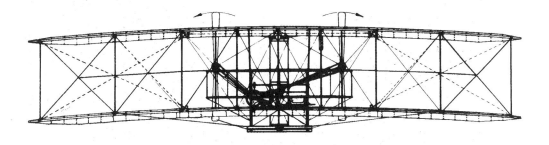

Wright Brothers did it become obvious that the constructive forms of *Avion III* had no significant function. We could say that the constructive forms of this non-functioning machine then reduced to artistic forms. But before we get to Ader we have to fly back once more to the Great Exhibition.

Constructing Space

The role of the *Crystal Palace* was important in shaping people's thoughts about technology and its possible beauty.[39] We could apply here the words of Le Corbusier and say that the *Crystal Palace* was revolutionary because it was "a machine for showing things in." The functional aspects alone would have been enough to make it a truly amazing building: its enormous size, the speed of its construction, and its cost-effiency were unseen before.[40] But beyond that the *Crystal Palace* was beautiful, like a visual miracle with "general lightness and fairy-like brilliancy never before dreamt of […]."[41] And clear light there was: the whole building was transparent and, according to a contemporary visitor, gave an impression of all materiality blending into atmosphere. The building appeared not only grand but also impossible to measure with the eye; "We see a delicate network of lines without any clue by means of which we might judge their distance from the eye or the real size. The side walls are too far apart to be embraced in a single glance. Instead of moving from the wall at one end to that of the other, the eye sweeps along an unending perspective which fades into the horizon. We cannot tell if this structure towers a hundred or a thousand feet above us, or whether the roof is a flat platform or is built up from a succession of ridges, for there is no play of shadows to enable our optic nerves to gauge the measurements."[42] Suddenly a temporary exhibition hall, designed by a mere gardener, had opened up a whole new way of seeing the possibilities of technol-

· · · · · · · · ·

39 On the aesthetic impact of the *Crystal Palace*, see Friemert 1984, pp. 39–41.
40 For statistics, see Gibbs-Smith 1981, pp. 23–25. The building was erected in four months and the greatest number of people to be inside it at one time was 93,244. The sheer profit made from the Exhibition exceeded the cost of the building and its fittings.
41 An article printed in *Ecclesiologist* in 1851, taken from the passage quoted in Chadwick 1961, p. 189.
42 Lothar Bucher in 1851, quoted in Benevolo 1971, p. 102.

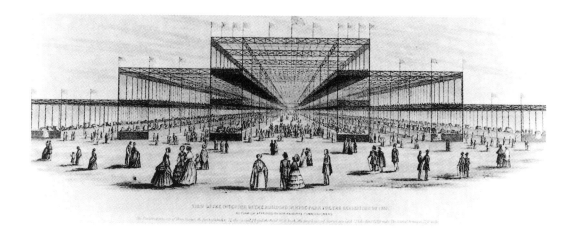

ogy.[43] Compared with all the buildings around it and with most of the exhibits inside it, the *Crystal Palace* itself was a vision of the future – a vision opening everywhere towards skylight.

Sigfried Giedion's assessment of Paxton's design is worth noting: "In the Crystal Palace an artistic conception outdistances the technical possibilities of the era – something which is very rare in the nineteenth century." Giedion saw, however, that the artistic quality was due to Paxton's familiarity with delicate plants rather than with rough machines: "The curious association of an unmistakable grandeur with a certain gentleness was never again to be achieved."[44] In its fragile glasshouse appearance the *Crystal Palace* remained unique but at the same time served as a powerful example for all further attempts to overcome the feeling of gravity in giant exhibition halls, such as the famous *Palais des Machines* (1889) designed by Ferdinand Dutert.[45] For some viewers the vast covered space in Paris again seemed endless; J. K. Huysmans for instance compared the *Palais des Machines* to a cathedral. He wrote about its suberb interior, taller than the highest of naves, its arches and its endless sky of glass. And this time there was even more than daylight: "At night, when the Edison lamps are lit, the hall appears to expand and become infinite [...]."[46] However, not every visitor was a poet, and for some it was enough to say that inside the building one's gaze can travel over half a kilometre of bright and empty space.[47]

The Crystal Palace as imagined by an artist before the construction work started. (Architectural Design 11/12 1987, p. 70.)

. . . .

43 Although Paxton is often remembered as the gardener for the Duke of Devonshire, he was in fact a man of many talents. See McKean 1994, pp. 13–15.

44 Giedion 1947, p. 189.

45 "The two most beautiful buildings of the period of the great exhibitions – the Crystal Palace and the Galerie des Machines of 1889 – have disappeared. [...] Only photographs and etchings remain as witness that the overcoming of gravity in apparently floating constructions (which is the essence of any solution to the problem of vaulting) was achieved in magnificient form during the nineteenth century." Giedion 1947, p. 183.

46 "L'interieur de ce palais est, en effet, superbe. Imaginez une galerie colossale, large comme on n'en vit jamais, plus haute que la plus élevée des nefs, une galerie s'élançant sur des jets d'arceaux, décrivant comme un plein cintre brisé, comme une exorbitante ogive qui rejoint sous le ciel infini des vitres ses vertigineuses pointes [...] Le soir, alors que les lampes Edison s'allument, la galerie s'allonge encore et s'illimite." J. K. Huysmans, "Le Fer" in *Certains*. Paris: Librarie Plon 1908, pp.179–180. The book was first published in 1889.

47 A contemporary comment as quoted in Benevolo 1971, p. 106.

Construction of a "Zeppelin." (Aviation. The Early Years 1997, p. 235.)

It is interesting that both these buildings, as well as the exhibition halls in Paris 1855, 1867, and 1878, were considered dazzling by the standards of their day: the contemporary spectators were not accustomed to the amount of light that was admitted.[48] This aspiration to open space, to lightness of construction, to free air circulation, and to the use of daylight (and in 1889 the electric lamps mentioned by Huysmans) can be discussed in purely architectural terms, but it also has a symbolic dimension. These exhibition halls were called "palaces" first because of the extraordinary appearance of the *Crystal Palace* and later for

· · · · · · · · ·

48   Commenting the *Palais de l'Industrie* of Paris 1855, Giedion 1947, p. 193.

the sake of tradition.[49] But there must have been something fairytale-like in them, after all they contained the great and valuable treasures of their time. According to a Victorian art magazine, the *Crystal Palace* "flashed on the eye more like the fabled palace of Vathek than a structure reared in a few months by mortal hands."[50] Miracles were part of the parcel: in the *Palace des Machines* the visitors could study the show from a *pont roulant*, an electrically powered gantry which transported them from one end of the hall to the other, moving high above the working machines like a flying carpet. It is then exciting to see how the structure and form of these "palaces," most of them purposely built just for displaying machines, were repeated and further developed in constructions related to movement – not only in the great railway stations of the early twentieth century but also in the airships and aeroplane hangars.[51]

Space Inside Out

The reference to airships is not coincidental: aviation and the exhibition buildings of London and Paris have a shared history. Already at the first industrial exhibition in Paris 1798 a balloon was one of the attractions.[52] No surprise, then, that on the first day of the *Crystal Palace* a balloon was ready to ascend as soon as the Queen declared the exhibition open.[53] Giffard's big hydrogen balloon was displayed at the *Exposition Universelle* of 1867, and the same year the famous photographer and balloonist Nadar took twelve visitors at a time up in his huge double-decker captive balloon *Géant* – the first time that the visitors had been able to have a live "bird's-eye view" of an exhibition and its buildings.[54] But things could be seen also from another angle. In 1859 Camille Vert changed the point of view from the open to the architectural space of the building by bringing his dirigible *Le Poisson Volant* inside the *Palais de l'Industrie*.[55] Likewise, Nadar's *Géant* was on display inside the *Crystal Palace* in 1863, and five years later the same place witnessed the first ever exhibition devoted to flying apparatuses.[56] The Aeronautical Exhibition with its seventy-seven exhibits,

· · · · · · · · ·

49 When the Americans wanted to have their own exhibition two years after London, the exhibition building in New York was named *Crystal Palace*. Likewise a building in Munich 1854 was called *Glas Palast*. See Hindle & Lubar 1986, pp. 267–268, and Benevolo 1971, pp. 102–103.
50 An article in the *Art Journal*, quoted in Briggs 1988, p. 59.
51 See for example the pictures of the frame of a Zeppelin and its hangar in *Aviation. The Early Years* 1997, p. 235, and the British airship R 100 on p. 298. On the link between bridge-building, aeroplane design, and lightness of construction, see Asendorf 1997, pp. 15–16.
52 See the picture in Giedion 1947, p. 178.
53 Beaver 1977, p. 35. In charge of the balloon was Charles Spencer, one of the best known aeronauts in Britain.
54 There is a painting of the exhibition by Manet, showing a balloon; see Giedion 1947, p. 197. On Giffard, see Fonvielle 1907, p. 61 and p. 63. On Nadar, whose balloon had several mishaps on these flights, Allwood 1977, p. 48; Fonvielle 1907, pp. 54–55; Kennedy 1982, pp. 27–30.
55 The photograph taken on this occasion is the earliest known to show a flying apparatus, see Dollfus & Bouché 1938, p. 100.
56 Organized by the Aeronautical Society of Great Britain, June 25 – August 5 1868.

Nadar's Géant on display at the Crystal Palace in 1863. In the cabin there was, among other things, a darkroom for developing photographs. (Kennedy 1982, p. 28.)

among them "two machines constructed with the view of enabling a man to fly by his own muscular power," became a social occasion: "The Exhibition attracted great numbers of spectators, most of whom gazed in bewilderment at the inventive projects which were alleged to open the new age of aerial navigation."[57]

After the Aeronautical Exhibition the *Crystal Palace* seems to have become for decades a popular context for different aeronautical programmes in London. In 1873 the French balloonist Duruof made a highly successful public ascent by the *Crystal Palace,* and when the first English airship *Nulli Secundus* made its unlucky maiden journey in 1907, the destination was clear: "It landed at the Crystal Palace where, buffered by strong winds, it had to be deflated, ripped up, and carted back to its factory at Aldershot."[58] The *Crystal Palace* was so much connected to the idea of aviation that even in the novel *The War in the Air* (1908) by H. G. Wells, the inventor Alfred Butteridge's aeroplane makes its debut flight from the *Crystal Palace* to Glasgow and back. Moreover, we are told that this marvellous flying construction was secretly built inside Paxton's building.[59] Wells did not have to use much imagination since in real life the common history of exhibition buildings and aviation had by then reached almost symbiotic measures. Both the spacious halls and the entertaining context had proved useful. The Lebaudy airship had used the *Palais des Machines* of Paris as a hangar in 1903, and a year later the flamboyant young pilot Hubert Latham

. . . .

57 Penrose 1988, p. 113. On the muscle-powered machines, see *Report of the First Exhibition of the Aeronautical Society of Great Britain.* Greenwich: Henry and Richardson 1869, p. 8. There were, of course, all kinds of shows in the *Crystal Palace* from roses to cats and dogs.
58 Goldstein 1986, p. 67. On the flight of the feeble *Nulli Secundus*, see Wallace 1958, pp. 60–64. According to Beaver, "generations of Victorian balloonists ascended from the Palace." Beaver 1977, p. 116.
59 Wells 1909, pp. 24–28.

The Lebaudy airship using the Palais des Machines as a hangar in 1903. (Fonvielle 1907, p. 245.)

made a successful Channel crossing balloon voyage to a suburb of Paris, starting off where else but from the *Crystal Palace*.[60]

The intertwining history of these great and airy buildings and the fragile flying apparatuses is interesting in itself, but I would go further and suggest a more specific reading. According to a contemporary article in the *Art Journal*, there was "a cause of insecurity" in the *Crystal Palace*, rising from the apparent lightness of its supports as compared with the vastness of its dimensions. The feeling was overcome, however, when the visitor was informed that the strength of every separate part had been tested.[61] This feeling of uncertainty, caused by a construction made according to an unfamiliar logic, reoccurred fifty years later with the flying machines. The argument of the structure's tested strength was commonly used with the early aeroplanes, as it seemed unlikely to many viewers that such fragile constructions could possibly fly to the great blue yonder. The contradiction between the structure and the space was again apparent. Despite its frail and insecure appearance, the Wright Brothers' *Wright A* functioned well and the answer given as an explanation was that its parts had been carefully calculated and tested.[62]

Something in the logic of the *Crystal Palace* and the *Wright A*, as it appeared to contemporary viewers, was going in the same direction. The "mechanic building" and the flying machine were based on the same ironclad laws of engineering. It is no coincidence that Gustave Eiffel became an important pioneer of aerodynamics; in order to make his Tower stand securely he had to calculate the wind pressures with great care. We could therefore say that when Le Corbusier in the 1920s introduced aeroplanes as examples for architecture to follow he

. . . .

60 On Lebaudy, see Fonvielle 1907, pp. 251–153, also a photograph p. 245. On Latham, see Wallace 1958, p. 101. Aviation was popular and the *Crystal Palace* was by no means the only place in London where balloons were seen. In my opinion, however, the symbolical importance of the *Crystal Palace* is unequalled.
61 Quoted in Briggs 1988, p. 59.
62 The *Wright A* is the machine Wilbur Wright demonstrated in Europe in 1908, while the Wrights' first flying machine of 1903 is commonly called the *Wright Flyer*.

Architecture of the
"flying machine."
The unsuccessful
Roshon multiplane.
(Aviation. The Early
Years 1997, p. 163.)

was actually re-inventing something. The space inside the *Crystal Palace* and the *Palais des Machines* and the space outside the *Wright A* had been formed and conquered with the same logic of constructive minimalism. It may even be that the comments on the beauty of these two machines – the building you could fly in and the aeroplane that could serve as a model for your building – are rooted in one and the same emotion.[63]

Nature's Good Design

The period from the Great Exhibition of London 1851 to the *Exposition Universelle* of Paris in 1889 was remarkable in two ways.[64] The first cause of amazement was what I call the "mechanic buildings," a whole new category of iron and glass structures, starting with the *Crystal Palace* and reaching its zenith

. . . .

63 I do not know if Charles H. Gibbs-Smith ever discussed the matter, but the fact that he wrote books both on the early aviation and on the Great Exhibition has been of heuristic importance to me.

64 The exhibitions in Europe between these two were Paris 1855, 1867, 1878; London 1862; Wien 1873. On the history of the universal exhibitions, see Allwood 1977; Schroeder-Gudehus & Rasmussen 1992.

in 1889 with the erection of the *Palais des Machines* and the *Eiffel Tower*. This aspect we have already discussed. The second phenomenon, and the one we should now turn to, was the concept of moving machines, the "beautiful machines" admired by the public. In the 1889 exhibition one of the most popular attractions was the whole new palace full of moving machinery. It was also to remain the climax of the trend which had started with the machine hall at the *Crystal Palace*. By the time of the next *Exposition Universelle* (1900) the machines had lost much of their magic, partly because new machines called automobiles were seen moving every day on the streets and roads of Europe. Yet parallel to the machine halls we find another manifestation of mechanical movement.

The beauty – or the alleged ugliness – of the new buildings was a matter of architecture. Even the latest constructions could be discussed within the art and could be seen against its history. The moving machinery did not have a similar framework. Mechanical function and necessary calculations could be presented in technical journals but there aesthetic arguments had little space. Therefore we come across the idea of beautiful mechanical movement more easily in the context of another kind of science, namely animal physiology. The exhibition year 1889 saw the publication of Paul Souriau's book *L'Esthétique du mouvement*, a philosophical treatise on the beauty of a rather neglected area of common experience. Souriau's aesthetics is based on organic movement, and I will here only briefly point to the second part of his book, *La beauté mécanique*, and especially the section *La locomotion aérienne*. In his argumentation Souriau adapts an old metaphor and compares the muscular machine to a steam engine or to a water-wheel.[65] However, this animalization of machines works both ways and we can read the argument the other way round, saying that the machine movement is beautiful when it has characteristics similar to animal and human movement. Parallel thoughts about machines can be found, for example, in the work of the philosopher Jean Marie Guyau from 1884, *Les problèmes de l'esthetique contemporaine*. According to Guyau, the machine which best resembles a living creature is also the most beautiful.[66] For Guyau and Souriau, expression of force, both in animals and machines, is something that calls for admiration. But while Guyau compares the machine to prehistoric animals, Souriau takes up again the steam engine and the water-wheel and moves from there, via natural phenomena, to great iron constructions, such as the *Eiffel Tower*, and sees that the aesthetic is the same whether a thing is organic, inorganic, or man-made. Flight and flying things are no exception. Souriau suggests that as we admire the line drawn on a paper by an artist's hand, we might as well admire the beauty of the lines of a bird's flight in the sky and consider them as a

. . . .

65 "La machine musculaire est comme une machine à vapeur dont les cylindres mal alésés laisseraient du jeu au piston; ou encore comme une roue hydraulique dont les auges fuiraient." Souriau 1889, p. 81.
66 M. Guyau, *Les problèmes de l'esthetique contemporaine*. Paris: Alcan 1891, pp. 116–117. The book was first printed in 1884.

work of art.[67] Since Souriau believes in man's chances of building a glider and learning to soar, it is easy to conclude that people one day would look at man-made lines in the sky as artworks.[68] No surprise, then, that Wilbur Wright was called a poet in 1909, or that Alvar Aalto in 1921 wrote about reading the pilot's feelings from the curves his aeroplane makes in the air.[69]

Writers like Souriau and Guyau did not invent the aesthetics of animated machine themselves, for at least two influential books had foreshadowed their argumentation: J. Bell Pettigrew's *Animal Locomotion* and Etienne-Jules Marey's *La Machine Animale*, both published in 1873.[70] The two scientists made extensive experiments with insects and birds in order to measure their wing movements. Marey also made some brief comments on building a flying machine, and Pettigrew included in his book a whole dissertation on *Aëronautics*. If we compare their books and the one by Souriau, we soon observe that all three writers had different views about artificial flying. Souriau believed in soaring – the other two options being *vol vibrant* (insects) and *vol ramé* (birds) – while Marey thought that more scientific research was needed; he mentions the ingenious experimenter Alphonse Pénaud, whose designs had a propeller. Pettigrew, however, was convinced that he had found the secret of a successful flapping-wing machine.[71] When Pettigrew and Marey were cutting the wings of insects and the feathers of birds, or when they attached the animals to their scientific apparatuses, they always considered the living creatures to be beautifully designed little machines. Marey begins his book by pointing out that the old comparison of animals to machines can now be used more aptly than ever. Seeing animals as machines is not only legitimate but also highly useful.[72] Because the animal, say a bird, is a machine that functions well in the work it is designed for, it is logical to study it closely and find out its mechanism. With the help of this information man can then build an analogous machine, a flying machine that really works.

This leads us back to the partially addressed question of functional beauty. We value a machine that works, we might even call it beautiful because of this. In this respect we are not very different from the scientists of the nineteenth century admiring the ingenious design of birds. But what about a machine that

. . . .

67 "Nous admirons une ligne tracée sur un feuille de papier par la main d'un artiste. Mais il peut y avoir, non seulement autant de grâce, mais de beauté veritable dans la courbe décrite dans la ciel par l'oiseau qui vole. Pourquoi ne dirions-nous pas que cette courbe, elle aussi, est une oeuvre d'art?" Souriau 1889, p. 161.

68 On artificial flying, Souriau 1889, pp. 157–159.

69 On Wright, see Wohl 1994, p. 27. On Aalto, see below p. 101.

70 Of the two Marey soon became internationally known. His name appears in wide range of texts from Verne's *Robur-le-Conquérant* to Bragaglia's "Futurist Photodynamism" (see Apollonio 1973, pp. 38–45.) Eadweard Muybridge, another important figure, published his photographic survey *Animal Locomotion* in 1887.

71 Souriau 1889, pp. 146–159; Marey 1873, p. 288; Pettigrew 1874, pp. 235–258. Marey's work may have overshadowed Pettigrew's ideas about organic movement. However, Pettigrew's design for a *Compound Wave Wing* comes closer to some later ornithopters, such as Tatlin's *Letatlin*.

72 Marey 1873, v–vi. "La comparaison des animaux aux machines n'est pas seulement légitime, elle est aussi d'une utilité extrême à différents points de vue."

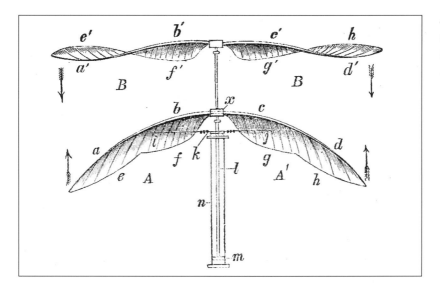

J. Bell Pettigrew's
Compound Wave
Wing. (Pettigrew
1874, p. 243.)

does not fulfil its function? How did people see a machine, animal-shaped or
not, when it proposed only a dream or could not keep its promise of functionality? Many of the technical examples discussed in this study fall into this
category of "underachievers," yet it would be difficult to argue that they were
therefore seen as ugly. For Wells ugliness may have been the measure of imperfection, but for anyone who has ever dreamed of breaking the bonds of gravity
even the unsuccessful contemporary proposals for an aeroplane are likely to
have been shapely. Imperfect, maybe, poor in their constructive thought, possibly,
but strangely beautiful without question. The beauty we are discussing here has
its own character. First of all, it does not carry with it a flavour of nostalgia. The
objects of this beauty are something new and contemporary, not yet abstracted
to a museological distance. [73] At the same time they are built to perform something that has never been done before. If they succeed, like the *Wright Flyer*,
then the simplicity of the technical solution adds to the amazement. If they fail,
as is the case with Ader's bat-analogous *Avion III*, the complicated technical
ingenuity and boldness of the original vision may nevertheless suffice to make it
beautiful, at least to some viewers.

. . . .

73   Much of machine aesthetics today is nostalgic. For the discourse of nostalgic beauty see any
     publication dedicated to old cars, trains, or aeroplanes. For an attempt to talk about *new*
     functional beauty, see for instance Gelernter, who writes about the beauty of computer
     programs: "The beauty of a proof or a machine lies in a happy marriage of simplicity and
     power – *power* meaning the ability to accomplish a wide range of tasks, get a lot done [...] I
     call this type of beauty 'machine beauty'." David Gelernter, *Machine Beauty. Elegance and
     the Heart of Technology*. New York: Basic Book 1998, p. 2.

Future and Machines

"It was not until the very end of the nineteenth century that Rudyard Kipling could advocate a new poetry celebrating the essential beauty of the machine," wrote Herbert Sussman in the 1960s.[74] His timing for the moment when Victorian poetry recognizes machines is most likely to be correct, yet hardly interesting news.[75] As Sussman himself later concluded, the deep-seated confusion about the aesthetic value of the machine was due to the traditional literary conventions.[76] The machine was not so much looked at as itself but as a symbol, something that suggests a complex meaning beyond itself. But even in cases where the literary conventions were radically changed, the role of the machine often remained confused.

When the Italian Futurists made themselves known to the world in 1909, they did it with words instead of art. The text of their manifesto was by Filippo Tommaso Marinetti, a poet who certainly understood the value of good rhetoric – deservedly his writing has been called a brilliant piece of strategy.[77] But the successful launch on the front page of *Le Figaro* entailed a problem: how to live up to promise. It was not as easy as the tall talk about burning the museums, and it actually took them several years to produce artworks matching their striking name. The best part of the fury of the Futurist manifestos was directed against contemporary academic art and its good taste, described as "nauseous." The Futurists shouted that they were bored with safety and stability, and longed for a faster and more dangerous life. It is still surprising, however, to see how the early Futurists wanted to express something dynamic in their art, not by painting cars or aeroplanes but horses instead (Boccioni, *The City Rises*, 1910–1911), or depicting, in a famous study on movement, a sausage dog walking (Balla, *Dynamism of a Dog on a Leash*, 1912). Although at times the Futurists have enjoyed a reputation for being among first artists to promote machines, around 1909 at least they did not understand very much about inorganic machines – moving or unmoving.

Futurism started as a literary movement, not as a technical club. But in the literary context their relation to machines may appear even less futuristic than in painting. In France, where Marinetti had studied, balloons and other flying apparatuses had appeared in literature from the 1860s onwards. Bicycles, too, had been turned into vehicles of narrative line, as in 1898 in Maurice Leblanc's *Voici des ailes!*[78] Finally in 1907 Octave Mirbeau dedicated his book *La 628-E-*

. . . .

74   Sussman 1968, pp. 2–3.
75   There is of course literature and art dealing with the new world already in the eighteenth century. A classic study on the subject is Klingender 1975. However, the eighteenth century poems on mines and cotton factories do not seem to talk about the beauty of the machines.
76   Sussman 1968, p. 229.
77   Martin 1968, p. 36. For a well contextualized history of Futurism, see Edwards 1987.
78   Jules Verne's novel *Cinq semaines en ballon* came out in 1863, but it was only ten years later that Verne himself flew with Eugène Godard's balloon. The story of a heavier-than-air machine *Robur le Conquérant* was published in 1886. On Leblanc's novel, see Carter 1992, pp. 58–60.

8 to his first automobile, to his "docile and precise instrument of penetration." For Mirbeau the automobile was not only an entertainment, but something bigger: "[…] she is my life, my artistic and spiritual life, just as much as my house, and even more."[79] What Marinetti in his turn introduced was a strong and breathless rhythm, not a fresh look at the machine.[80] Apart from its distinctive style, the first Futurist manifesto adds surprisingly little new on technology to the words of Thomas Carlyle who, describing his first train journey in 1839, had written: "We went over the tops of houses – one town or village I saw clearly, with its chimney heads vainly stretching up towards us – under the stars, not under the clouds but among them. Out of one vehicle into another, snorting, roaring we flew: the likest thing to Faust's flight on the Devil's mantle; or as if some huge steam night-bird had flung you on its back, and was sweeping through unknown space with you, most probably toward London."[81] It was also Carlyle who already in 1829 had described, himself more anguished than proud, the new feeling of omnipotence the machine had given to man, the feeling which we find later – with added cockiness and artistic bombast – in the manifestations of the Futurists: "We remove mountains, and make seas our smooth highway; nothing can resist us. We war with the rude Nature; and by our resistless engines, come off always victorious, and loaded with spoils."[82] Marinetti's descriptions of the contemporary technical world reveal a gap between poetry and provocation on the one hand and observation and analysis on the other. It is true that the first Futurist manifesto famously affirmed a racing car to be more beautiful than the *Victory of Samothrace*, and trains, steamers, and aeroplanes were mentioned together with places like railway stations, shipyards, and factories. And yet, if we study them closely, the first manifestos of 1909 and 1910 have nothing that would suggest a concentrated look at the machine, especially at the aeroplane.[83]

Some people have seen the matter differently, at least in passing. In the 1960s Reyner Banham wrote: "For aircraft there was not, and could not be, any comparable tradition of enthusiasm [as for locomotives]. The first demonstrably successful European machine was the Voisin Canard flown by Santos Dumont in 1906 near Paris. However, any widespread eye-witness experience of aircraft, such as Marinetti must have enjoyed in order to write a passage so conspicu-

. . . .

79 "[…] cet instrument docile et précis de pénétration que'est l'automobile […] elle est ma vie, ma vie artistique et spirituelle, autant et plus que ma maison." Octave Mirbeau, *La 628-E8*. Paris: Bibliothèque Charpentier 1910, ix–x. For a short survey of modern themes in French literature 1880–1930, see Nathan 1971.

80 It has been suggested that Marinetti's idiosyncratic rhetoric may have been directly influenced by the essays of the Italian critic Mario Morasso, who wrote about "The Aesthetics of Speed" and "The Heroes of the Machine" in the early 1900s. See Martin 1968, pp. 42–43.

81 Quoted in Sussman 1968, p. 25.

82 Quoted in Marx 1964, p. 171.

83 I am referring to the three first manifestos from February 1909 to April 1910. See Apollonio 1973, pp. 19–31. Robert Wohl's comment, that Marinetti shows little interested in or knowledge of the construction of contemporary aircraft, can also be extended to other machines. (Wohl 1994, p. 139.)

ously different from H. G. Wells's imaginative projections of aviation, must have waited on the Wright Brothers' European tour of 1908."[84] Banham's remark raises some questions. We can ask if Marinetti, whose Futuristic hero was an African giant with a sexual organ eleven metres long, really had to see an aeroplane in order to write differently from Wells, who had suggested that when the Martians come and conquer our planet they will first land in the Surrey countryside.[85] The sentence in the First Manifesto to which Banham most likely refers – in fact the only possible sentence – is the following: "[...] the sleek flight of planes whose propellers chatter in the wind like banners and seem to cheer like an enthusiastic crowd."[86] Is this really an eye-witness report of the most amazing machine of its day? Is the chatter of the propellers all that the grandiloquent poet has to say when he has watched the first flying aeroplane? Marinetti, for one thing, was not born to be mild, and in the light of his words it is difficult to believe that he had seen an aeroplane fly when he wrote the first manifesto. Instead it looks as if he had learned from the numerous newspaper articles that the propellers of the *Wright A* made a distinctive sound. It adds a nice contemporary flavour to the text but tells nothing of his personal interest in the machine.[87] The same can be said about the dedication of his 1909 play *Poupées électriques* to Wilbur Wright. The play has nothing to do with flying or aeroplanes, and the gesture of hailing the man of the moment only proves how acutely Marinetti wanted to be seen as a modern up-to-date author.[88] This is not to say that he was unaware of aeroplanes. The poet eventually flew as a passenger in September 1910, and in the following year he started to write the poem *Le Monoplan du pape* (1912). What the lively gestures of the Futurist may prevent us from seeing, however, is that there were artists who already before the first Futurist manifesto had a much closer relationship with machines, especially aeroplanes.[89]

. . . .

84   Banham 1967, p. 104, n. 5. There are some inaccuracies in Banham's note. Santos-Dumont's plane was his own design *14-bis*, not the *Voisin Canard*, which in turn was built in 1911. Wilbur Wright made the flights in France alone in 1908 while Orville was demonstrating their machine in the U.S.A.

85   Marinetti's novel *Mafarka – il futurista* [Mafarka the Futurist] was published in 1909 (Edwards 1987, p. 23), H. G. Wells's *The War of the Worlds* in 1898. Wells lived in Woking where the first Martians landed.

86   "[...] le vol glissant des aéroplanes, dont l'hélice a des claquements drapeau et des applaudissements de foule enthousiaste." The English translation as in Apollonio 1973, p. 22.

87   Robert Wohl has pointed out that the first manifesto came only six weeks after Wilbur Wright had completed his season of flights in Le Mans, and wonders if this is was mere coincidence. (Wohl 1994, p. 138.) Considering the news coverage, these things can be linked. Marinetti certainly had all reason to be sensitive to excitement about flying, but it is altogether another thing to conclude, as Banham did, that he had already seen an aeroplane in action.

88   According to Wohl, the dedication is to Wright "who knew how to raise our migrating hearts higher than the captivating mouths of women." *ibid.*, p. 2.

89   There is ample material supporting the Futurists' predilection for flying machines, but it seems that none of it was produced before 1912, and most of it later. See Bergman 1962, pp. 136–141. Also *Futurismo & Futurismi*. Milan: Bompiani 1986, p. 423. It should be also noted that in 1912 Balla painted not only the famous dog but also works entirely abstract.

Pilot Henri Farman painting.
(Collection de Mme H.
Farman.)

Learning to Fly

In the early stages of their careers, the Futurists did not aestheticize the mechanical movements of machines but those of animals, and as artist-admirers of aeroplanes they were already latecomers. Other artists had reacted much faster, and by 1908 some were already flying towards the future. After the first European flights of Wilbur Wright in 1908, the newspaper *L'Illustration* quoted the words of one eye-witness, Léon Delagrange: "If the machine is already amazing to look at in repose, especially when one knows it is an aeroplane, it is still more amazing to see it manoeuvre."[90] Delagrange was a professional sculptor who had ordered an aeroplane in 1907 and become one of the pioneering pilots in Europe. He also became one of the first to die in a "futuristic" accident when his plane crashed in Bordeaux in 1910. Delagrange, however, was not the only artist who bought himself wings. Henri Farman, the most famous pilot in Europe before Blériot, was a racing cyclist and a painter who, like Delagrange, had studied at the Beaux-Arts in Paris. Delagrange's fellow student, the sculptor Thérèse Peltier, became the first woman to travel in an aeroplane. But despite their youth these people were not young radicals. Their rather conservative artistic vision seems to have had little connection with the world of machines and the joys of aviation. Their background in art could be easily passed off as insignificant if there had not been so many others like them in the aviating community.

. . . .
90   *L'Illustration* 15 August 1908. Quoted in Gibbs-Smith 1974, p. 289.

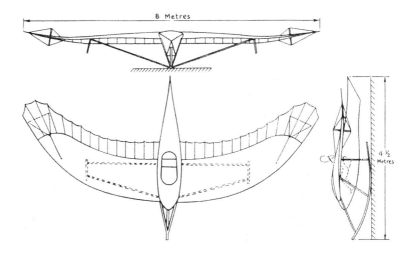

A glider designed by the painter José Weiss. (Welch 1965, p. 42.)

Artists and aviation had come together already in the 1890s, at the time of Otto Lilienthal's famous glider experiments. The German painter Arnold Böcklin, well known for his work *Toteninsel*, made plans for a flying machine, while his somewhat obscure Swiss colleague, Carl Steiger, published a surprising book on the same subject.[91] Of the two artists Steiger deserves the fuller study. His book is an exceptional piece of independent work and comes not only with calculations but with sixteen pages full of fine free-hand drawings, including bird anatomy and highly original aeroplane designs.[92] At the beginning of the twentieth century, flying machines attracted artists such as Czeslaw Tanski, an established painter who eventually became the father of Polish aviation, and the French-born landscape artist José Weiss, who lived in Britain and made extensive experiments with gliders. There was Henri-Marie Coanda, a student of sculpture from Rumania, who turned to engineering and built the prototype of an extraordinary "jet-plane" in 1910.[93] And in faraway Finland the

. . . .

91 On Böcklin's ideas, see Ferdinand Runkel & Carlo Böcklin (eds.), *Neben meiner Kunst. Flugstudien, Briefe und Persönliches von und über Arnold Böcklin*. Berlin: Vita 1909, especially pp. 197–216. Böcklin visited Otto Lilienthal in 1894; see Seifert 1992, pp. 109–110.

92 Carl Steiger, *Vogelflug und Flugmaschine*. München: G. Franz 1891. Twenty years later Steiger published another book on aeronautics (*Flugwiderstand und Segelflug*, Zürich 1911), but I have not been able to see it.

93 On Henri Farman, see Sahel 1936; Farman 1910, pp. 41–58; entries in Lassalle 1962 and Riverain 1970. On Léon Delagrange: *Dictionnaire de Biographie Française* (tome 10, col. 641). Paris: Libraire Letouzey 1965; entries in Lassalle 1962 and Riverain 1970. On José Weiss: Nahum 1995, pp. 245–247; Welch 1965, pp. 41–43; Peter Lewis. *British Aircraft 1809–1914*. London: Putnam 1962, pp. 520–525. On Czeslaw Tanski: Jerzy B. Cynk. *Polish Aircraft 1893–1939*. London: Putnam 1971, pp. 8–22.
Delagrange, Peltier, Tanski and Weiss are also included in the Thieme-Becker *Künstlerlexikon*. 37 vols. Leipzig: Engelmann & Seemann 1907–1950. Farman gave up art before he started his flying career, but it seems that Delagrange even exhibited one of his works beside his aeroplane in the eleventh exhibition of automobiles, cycles, and sports in 1908. The small work can be seen dimly in the photograph published in *Flight* 3/1909, p. 34.

first aeroplane was bought by Adolf Aarno, a sculptor whose artworks gave no indication that his last exhibition in 1911 would consist of nothing but a flying machine on a pedestal. His case will be discussed in detail in Part Two. What these people had in common was probably simply excitement, but contemporaries noted that their artistic inclination might also give them a different view on machines. Writing on Delagrange, the reporter François Peyrey suggested that the artist's eye, which usually caresses the harmonious curve of woman's waist and the roundness of her breast may also find the hard lines of engine's steel structure agreeable.[94]

Aviation was hugely popular and one did not have to be an artist to get excited about the subject. However, it seems that aviation attracted two kinds of artists. The well known names are those talented painters who during the 1910s and 1920s drew inspiration either from the forms and materials of the new inventions, Robert Delaunay and Fernand Léger for example, or from the spiritual aspects of ascension, as did Kazimir Malevich.[95] Then there were those lesser artists, like Delagrange and Farman, who gave up art to become pilots themselves. It is easy to find similar examples from literature. Aviation caught the imagination of some authors to such a degree that they actually bought themselves aeroplanes: the Russian Futurist poet Vasili Kamensky is the most famous example. Others went flying in someone else's aeroplane: Gabriel D'Annunzio is known for this, less well known is the young Hermann Hesse.[96] Some authors were excited by the flying machines and their brave pilots but remained firmly on the ground and reported their feelings. Franz Kafka wrote an article on the Brescia Airshow in 1909, while Marcel Proust incorporated his aeroplane enthusiast secretary into his *A la recherche du temps perdu*. Learning to fly solo the unlucky secretary first made a successful emergency landing in the sea, but sank with the plane a moment later.[97] In poetry in particular the pleasures and perils of flying proved to be a popular subject, not least because of the wealth of available metaphors.[98]

. . . .

94 "L'oeil artiste qui caresse la courbe harmonieuse d'une hanche ou la rondeur d'un sein, peut-il aussi se complaire à suivre les lignes arides d'une épure, à sonder les poumons d'acier d'un moteur!" Peyrey 1909, p. 284.

95 Léger's work will be discussed later in this study; on Malevich and Delaunay in 1910s, see the chapter "Painters take Flight" in Wohl 1994, pp. 157–200. Christina Lodder has recently argued that Malevich's ideas were not only spiritual but closely connected to the material side of flying, such as aerial photographs and images of flying aeroplanes. ("Malevich and Flight: Beyond the Spiritual," unpublished paper 2001.)

96 On Kamensky, see Wohl 1994, pp. 145–153; Wohl gives him the title "The first authentic aviator-poet." (ibid., p. 153.) On D'Annunzio, ibid., pp. 114–122. On Hesse, see Ingold 1987, p. 305 and 307.

97 Franz Kafka, *Die Aeroplane in Brescia*. On Kafka, see Wohl 1994, pp. 111–114. On Proust and aviation, see Carter 1992, pp. 133–205.

98 On aviation in literature, see for instance Goldstein 1986, and on poetry especially Felix Philipp Ingold, *Literatur und Aviatik (Europäische Flugdichtung 1909 bis 1927)*, Schriftenreihe der Eidgenössischen Technischen Hochschule Zürich, Poly 7, Basel-Stuttgart 1978. Aviation poetry was at times really popular. The first competition of "air poetry" was announced by the Académie Française in June, 1909. (See Lista 1973; Wohl 1994, p. 260.) According to one estimation more poèms were written about Charles Lindbergh and his flight than about any other personage or event in Western history (see Corn 1983, pp. 23–24.), but I suspect the calculation does not include Jesus or the Virgin Mary.

A 1851 machine built in the Egyptian style. (Pevsner 1951, p. 24.)

The pioneering and poetic years of aviation were short-lived and after the First World War the aeroplane was no longer a new curiosity causing amazement but a functional everyday machine carrying mail and well-to-do passengers. This did not necessarily diminish the aesthetic dimension of the aeroplane but it tended rather to underline its usefulness.

À Propos

The new attitude to the flying machine, as well as to other things discussed in above, is revealed in an essay by the painter Piet Mondrian from 1919–1920. In a few words Mondrian sums up a new twentieth-century conception of machine beauty. Reading it now we can sense the shift from the first expressions of fascination in the mid-1850s to a matter-of-fact statement of the 1920s: "The beauty of pure function is demonstrated by many objects of every day use. A simple drinking glass is beautiful, so is an automobile and an airplane. And, to cite only things of our own time, so are works of modern engineering bridges, factories, and so on, in metal or concrete."[99] Mondrian's neutral and impassive words may sound like the end of the matter, but that, of course, is an illusion. The discussion about simplicity of form and purity of function was far from over, and the vocabulary used by Mondrian was not to everyone's liking. In the late 1920s, the poet Ezra Pound was working on an essay on machine art. He

· · · · · · · · ·
99   Mondrian 1995, p. 64.

Ezra Pound's 1930 example of 'Gothic' form; the Kearsage crane. (Pound 1996, p. 99.)

found some contemporary machines still representing erroneous, almost Victorian ideas: "I am not so sure about the Kearsage crane. I chose it as an illustration of 'Gothic' form, I dislike the Gothic, and I believe, on perhaps the too flimsy basis of hearsay, that the Kearsage crane does not work to complete satisfaction. I suspect that cranes will be improved, and that their increasing effiency will bring them nearer to Egyptian or Roman form."[100] This shunning of Gothic and yearning for great classical simplicity – Pound clearly was not at home with the Greeks – is something that we also find reappearing in the 1920s texts by Le Corbusier and Amédée Ozenfant, who saw no difficulties in combining *esprit nouveau* and the *Parthenon*, that is, the machine and the utopian past. In 1924, the same, strange combination of new spirit and old ideals made the young architect Alvar Aalto describe his aeroplane voyage towards Venice, not as the most Futuristic, but the first Hellenic day of his life.[101] It was total victory for the *Victory of Samothrace*.

· · · · · · · · ·

100 Pound 1996, p.69. The text was written 1927–1930 and first published in 1987.
101 Schildt 1984, p.136. For the famous Greek temple, see *The Parthenon and its impact in modern times*. Athens: Melissa Publishing House 1994. A magnificent book with the interesting photographs: "Eisenhower inspects the Parthenon by helicopter in 1952" (p. 292) and "Junkers aeroplane demonstrated in Athens October 1930" (p. 295).

2.
Middle

■ Paris 1900: The Steam-Powered Bat

Remember that your flying machine must imitate no other than the bat, because the web is what by its union gives the armour, or strength to the wings. [1]

Leonardo da Vinci

Architecture was to be given up a few weeks after I had set eyes on Ader's Avion. [2]

Gabriel Voisin

We can imagine that there was something frightening in the appearance of the machine. It was beautifully constructed, no question of that; the precision of its strange and complex parts, the choice of the materials, their meticulous finishing, and the loving attention to detail were apparent, yet something in its giant bat wings and its eight sharp-edged propeller blades made one apprehensive. But was there really anything to be afraid of? Anyone could see that the large wings were covered with a fabric of silk, like skin or parchment, and the blades of the bamboo propellers looked like quill pens. Was not then the whole thing but one big fabrication, a weird tale written to scare an unsuspecting child? And still, it did not feel like fiction, quite the opposite. It was all too real, all too much a harbinder of the new time coming. As a long awaited flying machine it was a dream become a nightmare; a flyer with a fearful symmetry, a bat out of hell. Moments of reflection in the shadow of its sixteen metre wingspan gave many visitors the shivers; it was not a metaphor of one of them going up in the clear blue sky, but a metaphor of someone suddenly coming down from the dark clouds over them. It was a war machine.

. . . .

1   *The Notebooks of Leonardo da Vinci*, ed. Jean Paul Richter. New York: Dover 1970, vol. II, p. 278.
2   Voisin 1963, p. 106.

Attraction

On a warm and sunny day, at the age of fifty-nine, Clément Ader received his gold medal.[3] He was very proud of it, as were all the other 8,888 (eight thousand eight hundred and eighty-eight) individuals and companies who were given a similar *diplôme de medaille d'or* at the *Exposition Universelle* of Paris in 1900. Like all the previous universal exhibitions, it was a major event. Only this time it was something more: it was huge, enormous. A young student of architecture named Gabriel Voisin was employed as a draughtsman during the massive construction work and saw it all from the inside: "The work was being scamped in a gradually mounting disorder by men who were at the end of their tether. We were continually harassed because of the delays. The Universal Exhibition of 1900 was a hell alongside which Dante's seemed to me to be an elysian resting place."[4] Once open, the exhibition proved to be even more crowded than the pits described by Dante; during the six months from April till November it attracted over fifty million visitors.[5] If even half of them stopped and looked at Ader's award-winning invention, then he had certainly made his *Avion III* the best known flying machine in the world. The exhibition jury, on the other hand, had a very positive feeling about it – they were sure that Ader's construction attracted a glance from every visitor.[6] The only problem was that *Avion III* had never flown. Fifty million pairs of eyes were staring at a nonfunctional machine.

This was not the first time Clément Ader exhibited a flying apparatus. He was a recognized professional inventor with a well respected name in technical circles. Ader had started his career in the 1860s with a small innovation in railway technology but had later turned his attention to more delicate things. Ader was not only talented, he also had an eye for the coming trends: during the two following decades he made a fortune with his telephones.[7] What interests us, however, is that from 1870 onwards his mind was also occupied by the dream of flight. Ader may have caught the spark of interest from his friend Felix Tournachon, better remembered as Nadar, the famous photographer and well-known balloonist, who in the 1860s had promoted the idea of a heavier-than-air machine.[8] It was in Nadar's atelier that Ader in 1874 exhibited his first "bird," an

. . . .

3   It is not known to me on which day Ader received his medal. The idea of sun and warmth is based on the information of the meteorological averages in Paris on July 1900 (24 h temperature 21.56 °C, precipitation 33.3 mm). See *World Weather Records*. Smithsonian Miscellaneous Collections, Vol. 79. City of Washington: The Smithsonian Institution 1944, pp. 498–499.

4   Voisin 1963, p. 100.

5   The official number of visitors was 50,860,801. The number of the diplomas granted was 45,905, including the 8,889 gold medal diplomas. For these as well as for other interesting statistics, see Schroeder-Gudehus & Rasmussen 1992.

6   "[…] a certainement attiré les regards de tous les visiteurs." Printed in Gibbs-Smith 1968, p. 177. *Avion III* was classified in section VI *Génie civil, moyens de transport*, in the sub-section 34. *Aérostation*.

7   For a list of Ader's patents in France and abroad, see Lissarrague 1990, pp. 276–279.

8   See Nadar 1866.

Clément Ader's prize-winning AVION III. (Maurice Rheims, Kunst um 1900. Wien–München: Verlag Anton Scroll 1965, pic. 559.)

engineless model with wings made of goose-feathers.[9] In the course of the years the idea grew bigger and the plans became more detailed, until in 1882 Ader started to build his first motorized flying machine. The result of his toil, the steam-powered tractor monoplane *Éole*, was in turn displayed at the *Pavillion de la Ville de Paris* in October 1891, a year after Ader had managed to make a brief jump with it. Unfortunately, there seems to be very little information concerning the exhibition, other than what Ader himself wrote about it sixteen years later.[10]

Secret Weapon

The standard histories of early aviation have traditionally been interested in the flight attempts, not in the displays. Yet exhibiting was one important part of the development of these apparatuses, and it can be said with all fairness that Ader was neither the first nor the last engineer whose aeronautical inventions performed best when presented indoors.[11] This was true especially with the *Éole*. Ader had first thought about attracting publicity for his invention but the

. . . .

9   Gibbs-Smith 1968, p. 9. The same "bird" was shown later in 1883 in the Aeronautical Exhibition at the Trocadero.

10   Ader mentions the exhibition in his book *La Première Étape de l'Aviation Militaire* (1907); see Gibbs-Smith 1968, pp. 14–15 and 184–185, and Lissarrague 1990, p. 113. Ader's leap with his *Éole* on 9 October 1890 is generally accepted as the first piloted powered takeoff in history. Some French authors have even claimed that it was a flight.

11   In the studies of Ader's career in aviation Gibbs-Smith (1968) and Carlier (1990) briefly mention the exhibitions in 1898, 1900, and 1908, while Lissarrague (1990) does not pay any attention to them.

character of the exhibition changed when he managed to establish contact with the French army officials. The Minister of War himself arrived to see the machine. In his eyes Ader's distinguished career and long experience augured well for the exciting new invention, and the result of the display and the ensuing negotiations was that the work now continued as a secret project. Ader received a generous subsidy from the government and became an advocate of military aviation. However, the making of the flying machine progressed slowly, and it took Ader six years before he was ready to organize his next exhibition.[12] In June 1898, Ader printed special invitation cards for the first occasion of displaying his latest invention, the *Avion III*. This time he invited influential civilian guests, as well as representatives of the press, to a private view in his own workshop, rather grandiosely named *Laboratoire d'Aviation*.[13] Again, there was not much he could do with his machine except to display it.

The only attempt to make the *Avion III* fly had failed eight months earlier and Ader's career as an aeroplane designer had come to an abrupt end.[14] The contract Ader had signed with the French Ministry of War in 1892 for building a flying machine had guaranteed him a substantial income during these years, but soon after the unsuccessful secret test the officials decided to withdraw their liberal financial support.[15] It had finally occurred to the men at the Ministry of War that Ader would not be able to build them a machine to fly six hours at a height of several hundred metres, carrying either two men or one man and a bombload, as defined in the contract.[16] In retrospect it is easy to see more reasons behind the failure than just the client's unrealistic expectations. After all, the machine had not flown a single instant, with or without bombs.[17] Beyond doubt Ader was an excellent engineer and the small and powerful steam-engines he had built for his aeroplane were probably the best in the world, but at the same time he had paid very little attention to aerodynamics and had taken no notice of the discoveries of other aviation pioneers. Ever since his first

. . . .

12   After the contract Ader first started building a new single propeller plane, *Avion II*, but he abondoned it before it was finished and designed then the twin-engine *Avion III*.

13   Picture of the invitation card in Gibbs-Smith 1968, p. 27.

14   Ader's tests with his machines are not within the scope of this book. For detailed discussions, see Gibbs-Smith 1968, Carlier 1990, and Lissarrague 1990. They present slightly different versions of the activities and achievements of Ader. In France his reputation has been carefully protected and Lissarrague has done his best to refute Gibbs-Smith's claims that Ader fabricated stories about his flight tests. Whether or not Ader made one or two tests with his *Éole*, and whether or not *Avion III* was ever airborne is not important to us. It seems, however, that when Lissarrague talks about *un vol* he has one kind of criterion for Ader and another kind for foreigners.

15   Ader received at least 600,000 francs. It has been calculated (Lissarrague 1990, p. 132) that in 1990 francs it makes over 97 million! No wonder that he could have twenty-two employees working in his laboratory. See Carlier 1990, pp. 60–61.

16   It is difficult to say if Ader sincerely believed that he could build such a machine. For the details of the contract, see Lissarrague 1990, pp. 134–136.

17   Lissarrague emphatically disagrees: "Le vol de 300 mètres à Satory du 14 octobre 1897 est une certitude." Lissarrague 1990, p. 207. According to Carlier, the flight can be neither confirmed nor refuted, see Carlier 1990, p. 219. Gibbs-Smith 1968 is based on the argument that the flight never happened. This way or that, the result was that the machine broke down, the tests were ended, and the army lost its interest in the matter.

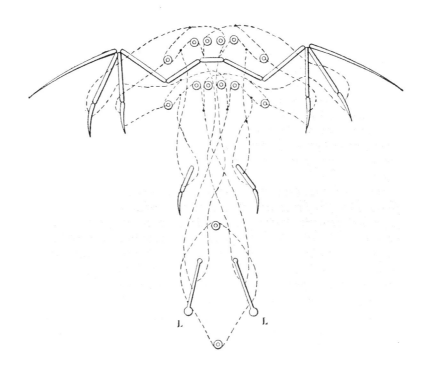

The system of "organic" movements in Ader's flying apparatus Éole 1890. (Gibbs-Smith 1968, p. 153.)

L   L

apparatus *Éole,* Ader had stubbornly imitated the form of a bat without really considering what a bat's flight is usually like.[18] Yet, it is interesting that in the design of the would-be war machine *Avion III* Ader was using a "biological metaphor" instead of a mechanistic one, thus reflecting the contemporary discussions on animal locomotion, as well as foreshadowing the twentieth-century *biotechnik* approach in solving mechanical problems.[19]

But the machine shown to a selected audience in 1898, and to the public at large in 1900, was not a solution to a problem. Like everyone else in the business, Ader could but tell the world that he had not found the secret of motorized flying – yet. As the contract with the army was dropped, Ader tried to lure wealthy investors – the private viewing of the *Avion III* in 1898 probably served

· · · · · · · · ·

18 The most diverting thing in both *Éole* and *Avion III* was the way their wings could be folded in for storage, just as bats do when they go to sleep. In Germany Otto Lilienthal used a very similar idea in the gliders he patented in 1894 and 1895.

19 The reference is not to gene technology but to machines designed following zoological ideas. On *Biotechnik* and flapping wing machines, see Nahum 1995. For the 'bionic' elements in Ader's construction, see Biruta Kresling's article and her excellent drawings of the details of *Avion III* and of the bones and strings of the 'flying dog' (*Plecotus auritus*). "La 'Chauve-souris' de Clément Ader," *La revue du Musée des arts et métiers,* No 13 December 1995, pp. 23–30. For pictures of Ader's constructions, see *ICARE, revue de l'aviation française.* No 134, 3/1990 ("Le Dossier Ader") and Pierre Lissarague, "Nouvelles photographies de l'atelier d'Ader," *Pégase.* No 68, Janvier 1993, pp. 12–120.
Avion III was simpler than *Éole,* which had proved very unstable. According to Gibbs-Smith: "The bewildering complexity of wing-movements on the *Éole* were included by Ader in order to reproduce mechanically as many as possible of the wing-movements of the bat […]." Gibbs-Smith 1968, p. 85.

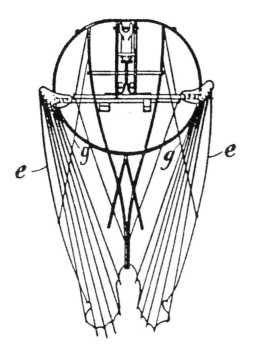

The method of folding wings. From Lilienthal's patent 20 August 1895. (Seifert & Wassermann 1992, p. 107.)

this purpose – but without success. Other attempts to generate interest were equally disappointing. One of the last hopes failed when Ader's brief note on the *Avion III* was presented to the *Académie des Sciences* in 1898 by its distinguished member Etienne-Jules Marey.[20] Marey had promoted the idea of *la machine animale* twenty-five years earlier. He had painstakingly photographed and measured the movements of flying birds, and was certainly one of the best experts in the world to evaluate whether the bio-technical concept of the *Avion III* was useful or not. But the response from the academic circles was deadly silence; it seemed that nobody had faith in Ader's machine. It was almost ready for the museum.

New Century

Although by 1900 the problem of motorized flying remained unsolved, the *Avion III* was indeed a memory from the past. Ader had given up his *recherches d'avionneur*[21] in 1897, but such was the progress made in aviation that only three years after its completion Ader's steam-powered machine started to look like an extinct animal or an archeological relic. It had been an exceptional

. . . .
20   The text read by Marey is printed in Gibbs-Smith 1968, pp. 175–176.
21   The word is one of Ader's neologisms. *Avionneur* – Qui travaille à l'avionnerie. *Avionnerie* – Art de construire les avions. *Avion* – Véhicule, appareil aérien ailé. (Carlier 1990, p. 61.)

construction from the beginning but now its formative idea was lagging far behind the progressive mainstream. The good thing in this was that Ader did not have to pay any admission fees for the *Exposition Universelle*, simply because his *Avion III* was taken in as a part of the retrospective exhibition.[22] Ader's machine had turned into a curiosity: it was an odd and scary looking machine but worse than that, it was now officially *passé*.

In the context of the great 1900 world fair both the appearance of *Avion III* and the stories of its shortlived history clearly represented an earlier period. The general atmosphere of the exhibition was quite different from the previous one eleven years earlier. There seemed to be changes in the novelty value of technology in general and even the more conventional machines were not met with the same enthusiasm as before. While the 1889 exhibition had been famous for its great technological achievements, the *Eiffel Tower*, the moving board walk, and the *Palais des Machines,* the public at the turn of the century was more concerned with new fashions and the new artistic style, *Art Nouveau*, than with heavy technology. Stuart Durant has pointed out that "The Universal Exhibition of 1889, far more than the Paris Exhibition of 1900, marked a turning point in our collective history. The prognostications of Jules Verne and H. G. Wells, and our subsequent obsession with the technological millenium, have their roots in 1889. For it was 1889, not 1900, that so many elements in the agenda for our own century – cultural, technical and architectural – were adumbrated."[23] Machines were shown, of course, yet their palace was no longer the main attraction but "was eclipsed by the plaster and ceramic rococo envelope of the *Chateau d'Eau*. Inside the machines had to share their glory with Menier chocolate, Champagne, Grey Poupon mustard, and Amiex preserves."[24] The 1900 exhibition launched consumerism instead of industrialism and came alive with electricity, not with steam engines. Amidst the flamboyant national pavilions and the general architectural chaos the focus of the exhibition was on the *Palais de l'Électricité* with its giant dynamos.[25] There were sown the seeds of the aesthetics of the future, from electric kitchen devices to colourful neon lights. The change in atmosphere was so dramatic that only nine years later the mighty iron and glass structure of the *Palais des Machines* would be demolished and lost forever.[26]

. . . .

22   The iniative for showing the machine had come from Ader himself, and the admission committee liked the idea: "Le Comité donne son accord il juge même que l'appareil *sera un des clous* de l'Exposition. Il est alors décidé de suspendre l'*Avion* au plafond de la galerie et de dispenser Ader des droits d'exposant, son appareil pouvant être considéré comme faisant partie de l'exposition rétrospective." Carlier 1990, pp. 98–99.

23   Durant 1994, p. 11.

24   *1900: The New Age*, p. 23. During the 1900 exhibition *Palais des Machines* was used mainly for the display of food products and machines were shown in the old *Galerie des Machines* designed by De Dion for the 1878 exhibition.

25   Many of the national pavilions were as far from the electric 1900 as possible: Belgium had a medieval town hall, Britain built a stately country house, Turkey a mosque, and Austria and Spain erected Renaissance palaces.

26   *Palais des Machines* was demolished in 1909 and was soon missed by many. Raymond Duchamp-Villon wrote about it in 1913: "Construite pour l'Exposition de 1889, son souvenir domine nos premières impressions de la vie collective, et je vois encore, très nettement, dans

Illusions of Flight

In all the previous exhibitions aviation had been present "live" in the form of balloons, such as Nadar's famous *Géant*, but by 1900 this was just too ordinary. This time the exhibition was characterised by illusion rather than by physical effort. Among of the most popular attractions were the *Maréorama*, a simulated sea voyage, and the "Trans-Siberian Express," a simulation of the Moscow-Peking train journey. But it was also possible to experience the excitement of flying in the form of an illusion. The first "flight simulator," the engineer Grimoin-Sanson's *Cinéorama,* was a bold example of state-of-the-art technology. The visitors stood on a platform resembling the gondola of a giant balloon (half the balloon was visible over their heads) and watched a multiprojector film panorama landscape around them, as seen on a flight at an altitude of five hundred metres.[27] What all these machines created, was of course an illusion of something already existing; there was nothing new or fantastic in boats, trains, and balloons.[28] Yet people loved these entertainments because the apparent realism gave everyone who had travelled a chance to compare the power of the illusion to the real thing. Alongside all the moving images Clément Ader's machine was rather different, but hanging with its wings spread from the ceiling of the newly built *Grand Palais* it nevertheless suggested an illusion of aviation. Apart from that the award winning *Avion III* did nothing at all – it could not and it did not have to. By simply floating over the heads of the millions of visitors it anticipated the approaching moment of true flying. It was an anticipation worthy of a gold medal.

The members of the jury were well aware that the *Avion III* was not a flying machine in the literal sense of the word. But they saw it as an example of brilliant craftsmanship, and, since it was by a Frenchman, they had little difficulty in deciding on the highest award. In its report the jury even confessed that "if the functioning of the *Avion* had responded to the hopes of its inventor, there would not have been a high enough award with which to recognise such merit."[29] The jury made an exquisite point in underlining the hopes of the inventor, but the actual argument for giving the medal was in the lightness, the strength, and the elegance of Ader's construction.[30] The first two things are

. . . .

la clarté de l'immense vaisseau, la promenade hallucinée du pont roulant, par-dessus les volants-tourbillons, les courroies-reptiles, parmi les grincements, les sifflets et les sirènes, surgissant du trou noir des disques, des pyramides et des cubes." Raymond Duchamp-Villon, *L'Architecture et le fer. La tour Eiffel.* Paris: L'Échoppe 1994, p. 8.

27   With its film technology *Cinéorama* was one step ahead of *Maréorama* and the Siberian train, which used large rolls of painted landscapes. However, *Cinéorama* was closed soon after its opening because of the fire risk caused by the projectors. See Erkki Huhtamo, *Elävän kuvan arkeologia.* Helsinki: Yle-opetuspalvelut, 1996, pp. 148–149. On *Cinéorama* also Asendorf 1997, p. 201.

28   The attraction which reached beyond the normal experience was *Le globe celeste* where the visitor could enjoy, in Richard Mandell's words, "a voyage in outer space accomplished with the help of a rolling canvas." Mandell 1967, p. 65.

29   Gibbs-Smith 1968, p. 29, with the original French text on p. 177.

30   "Tout cet ensemble constitue une merveille de construction légère, solide et élegante. . ." Gibbs-Smith 1968, p. 177.

essential for any aeroplane but for us it is the third criterion which is the most interesting. Following the admission committee's formulation, a contemporary exhibition guide described the *Avion III* as "a real attraction," at least for those who are technically minded.[31] But was it attractive? The jury had given it a prize because they thought it was elegant, but it would be interesting to know if the visitors at large saw it in the same way. In some respects the three year old *Avion III* must have seemed like one of the ancient "Egyptian" and "Gothic" machines of the 1850s rather than something for the twentieth century. Perhaps the machine's aesthetic quality was best recognized by those who knew the difficulties of the flying problem. François Peyrey, the leading aviation writer in France, agreed with the jury and praised the marvellous construction and its amazing details.[32] As real aviation progressed by leaps and bounds, the fascination of *Avion III* quickly wore off, however. When Peyrey encountered the machine again eight years later he felt it was surrounded only by silence, dust, and oblivion.[33]

In the 1960s the famous aviation historian, Charles H. Gibbs-Smith, wrote that Ader influenced nobody and nothing in aviation history.[34] One person whose testimony clearly speaks against Gibbs-Smith is the student of architecture who was building the Universal Exhibition, Gabriel Voisin. Here is his recollection of the first meeting with Ader's work: "A few days before the opening, I had to hurry to the transport section where I had to superintend the installation of the water system. I entered the gallery by a side door and I was at that very moment riveted to the ground by an unforgettable sight: a team of workmen was setting up, at the top of a passage, Ader's *Avion*."[35] Although Voisin and his brother had been playing with kites he was completely ignorant of Ader's research and had little knowledge of aeroplanes: "I had never seen a flying machine and I had no idea of the wonders which can be achieved by inspiration when it is associated with advanced techniques."[36] Voisin approached the workmen and was given permission by one of Ader's colleagues to sit in the cockpit of the plane. From then on he was hooked: "Often I have been moved; but on that day I was overcome by an enthusiasm which I had never known before. In my hands were the mysterious controls which could give life to this incomparable creation."[37]

. . . .

31 "[…] d'un intérêt absolument technique, offre un clou véritable: l'Avion." *Paris Exposition 1900*. Paris: Hachette 1900, p. 312.

32 "L'effort, cependant, est prodigieux, et la construction de l'artificielle chauve-souris une pure merveille. […] Tous les détails sont d'une infinie, d'une inouïe delicatesse […]." Peyrey 1909, p. 354.

33 "Sur l'*Avion* aux ailes immobiles, sur l'*Avion* au mécanisme figé par l'attente, tombait le silence, flottait un peu de poussière, de l'oubli […]." *ibid*, p. 356.

34 Gibbs-Smith 1985, p. 61. Gibbs-Smith may have given his judgement in haste. Not only Voisin but also Blériot experienced something in front of Ader's machine. "Dans un entretien accordé à la revue *Lectures pour Tous* de novembre 1909, Louis Blériot affirme que c'est la vue de l'*Avion* lors de l'exposition de 1900 qui lui donne la vocation." Carlier 1990, p. 203.

35 Voisin 1963, p. 100.

36 *Ibid.*

37 *Ibid.*

AVION III in the 'sleeping' position. (Dollfus & Bouché 1938, p. 140.)

Soon after the experience Gabriel Voisin brought his brother Charles to see the *Avion III*. This time, however, the aeroplane had to be studied from a different viewpoint: "This did not have the same effect on my brother as it had had on me. It was no longer near the ground in the conditions in which I had admired it before the opening of the Fair. Fixed high up in the gallery, and placed next to a partition, it had lost its three-dimensional appearance and looked more like an ornament than like a real creation."[38] But Gabriel Voisin had seen behind the ornamental appearance and could not get it out of his mind. He decided to abandon his studies at the Beaux-Arts and leave his trainee's post in an architectural office, and instead dedicate all his energy to aviation. He persuaded Charles to join him and in the following years the Voisin Brothers became the first commercial constructors of aeroplanes in Europe.[39] They worked for some time with Louis Blériot and designed and built the first planes for the two artists turned pilots, Léon Delagrange and Henri Farman.

. . . .

38 *Ibid.*, p. 107.
39 For a summary of their early career, see Munson 1969, pp. 170–172. (Munson's argument about the unreliablity of Voisin's memoirs does not affect our themes.) The young Jacques-Henri Lartique photographed the first flight of Gabriel Voisin's glider in 1904; see Borhan & D'Astier 1989, pp. 17–21.

Permanent Immobile

Clément Ader's invention is most likely the first non-functional heavier-than-air flying machine to have been officially declared elegant. This remained its best achievement. At the turn of the century it did not have to compete against functional aeroplanes, but as an engineer Ader was aware of the progress and he knew that even with the medal the *Avion* now had only historical value. The steam engines were outdated and the tailless construction and the bat-wings aerodynamically unsound. In 1903, three years after the *Exposition Universelle,* Ader donated his invention to the museum of the *Conservatoire des Arts et Métiers*, where it remains today just as much a masterpiece as it was in Gabriel Voisin's eyes hundred years ago.[40] However, the French aviation pioneers who had been inspired by the machine in 1900 wanted to pay homage to Ader, and in December 1908 the *Avion III* was delivered from the museum back to the *Grand Palais* for display to the eleventh exhibition of automobiles, bicycles, and sports.[41] For the first time the exhibition also included aeroplanes, and the historic *Avion III* was offered a place of honour on a pedestal surrounded by flowers. Another reason for Ader's second coming was his book *La première Étape de l'Aviation Militaire*, published in 1907. In it Ader claimed that he actually had flown with his *Avion III* in 1897, in other words six years earlier than the Wright Brothers, but that is another story.[42]

After the tens of millions of visitors at the *Exposition Universelle*, it is somewhat surprising to hear that to many aviators Ader's machine came as a revelation. The pilot Henri Farman's brother, Maurice, writing in 1910, stated that Ader, who was now in his seventieth year, was unknown to the general public, and even to the majority of French aviators, before his flying machine was exhibited in December 1908.[43] A description of the plane from 1908 makes one wonder if even the professional viewers were always aware what they were looking at. The correspondent for *Flight* noticed that the *Avion III* was brought to grace the exhibition and admired the elaborate framework of the wings, but thought that they were copies of a bird's wing.[44] There always was, however, one man who saw beyond the appearances and would continue to talk about the exceptional quality of Clément Ader's immobile flying machine. He was Gab-

. . . .

40 "The revelation which was made to me in 1900 by my first contact with the masterpiece [...]." Voisin 1963, p. 101. According to Lissarrague, Ader offered all his machines to the museum in 1902, but they accepted only *Avion III* and the engine of the never finished machine number 2. Lissarrague 1990, p. 227. The *Avion III* has gone through a major restauration and is in my mind the most stunning exhibit in the whole museum.

41 Sometimes this *Salon de l'Automobile* has been called also the first *Salon de l'Aéronautique*. See Gibbs-Smith 1985, p. 135. The first *salon* dedicated to flying apparatuses only was held in 1909.

42 For the history of Ader's claims, see Gibbs-Smith 1968.

43 Farman 1910, p. 32. His claim clearly states that many of the early pilots had started their careers around 1906 and after.

44 "The First Paris Aeronautical Salon," *Flight*, 2 January 1909, pp. 6–11. See also Gibbs-Smith 1968, pp. 163–164.

riel Voisin whose life had changed in 1900 because of a short moment inside the amazing *Avion III*. It was the same Voisin whose company in 1925 would lend their name and sponsorship to Le Corbusier's plan to re-organize the centre of Paris. Better than anyone else, Gabriel Voisin saw that Ader had not spent fifteen years of aeroplane building in vain. Compared with the haphazard experimentalists who succeeded in flying after a few years, many poorly designed planes, and several crashes, Ader had worked in a consistent way. The end product was not a functional aeroplane but surely a beautifully thought-out construction; "Any engineer can experience this same impression if he takes the trouble to go and see, at the Arts et Métiers museum, Ader's *Avion* and the aircraft of Blériot who made the Channel crossing. Twenty-nine years separate the two equally famous machines. But one of them, the *Avion*, is a highly developed creation while the other is an assembly, carefully contrived but primitive, owing its existence to improvisation."[45]

. . . .
45 Voisin 1963, p. 101. Voisin's argument holds good even today: in comparison with the restored *Avion III* the no-nonsense *Blériot XI* looks about to fall apart at any moment. How Voisin calculates the twenty-nine years separating the machines is a mystery to me.

■ Paris 1909: The Shiny Propeller

> *Airplanes by their nature are peculiarly and intensely thrilling to our modern spirits, and it may well be that in such typical products of our modern art we are approaching the degree of perfection in design achieved by certain craftsmen of the past.*[1]

Walter Dorwin Teague

The day was overcast with low cloud, but rain appeared unlikely.[2] At the *Grand Palais* the mechanics had had a busy morning dismantling the central showpiece of an extremely popular exhibition. Now they were carefully carrying it down the main staircase. Standing there under the grey autumn sky, with its separated wings folded on each side, the aeroplane looked so much smaller than the great historical reputation it had gained less than three months earlier. When the joyful yet dignified procession started to move along the Champs-Elysées and turned north towards the Place de l'Opéra, the technicians at the *Grand Palais* were already arranging another aeroplane on the central podium of the first *Salon de l'Aviation*. The organizers had decided to give this place of honour to *Antoinette*, the elegant plane which had competed against Louis Blériot's much clumsier design at Calais.[3] But elegance was not all that mattered in modern aeronautics; the unreliable engine of *Antoinette* had failed its pilot Latham twice during the competition and left him floating in the English Channel.[4]

We do not know if Guillame Apollinaire was standing in the cheering crowds who saw Louis Blériot's aeroplane pulled from the *Grand Palais* to the *Musée des Arts et Métiers* on 13 October 1909, but he nevertheless remembered this incident three years later when wrote: "Just as Cimabue's pictures were paraded

. . . .

1   Teague 1946, p. 102.
2   The average temperature in Paris during October 1909 was 11.7 °C and the monthly rainfall 105 mm. (*Worlds Weather Records.* Smithsonian Miscellaneous Collections, Vol. 79. City of Washington: The Smithsonian Institution 1944, pp. 497–499.) The photograph mentioned below (note 5) reveals that Blériot's plane did not cast a shadow and the street was not wet.
3   The change of planes can be seen from contemporary photographs. Most of them show Blériot in the centre (for example Prendergast, p. 73; Stoff, p. 45.) but at least one photograph (see *Aerospace*, May 1985, p. 30.) was taken after 13 October and shows the *Antoinette* on its place.
4   For the history of the first cross-Channel flight, see for example Prendergast 1981, pp. 35–47, and Chapter II in Wohl 1994. For an eye-witness report, see Harper 1929.

through the streets, our century has seen the aeroplane of Blériot, laden with the efforts of humanity made for the past thousand years, escorted in glory to the Arts et Métiers. Perhaps it will be the task of an artist as detached from aesthetic preoccupations, and as intent on the energetic as Marcel Duchamp to reconcile art and the people."[5]

At the Place de l'Opéra the buses and carriages came to a halt when people saw the *tricolore* leading the way in front of the world-renowned aeroplane. It was another great day for France and for Blériot – and for anyone who was interested in the new aesthetic role assumed by the flying machine. Apollinaire certainly was one of the very few who could conceive of comparing the ceremonial procession of Blériot's machine to the famous celebration of the new church paintings by Cimabue in Florence, almost six hundred years earlier. Apollinaire saw the symbolic value of the aeroplane clearly, but it seems that he did not look at the machine at all. His way of approaching the fuss about flying was sympathetic but literary. Aeroplanes may have poetic dimensions but poetry is about words, and there remained his real interest. It was, after all, Apollinaire the poet who in 1910 wrote a verse about Clément Ader's *Avion* – probably the first and last piece of poetry inspired by the name of a failed aeroplane – with a beginning and an ending like this: "Français, qu'avez-vous fait d'Ader l'aérien? Il lui restait un mot, il n'en reste plus rien."[6]

Taking Action to Rest

Let us proceed from the streets of Paris where people were watching Louis Blériot's aeroplane number XI on its way to the museum, less than a year after its construction.[7] We could say that it moved into its historical role much faster than it flew from France to England. After the sensational flight Blériot's conveyance ended its life as an aeroplane and immediately started a new one as an exhibition piece. Already at the landing site in Dover a tent was erected over the machine and a sixpenny entrance fee charged.[8] When the exhibit was later brought to Selfridge's department store in London for four days 120,000 people rushed to see it, compelling the store to remain open until midnight.[9] But what

. . . .

5   *Les peintres cubistes*, Paris 1913 (Apollinaire 1966, Vol. 4, p. 51.) The translation is from *Marcel Duchamp* 1993 (date 17.3.). For a picture of the plane's moving see Dollfus & Bouché 1938, p. 215. For the history of the man and his machines see *Blériot, l'envol du XXe siecle*, Paris: Maeght Éditeur 1994.
6   Apollinaire 1966, Vol. 3, pp. 565–566. The poem was probably written in 1910, and it is possible that Apollinaire sent it to the poetry competition of *l'Académie Française* with the theme "La Conquête de l'air." Considering the subject of his poem it is not surprising if we have not heard of a success. According to Lissarrague, the poem was first published in 1947; see Lissarrague 1990, p. 233. For a discussion of the poetry competition, see Lista 1973.
7   Blériot's plane earned its place in the museum very quickly indeed. In comparison, a much more radical machine, the world's first steam locomotive, designed by Cugnot, had to wait for thirty years. In the days of Blériot both the concept of the museum and the national interests were, of course, stronger.
8   Wallace 1958, p. 122.

did the machine look like? Was it beautiful in its beige cotton and spots of oil? What was it that people wanted to see? Flying itself was something only the rich could afford (royalty and the nobility from the King of Spain to the aristocrats of England had quickly flocked to fly with the Wrights in France), and since no-one was flying regularly in England in those days, the closest the London public could get to the real thing was to go and see Blériot's aeroplane.[10] For a moment the strange, travelstained construction outshone all the goods of the department store.[11]

The idea of displaying flying things on the ground was originally an English practicality; the first aeronautical exhibition was held in 1868 at the *Crystal Palace* in Sydenham. In this respect it was only natural to use the *Blériot XI* as an exhibit. What is interesting, however, is that the concept of showing the aeroplane which has crossed the Channel was invented before anyone had even tried his luck in the air. In August 1908 Lord Northcliffe, owner of the *Daily Mail*, tried to get Wilbur Wright to fly the Channel. Northcliffe promised him not only prize money, but also "half of the net receipts obtained by the exhibition of the Flyer at a great hall in London."[12] The generous offer was based on Northcliffe's accurate understanding of what a flight from the Continent over the Channel to England would mean. The feat, which Wright eventually refused and Latham later failed to do, was more than anything a symbolic act. It was the same Northcliffe who in November 1906 had proclaimed that England was no longer an island, and only because Santos-Dumont had made a hop-flight of a little over 200 metres in a park near Paris.[13] Thus when Blériot did succeed, he not only made aviation history but also fulfilled a prophecy. The performance of half an hour's flying soon turned into what Robert Wohl has called a social drama.[14] Many people in England and France, where the plane was first displayed outside the office of the newspaper *Le Matin*, came to see not only a vehicle of fearless sportsmanship but also a symbol of national feeling.[15] For some it symbolized danger, for others victory.

If Apollinaire really watched the procession of Blériot's aeroplane in October 1909, he saw something that was part of the public domain. The Channel crossing in July 1909 marked of course the heyday of aviation excitement in France, but both before and after that new flight records were set almost every

. . . .

9   *Ibid.*, p. 125.
10   The early pilots in Europe could afford to fly because they were either born rich (e.g. Santos-Dumont and Latham) or had accumulated enough money with other technical activities, often related to cars (e.g. Blériot and Farman). Blériot is said to have spent 800,000 francs on aviation by the time of his flight, see Wohl 1994, p. 63.
11   In retrospect it is always the *Antoinette* that has been called graceful and beautiful, not the frail *Blériot*. In 1909 the French journalist Fontaine, who witnessed Blériot's flight, called his plane "le bel oiseau de France," but here the emphasis seems to be on the country, not on the beauty of the machine. See Wohl 1994, p. 61.
12   Wohl 1994, p. 45.
13   Wallace 1958, p. 52. On Lord Northcliffe's interest in aviation, see Gollin 1984, pp. 186–197.
14   Wohl 1994, p. 66.
15   For a photograph of the machine outside the *Le Matin*, see Wohl 1994, p. 64.

week, and correspondingly the urge to see the flying machines was immense all over Europe. Between 22 August and 23 October 1909 people flooded to watch planes fly in aerial meetings at Rheims, Brescia, Berlin, Juvisy, Blackpool, and Doncaster. The audience over eight days at Rheims was estimated at half a million. Any exhibition of high culture whatsoever had difficulties compete with that.[16] The aeroplanes were exciting not only when they flew, but, as we have already learned, they were also interesting to see on the ground. Apollinaire was right about a shift in aesthetic ideas and his prediction about the future role of Duchamp shows a certain degree of foresight (even if we cannot say that Duchamp's work really reconciled art and the people). The flying machines looked good, and yet a comparison with contemporary cars or boats would quickly reveal them to be rather rough. It is telling that when Wilbur Wright spoke about beauty it was not near an aeroplane but in front of a Rolls-Royce *Silver Ghost*.[17] Compared with the shining luxury car the appearance of planes like *Blériot XI* was from another world. When it arrived in Calais to fly the Channel, the reporter Harry Harper took a good look at the plane: "A strange little machine it appeared when I first saw it in the railway goods yard at Calais. It was rather dirty, and built apparently in a flimsy fashion, and as it passed through the streets of Calais, towed behind a cart, it made a poor impression upon us as compared with the beautiful Antoinette."[18] Blériot's fabric was indeed soiled and the wheels of the undercarriage were caked with mud, while the *Antoinette* could compete with the finest vehicles with its polished brasswork and varnished cedar fuselage, a specimen of the work of master boatbuilders. But perhaps the magic of the aeroplanes was not at all in the nuts and bolts but in their apparent fragility. They captured the imagination of the viewers not with their force or speed but with their utter simplicity. Seen from afar an aeroplane was like a child's drawing. An interpretation of this fragility had already by 1908 found its way into works of art. There is something revealing in the fact that Douanier Rousseau, the grand old man of Paris avantgarde, had twice painted the *Wright A* when other artists only started to open their eyes.[19]

. . . .

16 The Armory Show in New York 1913 is said to have attracted 250,000 visitors in one month.
17 "She surely is a beauty," murmured Wilbur, "I guess we'll never be able to afford a car like this." Wallace 1958, p. 97.
18 Harper 1929, p. 64.
19 Rousseau based his picture on a photograph of Wilbur Wright's flight. The two paintings are: *Les Pêcheurs à la ligne avec aéroplane*, 1907–1908 (Keay 1976, pl. XXI; Wohl 1994, p. 181.); *Vue du Pont Sèvres et des coteaux de Clamart, St. Cloud et Bellevue*, 1908 (Keay 1976, pl. XXIV).

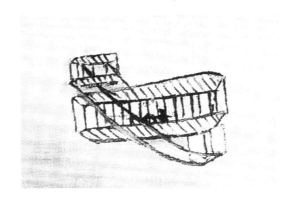

The Wright Flyer in Henri
Rousseau's painting 1907–
1908. (Wohl 1994, p. 181.)

Fascinating Display

Blériot's aeroplane was moved to the *Arts et Métiers* on the eleventh day of the
Salon, or more officially *Première Exposition Internationale de Locomotion
Aérienne,* before the eyes of Paris. The exhibition had been an unprecedented
success. Only the huge universal exhibition of 1900 had seen more people
crowding into the *Grand Palais.* During the first three days the salon had
attracted over 100,000 visitors.[20] Everything was set out in such style that the
reporter of the English magazine *Flight* wrote about "an artistic and fascinating
display," and continued: "Under the heading of the attractive and typical French
touches may be mentioned the rationally cheap, exceedingly artistic and
splendidly effective uniform scheme of stand decoration."[21] The aviation show
had many attractions but in the centre of the attention, framed in flowers, was a
podium for Blériot's famous monoplane. In the big exhibition hall around it
were twenty-five more aeroplanes on view, among them all the latest models by
Santos-Dumont, Voisin, and Farman. Professionally orientated visitors like
Herbert F. Lloyd, who reported on the show in *The Aeronautical Journal,* were
very interested in Henri Farman's new plane and especially in its engine, the
rotary 50 h.p. Gnome, which had earned him the Grand Prix for distance flying
at Rheims five weeks earlier.[22] And as if the heavier-than-air-machines were not
enough, there were several balloons beautifully displayed hanging from the
ceiling. One of them was a scale reproduction of the original Montgolfier.[23] The
reporter for *Flight* noticed the balloon too: "[…] looking on them merely as
features of the decoration, quite one of the most beautiful things being the very
faithful reproduction in light brown and dark blue of the Montgolfier."[24] A look
through contemporary photographs proves the reporter right; none of the later
exhibitions could compete with the aesthetic impact of the 1909 *Exposition.*[25]

. . . .

20 Prendergast 1981, p. 72; *Flight* 40/1909, p. 610.
21 *Flight* 40/1909, p. 610.
22 Farman's achievement on August 27 was a flight of over 100 miles, lasting over three hours.
23 On Gnome, Lloyd 1909, p. 122, on Blériot and the Montgolfier, p. 118.
24 *Flight* 40/1909, p. 610.
25 The only exception is the 1937 World Exhibition in Paris, where the stunning *Palais de l'Air*
    was decorated by Robert and Sonia Delaunay.

A view from the Aviation Salon of 1909. Note the balloons and the replica of the first Montgolfier. Blériot's plane front left. (Prendergast 1981, p. 73.)

In 1909 people's interest in aviation exceeded their interest in art. This holds true also for the aviation exhibitions. In the words of one historian: "By 1909, news of flying machines monopolized a good part of the daily newspaper. The aeronautical exhibition attracted crowds far greater than any of the artistic salons."[26] The comparison here is interesting and not at all accidental, since the great aviation exhibition of 1909 was held at the *Grand Palais* during the first two weeks of October, coinciding with the *Salon d'Automne*. To be more precise, the *Salon d'Automne* was held in the very same building.[27] Among the

. . . .

26   Sherry A. Buckberrough, *Robert Delaunay – The Discovery of Simultaneity*. Ann Arbor: UMI Research Press 1982, p. 37.
27   *L'Exposition Internationale de Locomotion Aérienne* was open 3–17 October. *7e Salon d'Automne* was open between 1 October and 8 November 1909.

artists who participated in this salon were three young men, whom we will soon discuss: Constantin Brancusi, Marcel Duchamp, and Fernand Léger. In the following I will argue that they also visited the aeronautical exhibition in 1909, not in 1912 as is usually thought.[28]

Three Men and a Propeller

In an interview granted to Dora Vallier in 1954, Fernand Léger recounted an anecdote widely quoted ever since. He recalled a visit to an aviation show in Paris before the First World War, together with Constantin Brancusi and Marcel Duchamp. Now, over forty years after the actual incident, Léger remembered Duchamp suddenly saying to Brancusi: "Painting is over. Who'd do better than this propeller? Tell me, could you do that?"[29] Duchamp, for his part, failed to remember the occasion when asked, and Brancusi came up with a totally different version of the conversation, but this has not diminished the popularity of Léger's story.[30]

While the story has become, in Ann Temkin's words, "a legend of modern art," there have been few attempts to fully investigate its background. Léger tells us that before making his comment to Brancusi "Duchamp wandered amidst engines and propellers, keeping silent."[31] As the silence of the sage has left many commentators content, questions like "What did these three artists really see?" or "How, if at all, did the show inspire them?" have barely been asked. Neither has the timing of their visit been fully established.

Of course, what makes the famous visit of Brancusi, Duchamp, and Léger worth re-examining is the possibility that they recalled the theme of aviation later not only in their words but also in their works, each one in his own way.[32] And even if we excluded the aviation aspect of the story, as many art historians have done, an aesthetic reaction in front of a ready-made object like a propeller is interesting enough in itself. But before we move on to the reactions of these three artists, perhaps we should recall that despite the aeroplanes had a huge novelty value for many years, they were not necessarily admired by everyone, especially when the surroundings changed from a happy exhibition to battle-

. . . .

28 For a look at the ways the story of their visit has been told in art historical literature, see Appendix.

29 "C'est fini la peinture. Qui fera mieux que cette hélice? Dis, tu peux faire ça?" Vallier 1982, p. 63. The interview was originally published in *Cahiers d'Art*, 1954, II. Translation here from Camfield 1991, p. 149.

30 "According to certain sources this statement was made by Duchamp to Brancusi and Léger in the course of a visit to the Salon de l'Aviation in Paris. However, Duchamp does not remember the circumstance." Schwarz 1969, p. 595. Brancusi's version will be discussed later.

31 "sans dire un mot" Vallier 1982, p. 63; English version in Camfield 1991, p. 149.

32 Asendorf thinks that this was the case: "All three artists were to return in later years, and in very different ways, to this impression." Asendorf 1994, p. 203. According to Varia, whose account is among the least convincing, the visit was no less than "of considerable consequence for the future of modern art." Varia 1986, p. 47.

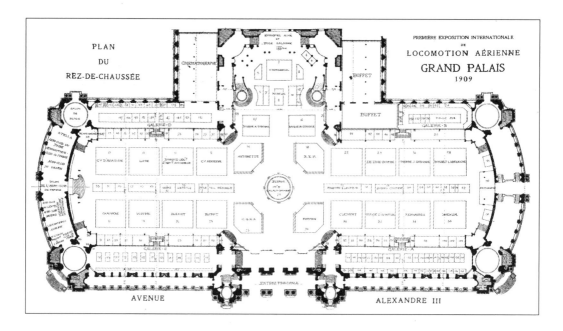

PLAN DU REZ-DE-CHAUSSÉE

PREMIÈRE EXPOSITION INTERNATIONALE
DE
LOCOMOTION AÉRIENNE
GRAND PALAIS
1909

AVENUE ALEXANDRE III

fields. Paul Klee, for example, had a good opportunity to see many of these heavier-than-air machines during his military service, but the most that he notes in his diaries from the period is: "I hadn't missed the noise of propellers." Instead of writing down any kind of aesthetic evaluation of aeroplanes Klee lists almost all the food he can lay his hands on and remembers to mention many nice restaurants.[33] Judging by the popularity of the *Salon de l'Aviation*, however, reactions like Paul Klee's were unknown in 1909. The *Grand Palais* flooded with people excited to see the flying machines, and the three hundred and thirty-three exhibitors guaranteed that there was value for the ticket. There were famous machines and unknown ones, machines with fixed wings, flapping wings, or even without wings. There were shiny propellers and polished engines, rubber tyres and special fabrics; some of them had been tested in the air, some not. There were hopeful inventors and interested businessmen, and there were rich people from all over Europe making orders for aeroplanes. For no obvious reason in one of the corners near the staircase was standing a lonely sailboat.

One interesting thing with this exhibition is that none of the machines was actually in the air. Only balloons floated in mid-air under the same steel and

The ground plan of the Aviation Salon of 1909. Gnome's stand on the left centre aisle. (Catalogue officiel de l'Exposition internationale de locomotion aérienne, 25 sept. – 17 oct. 1909.)

. . . .

33   Klee 1964, p. 369. The note is from 22 March 1917. Five days later Klee repeats the same lines in his letter to Lily Klee, only changing *Propellergeräusch* for the softer *Propellergesurr*. Paul Klee, *Briefe an die Familie 1893–1940*, Band 2: 1907–1940. Köln: Du Mont 1979, p. 859. In a diary note from November 1916 Klee mentions a Zeppelin manoeuvering gracefully above a town (Klee 1964, p. 350.), but in general he seems to have had no interest in aviation. Many of his works reveal that he liked birds, though. It is somewhat surprising that a similar attitude emerges for all major artists of the Bauhaus. As far as I know none of them gave aeroplanes any role in their modernism. Reyner Banham has noted that the Bauhaus masters did not posit any formal resemblance between machinery and the bare, spare rectangular architecture they produced. Banham 1981, p. 44.

Gnome stand at the Aviation Salon of 1909. (Photograph RAeS, London.)

glass arches where Clément Ader's inert *Avion III* had been hanging nine years earlier. All the aeroplanes stood firmly on the ground or on a pedestal, and could only suggest the possibility of overcoming gravity in their form. The best known aeroplanes were probably the most convincing looking; "Already tired of rest, ready to take flight again tomorrow," one observer described them.[34] With some other machines it was only a matter of make-believe; although the progress made during the past year had been remarkable, aviation was still at a fragile stage and most of the audience had no way of telling which machine was really capable of flying, and which one simply looked efficient. The *Blériot XI* had, of course, proved its capability, as had the *Antoinette* and Henri Farman's plane. But there were all kinds of other contraptions on display too. For instance, the engineless helicopter in Louis Vuitton's stand may have looked slightly suspicious, while the Lioré machine facing it was just like a real aeroplane. During the exhibition at least, the beauty of these apparatuses did not depend on their functionality. Both were to be earthbound forever. At their best (or worst) the more speculative exhibits were simply skillfully executed and elegantly displayed objects, and usually we lose sight of them after the exhibition. But let us now turn to the three young men who are, let us imagine, walking along the main aisle and seem to stop at the Gnome stand, only a few steps from Louis Vuitton's non-functional helicopter.

· · · · · · · · ·
34   A quotation in Prendergast 1981, p. 77.

Gnome engine being tested in 1908. (Dollfus & Bouché 1938, p. 204.)

Gnome engine being tested in 1908. (De l'Éole à Hermès: cent ans de moteurs dans le ciel. Paris: Musée des Arts et Métiers 1990, p. 13.)

Duchamp and the Spin

In his later years, Marcel Duchamp had no recollection of visiting an aviation show. Yet even an un-remembered visit may have all kinds of effects on one's personality. I cannot rule out the possibility that Duchamp's visit contributed to his concept of readymades, as has been suggested, even if any visit to the iron-monger's could have contributed much more, and even if none of Duchamp's readymades have links with aviation.[35] Except for those words reported for us

. . . . . .

35 On the alleged influence, see Appendix. André Gervais believes that Duchamp made works inspired by flying, and sees the *Bicycle Wheel* prefigured in the three aeronautical events he

Duchamp demonstrating his Rotary Glass Plates (Precision Optics). Man Ray's photograph from 1920. (Postcard, Moderna Museet, Stockholm)

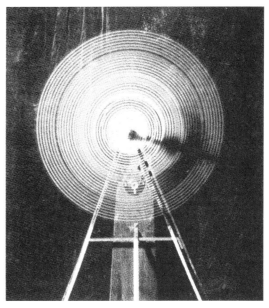

Duchamp's Rotary Glass Plates (Precision Optics) being tested, early 1920s. (Arturo Schwarz, Marcel Duchamp. New York: Harry N. Abrams, Inc. 1975, p. 133.)

. . . .

wishes to link. According to him they are "authenticated events," yet he does not explain who has authenticated the dating of the visit to Salon de l'Aviation as 1912. Gervais "might also want to associate the shape of a propeller blade to that of a tube of paint, or of two tubes of paint [...]." Gervais 1991, p. 403. Here, in my opinion, Gervais' associative want far exceeds his critical calm.

by Léger, the aviation show seems to have had no relation to Duchamp's artistic activities. But let us not give up too easily. Constantin Brancusi once made an interesting statement about movement: "The wheel, turning at the highest speed, gives an impression of immobility. It is only when the wheel is still you can see the spokes."[36] All this, however, seems to have more to do with Duchamp than with his own work. The spokes first bring to mind the *Bicycle Wheel*, but perhaps it did not turn "at the highest speed." There is, however, another work by Duchamp that comes closer to Brancusi's description, namely *Rotary Glass Plates (Precision Optics)* from 1920. It is very likely that Brancusi saw photographs of it at Duchamp's place – and heard how it had almost killed their mutual friend Man Ray – during his visit to America in 1926, when he also gave the above quoted interview.[37]

Rotary Glass Plates is a motorized work made of five rectangular glass strips with painted stripes on them. An electric motor makes the plates whirl around and the painted stripes create an illusion of many immobile concentric circles, matching up with Brancusi's words. The work itself and Duchamp's motives have not been very well explained, although references have been made to his interest in optics, which goes no further than the title of the work. I can offer no explanation either, but there seems to be, in my opinion, no real point in comparing the work to a propeller, as has been done.[38] Instead, I should like to draw attention to a photograph showing an aeroplane engine being tested. This is a machine we have already met, the famous seven-cylinder Gnome that had an almost revolutionary impact on early aviation.[39] The novelty of the Gnome was in its rotary concept, meaning that its cylinders revolved together with the propeller with a maximum speed of 1300 r.p.m. thus air-cooling themselves effectively during the flight. The picture of the engine's testing was first published in 1908 in the Paris journal *l'Illustration* and the actual machine was on display in *l'Exposition Internationale de Locomotion Aérienne* held at the *Grand Palais* in October 1909. In this show the fifty horsepower Gnome motor, already successful in the latest *Farman* biplane, was one of the state-of-the-art pieces that attracted much attention from the aeronautical public. Whether or not Duchamp was aware of it, the similarity between a rotary Gnome aeroplane motor running and his own *Rotary Glass Plates* whirling is surprising. Not only do both machines create an optical illusion but the period photographs of the rotating engine and the plates also have a strong resemblance.

. . . .

36 In Dorothy Dudley's article "Brancusi", published in the New York magazine *Dial* in 1927, quoted in Spear 1969, p. 18.
37 The work itself was purchased from Duchamp for the collection of the *Société Anonyme* in 1925 but kept in a box until 1935.
38 By such logic anything that goes round would remind us of a propeller. The reference is a lonely one, but quoted in Asendorf 1994, p. 208.
39 "[…] in its day, and for a time, the Gnome was supreme. The rest were nowhere. If you did not have a Gnome you could hardly be said to fly, because after little more than a brief 'hop' you were almost sure to come down with mechanical trouble of some kind or another." Harper 1929, p. 96.

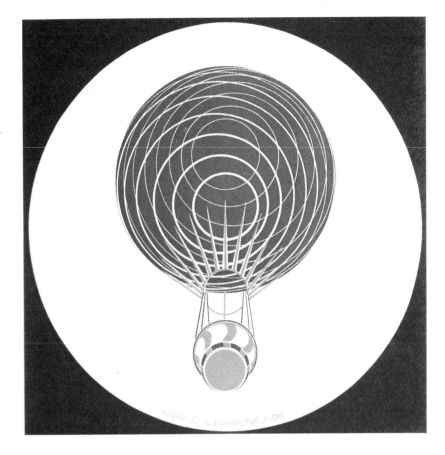

Duchamp's Rotorelief No 9, "Montgolfière." (Arturo Schwarz, Marcel Duchamp. New York: Harry N. Abrams, Inc. 1975, p. 177.)

Now, let us leave the engine spinning for a moment and take another look around the artworks. The only clear reference to aviation in Duchamp's corpus, apart from the small drawing *Aéroplane* (1912), is Rotorelief No. 9, titled *Montgolfière*. It is part of a multiple series of Rotoreliefs from 1935, a package of round doublesided cards meant to be placed on a gramophone turntable and then observed going around at 33 r.p.m.[40] Most of the pictures printed on these boards are abstract optical images, while *Montgolfière* shows a balloon and its basket seen from underneath. The subject matter has no connection with the drawings on other Rotoreliefs, and seems to constitute a mystery. Or could it be that the balloon and the image of a rotating aeroplane engine are distant memories from the same occasion, namely the 1909 Salon?

· · · · · · · · ·

40 According to Schwarz. In the 1930s, 78 revolutions per minute was still the standard in gramophone records. However, large 33 r.p.m records had been used with the first sound films in the 1920s. In 1931 RCA tried to market the 33 r.p.m "long play" record in the USA with poor success. Duchamp had a stand for the Rotoreliefs in a Paris exhibition for inventors and small manufacturers in 1935, but his invention went unnoticed. For a discussion of Duchamp's drawing *Aeroplane*, see Appendix, pp. 181–182.

Brancusi and the Bird

Constantin Brancusi in his later years used to tell a story about the visit to the aviation show similar to that told by Léger, but with a totally different emphasis. Instead of the dry and witty Duchamp it is now Brancusi himself who scores the points; "It was about this time that he had the 'revelation' he so often told us about. While visiting the Paris Air Show (1912) with Léger and Duchamp, he noticed a propeller. 'Now that's what I call sculpture!' he exclaimed, wonder-struck. 'From now on, sculpture must be nothing less than that.'"[41] Dumitresco and Istrati, to whom Brancusi told the story, also repeat the alleged lines of Duchamp, but in their version it is all thanks to Brancusi's clear sight that the propeller was noticed. According to Dumitresco and Istrati, the experience strengthened Brancusi's resolve to bring modern form to perfection. The difference between these two versions of the story is interesting. Instead of Duchamp's negative reaction (art is impotent) we now have a strikingly positive one by Brancusi (art is vital). To decide which version comes closer to the truth is not relevant since the variations display not so much facts as a difference in artistic character.[42]

When it comes to works of art, it is Brancusi who in this trio has produced the closest examples of propeller-like shapes. Although his Birds from 1923 onwards have a profile that might be likened to those of early propellers, and even if this has been voiced by journalists, it proves very little.[43] To speak about a concrete object like a propeller in particular and to speak metaphorically about flying in general are two different things. Many of Brancusi's works, but especially the Birds allow themselves to be described with metaphors of flight, as proved by Pontus Hulten ("Always oriented toward the sky, never toward the ground [...] a rhythm from bottom up that seems to defy gravity. [...] the moment of wrenching free, the moment of taking wing, of 'lift-off' to the sky.") and Mircea Eliade ("[...] flight is an equivalent of happiness because it symbolizes ascent, transcendence, a farewell to our human condition. Flight proclaims that weight has been abolished, that an ontological mutation has taken place within man's very being.")[44] All this is very beautiful and true, especially when Brancusi's own words lead one to favour these interpretations: "I have been searching a whole lifetime for only one thing: the essence of flight

. . . .

41 Hulten, Dumitresco & Istrati 1988, p. 92.
42 Ann Temkin describes Duchamp and Brancusi respectively as "Cartesian skeptic and mystic peasant." Bach, Rowell & Temkin 1995, p. 50.
43 During the lawsuit against the US Customs in 1927–1928 the bronze *Bird in Space*, or, more likely, a photograph of it, was described by *New York American* looking "[...] like nothing so much as, say, half of an airplane propeller." Quoted in Chave 1993, p. 201. According to Spear, *Bird in Space* has been compared to propellers, torpedoes, and rockets. She also talks about the formative period of modern ballistics and the Zeppelin airships. Spear 1969, pp. 36–37. In Lewis Mumford's opinion the bird is polished "as if it were the piston of an engine," but at the same time, "looking at the bird, one thinks of the shell of a torpedo." Mumford 1963, p. 337.
44 Hulten, Dumitresco & Istrati 1988, p. 38 and p. 51. Eliade 1982, pp. 200–201.

. . . Flight, what happiness!"[45] But is this a link between the Birds and the propeller he saw in an aviation show?

While no art historian today would claim that the Birds were copied from a propeller, there are still some misunderstandings when it comes to writing about the aviation side of the story.[46] Ann Temkin, for example, is clearly unaware what the early *hélices* were made of and she imagines the artists observing "a shiny metal propeller."[47] Léger tells explicitly that the propellers at which they were looking were made of wood: "Personally I was drawn towards the engines, towards metal rather than to the wooden propellers. . . But I still remember how stunning they were. God! They were marvellous."[48] And Léger was not the first to notice their beauty. Already in the combined automobile and aviation exhibition of 1908 the reporter for *Flight* made the same observation: "Wood is finding favour as a material for propellers with many experimenters, and there are some examples of very high-class work to be seen at the Salon. Properly made, a wooden propeller has a beautifully smooth polished surface."[49] The leading French maker of wooden propellers was Lucien Chauvière, whose company had previously manufactured wooden toilet seats. Smooth finish was appreciated in both products.[50]

In the light of his own words – if we are to believe Dumitresco and Istrati – Brancusi's revelation was not about flying but about pure plastic form. Indeed, if it had been only flying that he was interested in, why then wait until October 1912? Aviation had been in the headlines of every Paris newspaper ever since Wilbur Wright made his first flights in France in August 1908 and triggered a real flying fever. This turned into a huge national celebration when Louis Blériot won the competition to fly across the Channel in July 1909, a happening of which no-one in Paris was unaware. We have no original statement saying that Brancusi was especially interested in flying at that time, and indeed,

. . . .

45 Eliade 1982, p. 200. Another translation in Miller 1995, p.156.
46 It is tempting to imagine a correlation between the polished propellers and the polished sculptures of Brancusi, but is there any proof to support such an idea? Sanda Miller believes that "there is little doubt as to the two events which triggered Brancusi's interest in flying," and names them as "the simultaneous advent of Futurism and the Salon d'Aviation de Paris." If the advent of Futurism was the First Manifesto published in February 1909 and the Salon de l'Aviation which Brancusi visited would have been the one held in October 1912, as many writers seem to believe, it is not exactly on the spot to call them "simultaneous." Miller does not take her own stand in favour of any one of the datings, thus making her claim for the two events even more unclear. Miller also misreads Brancusi's attributed words in front of a propeller for those of Duchamp: "Duchamp apparently exclaimed in front of a propeller: 'En voila une sculpture!'. . ." Miller 1995, p. 154. My suggestion that the visit to the aviation show took place in 1909 could of course be used to support Miller's hypothesis.
47 Bach, Rowell & Temkin 1995, p. 51.
48 Vallier 1982, p. 63. The English translation as given in Chave 1993, p. 160. Metal propellers did exist, however. In the 1909 exhibition in Paris three machines (*Antoinette*, *Voisin*, and *REP*) were fitted with metal propellers, but their shape was quite different from the wooden ones, resembling more a pair of canoeing paddles than present day propellers.
49 *Flight* 2/1909, p. 23.
50 See Prendergast 1981, p. 67. In 1909 Chauvière could advertise his products by claiming that "Tous les Records sont battus avec l'hélice *Intégrale*." The recordholders Blériot (distance), Farman (duration), and Santos-Dumont (speed) had all used his propellers. For an advertisement, see Peyrey 1909.

concerning the evidence available, it might be more reasonable to conclude that he was not. Yet it is fairly common to write about Brancusi's Birds with a passing reference to his visit to an aviation show in the company of Duchamp and Léger. Usually no harm is done, but a closer look reveals that many interpretations are based on the uncritical use of testimonies from different decades, as well as making no distinction between the uses of metaphorical and common language. In some cases writers even invent new lines and place them in the mouth of the artist, as is done by Radu Varia. His Brancusi is standing in front of the propeller "in ecstatic contemplation," and says: "I shall do something else. And do it better."[51]

Whatever the date of the aviation show, none of the artists spoke about it in public before the 1950s. It is very likely that Brancusi produced his own comment after Léger's published interview, possibly because someone asked him about the incident, just as Duchamp was asked by Schwarz. It was also long after the visit that Brancusi spoke about his "lifelong search for the essence of flight."[52] Both comments come from the mouth of an old man at the end of his life's work, and they have little if anything to do with the thoughts of an artist who around 1910 was only on the threshold of his career. To point to the birth of the Birds with something that was said long after they were done strikes me as anachronistic, especially when other, more plausible interpretations are available. A good detailed study of Brancusi's Birds was undertaken by Athena Spear in the 1960s. She was probably unaware of the whole aviation story; at least she does not mention it. Yet she produces a very reasonable and coherent view of the Birds, not as "ultimate expressions of flight" but as a chain or series of one slowly transforming work starting from the first *Maiastra* in 1910(?). The problem for Spear is not where the spark for *Bird in Space* comes from but how Brancusi came up with the first *Maiastra*. Spear holds it that "no logical iconographic development led to the Maiastra." Instead, "it must have been a particular event which gave the sculptor his idea. And indeed an event, or rather two events, occurred."[53] However, it is not within the scope of this text to discuss the two events mentioned by Spear (the publication of the Rumanian poem *Pasarea Maiastra* and the première of Stravinsky's *L'oiseau de Feu*). But if the visit to the aviation show took place in 1912, the first *Maiastra* was already completed. And if the revelation in front of an aeroplane propeller really was as radical as the artist later suggested, it certainly took a long time to reveal itself it in his sculpture. Instead of a sudden change *Maiastra* goes through a series of step by step alterations and first becomes known as the *Bird in Space* in 1925,

· · · · · · · · ·

51   Varia 1986, p. 47. Since Varia does not explain where these words come from I can only read them as an example of his rather melodramatic imagination. In Varia's mind Brancusi was "Captivated by the beauty and originality of these new machines which, through their technical perfection, triumphed over gravity." *ibid.*
52   Printed in Giedion-Welcker 1958, pp. 198–199. The date given for Brancusi's words is June 1934.
53   Spear 1969, pp. 9–10.

The aeroplane in Brancusi's drawing
"Three Cows in a Meadow," 1929.
(Hulten, Dumitresco & Istrati 1988,
p. 64.)

when Léger is already promoting a *new spirit*, with a particularly strong emphasis on aeroplanes. Instead of sticking to the story of a revelation in 1912 we should consider the possibility that Brancusi came to name his slowly evolving *Maiastra* as *Bird in Space* under the direct influence of *l'esprit nouveau*. He may even have found it from the poem by Guillaume Apollinaire we mentioned earlier: "L'avion." The nineteenth line of this poem reads: "La plainte de la brise, un oiseau dans l'espace."[54]

To the best of my knowledge Brancusi produced only one work depicting an aeroplane. This is a funny little drawing from 1929, showing three cows in a meadow. In the sky above them we see a smiling sun and an aeroplane. Everything is sketched with a quick hand and the flying machine is but a few lines, yet recognizably a biplane. Now, it would be possible to turn the plane upright and say that it brings to mind the shape of *Bird in Space;* similar comparisons have been made between the sculpture and the abstract birds in *Snails and Birds*, another Brancusi drawing from 1929.[55] As tempting as these deductions may be, they do not help us in solving the problem of the visit to *Salon de l'Aviation*, in 1912 or some other year. On the contrary, the drawings seem to suggest that Brancusi was thinking about flying only after 1925, when the name *Bird in Space* was adapted for the work growing out of the former *Maiastra* series. Brancusi had certainly started his "research for the aerial," as Ezra Pound put it, earlier than 1925, but I believe it was the novel spirit of that time that gave his work a new, more abstract meaning.[56]

. . . .

54 According to Temkin (Bach, Rowell & Temkin 1995, p. 202), the name *L'Oiseau dans l'espace* first appeared at the exhibition *Art d'Aujourd'hui* in Paris in December 1925, and the English version *Bird in Space* at the Wildenstein Galleries exhibition in February 1926. At that time Apollinaire's poem had not yet been printed but Brancusi may have known about it. Moreover, let us not forget that it was Apollinaire who in his talk in 1917 introduced the expression "esprit nouveau" as a systhematic term. (See Wijk 1982; for the earlier history of this expression, *ibid.* pp. 34–42.)

55 The picture *Three Cows in a Meadow* can be found in Hulten, Dumitresco & Istrati 1988, p. 64. For *Snail and Birds*, see Brezianu 1976, p. 245, with comments on later gouaches with similar abstract birds. Also Bach, Rowell & Temkin 1995, p. 311.

56 Ezra Pound's article "Brancusi" in *The Little Review*, Autumn 1921. Reprinted in *Ezra Pound and the Visual Arts*. New York: New Directions 1980, pp. 211–214.

Léger and the War

Unlike Brancusi and Duchamp, Fernand Léger had an unquestionable enthusiasm for aeroplanes. The story of the visit to *Salon de l'Aviation* "avant le guerre de 14" is only one of many recollections. In his famous essay "The Machine Aesthetic: The Manufactured Object, the Artisan, and the Artist" (1924) Léger tells another story of a visit to an aviation show: "I will always remember that one year, showing at the Salon d'Automne, I had the advantage of being next to the Aviation Show, which was about to open. Through the partition, I listened to the hammers and the mechanics' songs. I jumped over the barrier, and never, in spite of my familiarity with these spectacles, had I been so impressed. Never had such a stark contrast assailed my eyes. I left vast surfaces, dismal and gray, pretentious in their frames, for beautiful metallic objects, hard, permanent, and useful, in pure local colours; infinite varieties of steel surfaces at play next to vermilions and blues. The power of geometric forms dominated it all."[57] Again Léger fails to tell us which year he is talking about.[58] The aesthetic impact may have been at its highest, but what makes his account particularly enjoyable is the part where he describes the mechanics in their turn visiting the *Salon d'Automne:* "[...] these worthy men, who had never seen an exhibition of painting in their lives, who were clean and fine, brought up amid beautiful raw materials, fell into raptures over works that I would not want to comment on." Léger ends his essay adoring the brightly coloured clothes of a sixteen-year-old mechanic who is "blissfully contemplating the nude women in gold frames."[59] New spirit or not, machine aesthetics had not captured everyone's imagination.

Léger probably never thought that in the future he would have to see these two objects of aesthetic experience – aeroplanes and images of nude women – coming together. The combination had a history in the symbolic statues which decorated the entrance of the *Palais des Machines* in 1889, but it was later undone by the Futurists who at least claimed that the machine was a new symbol for beauty while a naked woman was an unworthy subject to paint.[60] It was, then, a strange irony that many of the American bombers which pulverized ancient European cities during the Second World War – very much fulfilling the original Futuristic wish of getting rid of the dusty old museums and libraries – were decorated with painted pin-up images.[61]

In 1937, in an essay entitled "The New Realism Goes On," Léger makes a straightforward allusion to propellers and sculptures, possibly to those of

. . . .

57   Léger 1973, p. 60.
58   See Appendix.
59   Léger 1973, pp. 60–61.
60   In their *Technical Manifesto of Painting* (1910) the Futurists proclaimed: "We combat the nude in painting, just as tiresome as adultery in literature." Apollonio 1973, pp. 30–31.
61   For naked women and WWII aeroplanes see, for example, Gary M. Valant, *Vintage Aircraft Nose Art.* Osceola: Motorbooks International 1987.

Brancusi: "Hanging on the wall in the popular bals-musettes, you will find aeroplane propellers. They strike everyone as being objects of beauty, and they are very close to certain modern sculptures."[62] This is all very interesting, but once again we should note the year. This time it is thirty-five years after the presumed visit and seventeen years after the launch of the magazine *L'Esprit Nouveau*. The *Machine Art* -exhibition of 1934 at New York's MoMA had included an aeroplane propeller mounted on the wall, so the "bals-musettes" come as no surprise. Judging by his writings aeroplanes seem to have been important to Léger, yet a survey of his works tells a totally different story. No matter how inspiring he found them, aeroplanes play no role in his art as a subject to paint. His painting *Les Hélices* from 1918, used as an example by Asendorf and Sochor, was not inspired by an aviation exhibition but by the propellers of a ship.[63] The only works actually showing an aeroplane are the two small watercolours he made during his military service in 1916.[64] These works underline the fact that Léger was not fascinated by the flying machines as such. As with all machines, Léger thought not about their function but about their forms, materials, and colours.[65] For this purpose a crashed aeroplane was just as good as a new one.

Unlike Duchamp and Brancusi, Léger served in the military during the First World War. The very same interview that established the story of the visit is also a strong testimony to the tremendous impact the war had on Léger. He speaks about its superpoetic atmosphere and excitement, something that made him learn in two months more than he had learned in his whole life. While others may have experienced war as an empty interval, Léger felt it was in its all savage activity something that enabled him to foresee what would be the style of his own era, a style of machines.[66] The fact that Léger made his only paintings of aeroplanes during the First World War reveals its importance later in 1939-1940 when he was commissioned to do decorative work for the civil aviation centre of Briey, near Nancy. The project was eventually cancelled because of the outbreak of another war, but Léger produced some sketches and paintings, usually titled *Avion dans le ciel* or *Hommage à l'aviation*.[67] All these works

. . . .

62 Léger 1973, p. 116. The connection between industrial objects and art was seen slightly differently when the speaker was an industrial designer: "Any deviation from purely functional form is disastrous and the engineer is forced into functional design because he has no choice. In machine parts, too, the same compulsion operates and we have the marvellous abstract perfection of these forms – a beauty which makes Mr. Brancusi's sculpture seem somewhat trivial." Teague 1946, p. 68.

63 See Asendorf 1994, p. 207; Sochor 1982, p. 80.

64 "In two watercolours, *La Cocarde* and *L'Avion brisé* Léger took a crashed aeroplane as subject." (Francia 1983, p. 33.) According to a different calculation Léger made yet another work: "The Wrecked Aeroplane is one of three vigorous watercolours inspired by the arrival of French military aircraft." (Cassow & Leymarie 1973, p. 34.)

65 Blaise Cendras wrote about Léger in 1919 that his eyes wonder from a toiletkey to a Zeppelin. According to a later comment: "For him a machine did not serve – as in the case of Picabia, Max Ernst, or Marcel Duchamp – as an outlet for irony, rebellion or sexuality, but as a vehicle with which to express his admiration for the period." Gaston Diehl, *Fernand Léger*. Naefels: Bonfini Press 1985, p. 23.

66 Vallier 1982, pp. 62–63.

67 Laugier & Richet 1981, pp. 114–117.

show a group of circles like a big sun seen through drifting clouds of smoke and forms resembling violently broken tree trunks. The associations are not easily linked with the pleasures of civil aviation but bring to mind the mutilated landscape of war and destruction. The works cannot help expressing the first-hand knowledge Léger had about modern warfare and the role that once beautiful aeroplanes now played.

Fernand Léger, "Avion dans le ciel," 1940. (Laugier & Richet 1981, p. 117.)

■ Tampere 1911: The Machine on a Pedestal

> *The French wondered alternately about the unaffected man and the simplicity of the aeroplane. Indeed, in comparison with many other machines, this plane leads one to think: "Oh, is it not anything more complicated? And so clear-cut! Well, anyone should be able to make that!" Oddly enough, a good artwork often affects us in the same way.*[1]

Venny Soldan-Brofeldt

Spring was late that year. In the past days temperatures had varied and made the land wet and icy by turns. The 8.08 p.m. post train from Helsinki was facing westerly winds and clear skies, as it crossed the newly frozen territory.[2] Three or four carriages and a lingering cloud of smoke followed the engine. The sun had already set but perhaps the passengers could see the approaching silhouettes of factory chimnies. Against the dark sky they stood higher than any of the steeples. As the train arrived people busied around the Tampere station as usual, on a cold spring evening. Adolf Aarno must had arranged for someone to meet him at the station. He did not travel light, not this time. The wooden box he had with him was big and sturdy, perhaps even decorated with original French factory labels. Aarno and his helpers lifted it carefully onto a waiting horse-carriage, and that Aarno sat by the driver as they drove slowly down the main street. They had to cross the bridge and the running water underneath certainly made the air feel even colder. Under an electric streetlamp they stopped in front of the old pump room. It was getting late and after the long journey Aarno may have felt hunger, but he had to give in to his curiosity; as soon as the men had moved the box inside Aarno took the crowbar and forced the top of the box open.

Adolf Aarno was a bachelor and thirty-one years old. A self-made man, a well known sculptor, and now also the proud owner of a stone-mason's workshop.[3]

· · · · · · · · ·

1 "Ranskalaiset ihmettelivät vuoroin miehen, vuoroin koneen koruttomuutta. Kone onkin verrattuna moneen muuhun semmoinen, että tulee ajatelleeksi: vai eikö se olekaan sen kummempi? Ja niin selväpiirteinen! Tuommoisenhan kenen tahansa pitäisi osata tehdä! Omituista kyllä vaikuttaa hyvä taideteos useimmiten juuri näin." Soldan-Brofeldt 1910, p. 58. The description of Wilbur Wright and the *Wright A.*

2 The temperature in Tampere, Finland in the morning of 30 March 1911 was − 9.6 °C and twenty-four hours later + 2 °C. In the evening of 31 March wind blew 15 m/s from WNW. *Meteorolologisches Jahrbuch für Finnland 1911.* Helsinki: Meteorologinen keskuslaitos 1914.

3 Adolf Aarno was born in the village of Roismala at Tyrvää on 29 September 1879. He was christened Kaarle Adolf Virtanen and adapted the more artistic family name Aarno in his early twenties. He spent the obligatory four years at elementary school and then went to work.

The town of Tampere around him was small but bound to grow. Forty-five thousand inhabitants with more moving in. Industry took care of that; factories needed workers and workers needed houses. Tens of new buildings were erected every year. This was the time of expansion and speed. A train to Helsinki took only five hours and the city fathers of Tampere had plans to build tramlines. Bicycles had become popular, but Aarno knew of something even better. Later in the spring, weather permitting, he would take out his motorbike and drive down the cobbled main street. It was a rather noisy machine, often frightening both people and horses. There were over two hundred registered horsedrivers in the town.[4] And now, in the big French box he just had opened, one aeroplane.

Sculpture and Culture

Adolf Aarno made his public debut in 1904 at the annual exhibition of Finnish Artists, but it was at the exhibition the following year, when he showed a sculpture called "Bust," that he was first noticed.[5] The work was not an innocent piece *sans titre* but a small plaster portrait of Eugen Schauman, the "national hero" who had shot the oppressive Russian governor Bobrikov – and after that himself – in Helsinki only a year earlier. It was because of the daringly nationalistic and political subject, rather than for sculptural merits, that Aarno's work was well received in the newspapers. He was soon able to give up his job as a schoolteacher and concentrate solely on art. He modelled a new life size version of the Schauman bust and worked with other portraits, showing them the following autumn with reasonable success. Having made himself a name in the local art world Aarno did what many of his colleagues had done before him: he moved to Paris. Aarno started his studies at the *Académie Collarossi* in Paris in autumn 1906 and remained there until the following summer. By the end of 1907 he moved to Berlin to study at the strictly academic *Köninglichen akademischen Hochschule für die bildenden Künste* (Royal Academy of Art).[6] Unlike many of his colleagues who travelled in search of experiences, Aarno

. . . .

At the age of fourteen he left home, travelled to Uusikaupunki on the westcoast of Finland and became a baker's apprentice. A couple of years later, however, Aarno gave up this profession and began his studies at the Jyväskylä Seminary in order to become a teacher. Adolf Aarno graduated from Jyväskylä in June 1902 and the following autumn he worked as a schoolteacher in Helsinki. But the major reason behind his move to the capital seems to have been art, as already on the first of September 1902 he was a student at the Finnish Art Society's school. Aarno settled to Tampere in late summer 1908, working first as a teacher in the local Swedish-speaking school. See Ahonius 1961, pp. 29–36.

4   Tampere had a little over 45,000 inhabitants in 1911. For this and other statistics, see Eino Jutikkala, *Tampereen historia III. Vuodesta 1905 vuoteen 1945*. Tampere: Tampereen kaupunki 1979.

5   See the catalogue *Luettelo Suomen taiteilijain näyttelystä 1905 Ateneumissa*. Helsinki 1905, and the review in *Hufvudstadsbladet*, 31 December 1905.

6   The place in the higher course of the Berlin Academy was a competitive one. Aarno was the only foreigner among the seven applicants. *Hufvudstadsbladet*, 10 December 1907.

really seems to have worked hard during his two years abroad, so much so that he even participated in the annual exhibition in Finland autumn 1907 with three new works.[7] Aarno's art was from the beginning very conventional and the years in Paris and Berlin seem to have changed little or nothing. He followed the academic mainstream and showed no interest in the radical or innovative tendencies of art. But, then again, how likely was it that a lonely visitor from Finland, still a Grand Duchy of the Russian Empire, would have known about the extremes of art?

Finland had acted independently of Russia and organized its own pavilions in the Universal Exhibitions of Paris in 1889 and 1900. Both enterprises proved highly successful, and especially the pavilion of 1900 was recognized as the pearl of the whole exhibition. Then and there Finnish art made a fresh impression, but on its next visit to Paris eight years later it was already considered rather dull and old fashioned.[8] European art had changed its course, but Aarno, like most of the Finns studying abroad at the time, was not attracted to avant-garde of any sort.[9] At home art had functions other than mere aesthetic pleasure, as the Schauman bust had proved. The nation striving for independence needed a vital culture of its own, and this by definition could only be something already accepted as culture by other respectable nations. In 1907 a traditional piece of sculpture by an artist of Aarno's calibre, say a bust or, perhaps, an allegorical representation of something in the form of an unclothed woman, certainly came closer to that definition than Picasso's and Braque's early experiments with cubism, for example.

Picasso and Braque actually met first in Paris in 1907, when Adolf Aarno was studying there. Among foreigners visiting Paris the same year were also Wilbur and Orville Wright.[10] They were trying to sell the world's first functional aeroplane to the French Army, and later to the Germans, but had to sail home without success – only to see Wilbur return the following year with the magnificent flying machine that would turn the heads of all sceptics. The French ever since 1903 had been unimpressed by the Wrights' flight claims, and their visit in 1907 passed unnoticed by most people. But even without the Americans, Paris was already full of aeronautical activity and the news coverage can hardly have escaped Adolf Aarno's attention. Many of the now classic attempts were made as the pioneering generation of European aviation – Santos-Dumont, Blériot, Delagrange, Farman – learned to fly the hard way.[11] In August 1908, when Aar-

. . . .

7   *Luettelo Suomen taiteilijain näyttelystä 1907 Ateneumissa.* Helsinki 1907.
8   Nearly two hundred works by Finnish artists were displayed in a separate exhibition in the *Salon d'Automne* 1908. On the reception of the Finnish exhibition, see Riitta Ojanperä, "Suomen taide Pariisissa 1908" in *Varhainen modernismi Suomessa 1890–1920* [Early Finnish Modernism, 1890–1920]. Helsinki: Ateneumin taidemuseo 2001, p. 370.
9   There were exceptions of course. The young Finnish-Swedish architect Sigurd Frosterus was one of them, but unlike the small farmer's son Aarno, Frosterus was "entirely cultivated and from one of Finland's best families [...] His parents are, I believe, remarkably wealthy." An early twentieth century description, as quoted in Sarje 2000, p. 117.
10 On the Wrights' trip to Europe in 1907, see for example Gollin 1984, pp. 250–265.
11 On the aeronautical year 1907, see Gibbs-Smith 1985, pp. 121–127.

no had already returned home from Berlin, the news of Wilbur Wright's sensational flights in France were published all around the world, including Finland. It may be that on his journeys sculptor Adolf Aarno had not learned about new art but he certainly came home with a fascination for the new technology and speed.

New Machines

There were no automobiles in Finland at the end of the nineteenth century, and if one bought such an expensive machine in the early 1900s, it usually remained a rarity for a long time and accordingly treated with great respect, especially in the rural areas. When the estate-owner Linder's automobile in 1902 accidentally slipped into a ditch – despite the specially employed French driver – the workmen who came to help had to wait for towels from the manor house before they got permission to lift the car. It was an utter impossibility that ordinary country workers would be allowed to touch the modern French machine with their dirty bare hands. In the cities some people were just as careful to keep their new status symbol in immaculate condition. Before every drive Sergei Nikolajeff of Helsinki examined his automobile with a pair of chamois gloves on his hands and made sure that there was no dust under the wings. Linder and Nikolajeff at least thought that the new machines were meant to be taken seriously.[12]

As soon as automobiles and motorcycles came into general use in the largest Finnish towns respect gave way to a more practical attitude. People who had visited a busy European metropolis understood the first Finnish signs of a modern twentieth-century lifestyle and saw the possibilities for a rapidly growing business. The chamois-gloved Sergei Nikolajeff made an early move and started importing automobiles, establishing himself in a couple of years as the leading dealer in Finland. Because of his business it was usual for Nikolajeff to travel abroad, but one of his trips is of particular interest. When he headed for Paris in the autumn 1909, making orders for new automobiles was not the foremost thing in his mind. No, this time Sergei Nikolajeff of Helsinki was on his way to the *Grand Palais* to see the big *Salon de l'Aviation* and to buy himself an aeroplane. He had previous contacts with the Clément-Bayard automobile factory and at their stand in the *Grand-Palais* he now ordered one their latest products, the Santos-Dumont No 20, better known as *Demoiselle*. According to a contemporary report the elegant machine formed "the centre of attraction to most of the visitors to this exhibition."[13] Indeed, the aeroplane's sporty appear-

. . . .

12   Stories about Linder and Nikolajeff as cited in Salmi 1996, p. 122. It should be noted that the Linder accident has a strong proto-Futuristic flavour. As is well known, the first Futurist manifesto begins with a description of an automobile drive ending in a ditch. (See Apollonio 1973, p. 20.) Linder bought his car in 1900 and it was the second in Finland.
13   Lloyd 1909, p. 120.

The Demoiselle as Sergei Nikolajeff saw it displayed at the Grand Palais in 1909. (Nicolau 1997, p. 104.)

ance and its competitive price at 7,500 francs made it a popular choice and Nikolajeff had to wait for more than six months before the plane arrived in Helsinki.[14] By then it had occurred to him that he would never be able to fly with his machine; the small and light-weight *Demoiselle* was designed to carry barely sixty-five kilograms and Sergei Nikolajeff weighted at least eighty. The first aeroplane in Finland therefore remained in its box and waited for a small enough buyer.[15]

Nikolajeff was not the only Northern automobile dealer who in 1909 was attracted to flying. His Swedish colleague, Baron Carl Cederström, owner of the Stockholm-based company Bilaktiebolag or *Bil-Bol*, had a similar inclination. The baron was so determined to learn the new art that in the spring 1910 he travelled with his friend Count Nils Barck to Pau to study aviation in Louis

. . . .

14   Santos-Dumont did not claim any patent for his design but considered it public domain. *Demoiselles* were manufactured at least by two factories, Clément-Bayard and Morane & Saulnier. The production number of Aarno's aeroplane was 109. (Ahonius 1961, p. 51.) It is possible that this is a running number for all the machines made by Clément-Bayard, or then the plane may have been number nine. Charles Munson has estimated that no more than ten to fifteen *Demoiselles* were ever built. (Munson 1969, p. 162.) He may have taken it from Wykeham who gives the same number, (Wykeham 1962, p. 236.) but apparently the estimation is much too modest. It appears that forty *Demoiselles* had been sold by the end of 1909. (Prendergast 1981, p. 85.)

15   On Nikolajeff, see Ahonius 1961, pp. 25–28. With his fifty-five kilograms *Demoiselle's* designer Alberto Santos-Dumont truly was a flyweight aviator. On his glorious career, see Wykeham 1962, and Nicolaou 1997.

Flying with automobiles. Nikolajeff's machines head for heaven, Söderström's hurtle towards hell fire. Both posters by the Finnish artist Akseli Gallen-Kallela, 1907. (Akseli Gallen-Kallela. Helsinki: Ateneum 1996, pp. 282–283.)

Blériot's famous flying school. Here Cederström certainly showed better judgement than Nikolajeff, who had bought his plane without receiving any training at all. Moreover, a *Blériot* was also able to carry a heavier load than the small *Demoiselle* and did not impose similar weight restrictions on the pilot. But the road ahead of Cederström – even if he was good at gymnastics and dancing and grasped aerial balancing much more easily than many others – was not

smooth.[16] In those days learning to fly was an expensive test of patience in rather primitive conditions. The students were expected to pay for the damage they caused to the school's aeroplanes, which, needless to say, was considerable. It also turned out that lodging was difficult to find in Pau and the two Swedish noblemen had no alternative but to live for eight weeks in one of the big wooden boxes used as packing for the aeroplanes. But perhaps this voluntary humility only gave the new sport the right kind of aura. After all, during his spectacular flight season in 1908 Wilbur Wright had become known for his Spartan lifestyle, turning down free hotel accommodation and preferring the conditions of the bare wooden shed where his aeroplane was kept.[17]

. . . .

16 An article from the previous year gives a list of what is needed: "This art, more than any other, will require active energy, courage, decision of purpose, a quick eye and clearness of judgement, utmost presence of mind; also an enormous amount of patience, assiduity and perseverance, and finally, efficient training and physical dexterity." (Silberer 1908, p. 51.) Blériot's name attracted students, but he was himself a dreadful pilot and crashed numerous planes. See Prendergast 1981, p. 22.

17 On Baron Cederström's training in Pau, see Wennberg 1999, pp. 59–65. Cederström became the first Swedish pilot and made a fine career in flying. He died in a flying accident in the Finnish archipelago in 1918, when delivering an aeroplane to Finland. On Wilbur Wright's character, see Wohl 1994, pp. 23–28.

Aviation and architecture. Count Barck, Baron Söderström, and their apartment-box in Pau 1910. (Wennberg 1999, p. 61.)

Beautiful Constructions

Finland, too, had rough conditions but was short of noble pilots. Nikolajeff often advertised his flying machine in the newspapers, but finding a buyer for such an exotic vehicle in the Northern country proved complicated. There were certainly enough articles about flying in the Finnish press to trigger the excitement of would-be pilots, but it seems that the price of the aeroplane and the news of the fatal crashes in France effectively discouraged everyone.[18] During the autumn of 1910, when the *Demoiselle* was still waiting in its box in Helsinki, two Finnish books on aviation were published. One of them has a special relevance to the present study, since its author was an artist. Venny Soldan-Brofeldt was a talented painter and married to the famous Finnish author Juhani Aho. *Kuinka on opittu lentämään?* [How has man learned to fly?] was her first book and she drew some of the illustrations herself. We do not know for certain what aroused her interest in aviation, but as a well educated

. . . .

18   The following informative and illustrated articles deserve mention: "Lentokoneista," *Aika* No 19, 1909, pp. 652–664; "Ohjattavista ilmalaivoista ja lentokoneista," *Koneteollisuus* 10/ 1909, pp. 109–116 and 12/1909, pp. 143–146 and 12/1910, pp. 133–140; "Muutama sana lentokoneen vaiheista," *Luonto tieteen valossa I*, WSOY, Porvoo 1908, appendix pp. 33–39; "Ilmojen kautta, lintujen teitä," *Luonto tieteen valossa IV*, WSOY, Porvoo 1911, pp. 46–72. There were 32 aviation fatalities in 1910, including the crash of one of the famous pilots, sculptor Delagrange. (Gibbs-Smith 1985, p. 248. See also Soldan-Brofeldt 1910, p. 75.)

and travelled person she had had opportunities to see such machines and read about them from continental journals and newspapers.[19] It is probable that she walked underneath Ader's *Avion III* in 1900, while visiting the Paris *Exposition Universelle* where she received a bronze medal for her painting.

Soldan-Brofelt's background in art reveals itself in her book; a perfect example is the passage where she discusses the *Wright A* aeroplane. She is using the same source of information as the author of the other Finnish book, Kaarlo Suomalainen, but does not draw the same dull conclusions. Both writers explain how clear and simple the construction of the Wrights' machine was, unlike many other aeroplanes. It is so simple, say both, that it makes one think: "Well, anyone could make a thing like that." The technically minded Suomalainen then underlines that behind every detail there is much careful planning and several years of experimentation.[20] Soldan-Brofeldt, however, points out that the feeling "I could do this" is strangely similar to the way a good artwork often affects us.[21] The idea of art which lies behind her interpretation is interesting and surprising. In her eyes the outermost simplicity of the early aeroplanes was not a sign of insufficient skill but of ingenious thinking. This was beauty as seen by the *Le Figaro* reporter Franz Reichel in August 1908, and simplicity similar to the impression of the British aviator Claude Grahame-White, now reading like a description of a collage: "I think that what struck me most was the apparently simple mechanism, the crudeness of the materials employed in its construction, and the rough-and-ready way which they had been put together."[22] But in some viewers' minds simplicity and crudeness were never far from the unaesthetic. The architect Sigurd Frosterus, the leading Finnish-Swedish theorist of modern-

· · · · · · · · ·

19 According to the art historian Riitta Konttinen, the reason for writing the book was that Soldan-Brofeldt had two young sons who were interested in the subject. At their summer place in 1909 the family played and experimented with small balloons and kites. (Riitta Konttinen, *Boheemielämää. Venny Soldan-Brofeldtin taiteilijantie.* Helsinki: Otava 1996, pp. 338–339.) Two years earlier Juhani Aho had translated Selma Lagerlöf's book *Nils Holgerssons underbara resa,* which, of course, is about flying.
20 Suomalainen 1910, pp. 114–115.
21 Soldan-Brofeldt 1910, p. 58.
22 As quoted in Phil Scott, *The Pioneers of Flight. A Documentary History.* Princeton, N.J.: Princeton University Press 1999, p. 166.

ism, wrote in 1908 complaining that Henri Farman's aeroplane was lacking in all traces of elaborate form and elegance. Instead, said Frosterus, the machine looks like a plan of a bird with outspread wings, projected onto a piece of paper by a child's untrained hand.[23] Frosterus' article came out one week before Wilbur Wright demonstrated his machine in France, and we do not know what the architect would have made of the expedient forms of the *Wright A*. In his machine aesthetics Frosterus presupposed both form and functionality, and it seemed to him that all early aeroplanes were unsatisfying in comparison with the most developed machines, such as dreadnoughts. A couple of years later Frosterus found the monocoque *Deperdussin*, the speed-record holder of 1913, worthy of some acclaim; this aeroplane was in his mind more like a living being or a strong prehistoric bird. According to Frosterus, the *Deperdussin* was still a machine without charm and grace, but at least suited to the element of air.[24] And yet it is possible that on functional grounds the critical Frosterus might also have found something good in the transparent *Wright A* of 1908. Many commentators had pointed out that the American machine not only flew better but needed merely half the horsepower of a *Voisin* or a *Farman*, and was for that reason considered more elegantly built.[25] But then again, the impact of pioneering aviation was so great that for a time almost any machine capable of flying qualified as an artwork. In the words of an anonymous author, who around 1910 compared Blériot's aeroplane to its famous rival: "This bird is beautiful when it soars in the heights, but the *Antoinette* creates an even more artistic impression [...]."[26] And as the machines were like works of art, it comes as no surprise that their pilots were called artists.[27] Especially those who followed the first constructor-generation were happy to accept the title. According to Torsten Gullberg: "These newcomers were never constructors, nor were they called aviators or pilots. Not yet. They were entitled *flight artists*. With that name they were known all around the world, as was right. And as artists do, they gathered mainly in France, where the creative pulse of art beats hard, where the results are seen from the perspective of upspringing, where success can be greeted with humane enthusiasm instead of crushing it with unclear practical

. . . .

23 "Farmans flygmaskin saknar varje spår av utarbetad form och elegans, och likväl påminner *planen* om en fågel med utbredda vingar, projicierad på pappret av oövad barnahand." Frosterus 1908, p. 4. Frosterus saw that aviation was at its very beginning and only whispered of limitless potential. However, he underlines that the beautiful and undisputed results of Farman and Delagrange should not make us blind to the defects of present aeroplanes.

24 Frosterus in his book *Moderna vapen* [Modern weapons] from 1915, as quoted in Sarje 2000, p. 95. On Frosterus' machine aesthetics, *ibid.*, pp. 86–97.

25 "Wrights aeroplan är betydligt elegantare byggt än Voisin eller Farman." C. H. Hermodsson, *Flygkonsten II*. Verdandis småskrifter 169. Stockholm: Albert Bonnier 1910, p. 26. Hermodsson's text is based on earlier French books.

26 "Kaunis on tämä lintu, kun se korkeuksissa liitelee, mutta vielä taiteellisemman vaikutuksen synnyttää Antoinette-kone [...]." *Luonto tieteen valossa IV*, WSOY, Porvoo 1911, p. 70. The text appears to be a translation from a Swedish or Danish original.

27 "It is, however, an art that is still in its very earliest infancy, an art whose greatest artists are but too well aware that they have yet everything to learn [...]." Silberer 1908, p. 50.

possibilities and dim thoughts of the present moment."[28] As the first decade of the twentieth century was closing, these "artists" toured Europe and charmed audiences in many countries.

Wonder and Disappointment

As the year 1910 ended, Sergei Nikolajeff's *Demoiselle* was still sleeping in its box and no-one had seen an aeroplane in Finland.[29] Therefore the excitement was high when the newspapers announced that a real "flight week" would take place in Helsinki at the end of January 1911. In Sweden and Norway this kind of happening had already been arranged with great success. Over 50,000 people witnessed every flight in Stockholm in September 1910, and a month later in Oslo the atmosphere was even more enthusiastic than in Sweden and the crowds nothing short of enormous. The organizers in Finland were now hoping to see similar masses queueing at their ticket booths.[30] At first nearly "all of Helsinki" – possibly 20,000 people – came to see the greatest wonder of the twentieth century, but it soon became apparent that it was not going to be an easy task to fly in the freezing temperatures, or even take off from the windy and otherwise unsuitable "airfield." While the Danish pilot Knut Thorup was waiting for better weather, the situation allowed people to study a real aeroplane on the ground for the first time. A reporter from the paper *Helsingin Sanomat* was among the first to get a good look at the machine-bird, Thorup's rented *Blériot-Nyrop*. In front of the construction the reporter shared a similar feeling of simplicity as Soldan-Brofeldt had discussed in her book, but he also expressed alarm about the construction's weakness just as the anxious nineteenth-century visitors had when looking at the space covered by the *Crystal Palace*. In the early aeroplanes this relationship between the weak looking structure and the vast space was reversed while the logic remained the same. Will the construction stand up to the vast space? The way the Finnish reporter refutes his own anxiety is the same as that used in 1851: "When one looks at the machine, the weak, delicate rods, the criss-crossing steel wires, one is forced to think: 'that is not going to stand anything.' But despite all the doubts it will. The way every part of the plane is

. . . .

28 "Dessa lärjungar voro icke alltid konstruktörer, de kallades inte heller aviatörer eller piloter. Inte ännu. Deras benämning var 'flygkonstnärer'. Under det namet gingo de i hela världen, och det var riktigt. Och såsom konstnärer samlades de huvudsakligen till Frankrike, där i konstens livsluft skapandets puls sår starkt, där ett resultat ses i tillblivandets perspektiv, där en framgång kan hälsas med enthusiasm av ett stycke mänsklighet utan att söndermulas av ögönblickets oklara praktiska möjligheter och dimmiga betänksamhet." Torsten Gullberg, *Svenska vingar. Pioniärskedet 1900–1930.* [Swedish Wings. The pioneer period, 1900–1930] Stockholm: Holger Schildts Förlag 1929, p. 32.

29 In the neigbouring Sweden and Russia the first flights had taken place in the summer 1909, and in May 1910 there was a meeting of six pilots in St Petersburg. See Dollfus & Bouché 1938, p. 201.

30 On these flight weeks in Stockholm and Oslo where Baron Cederström starred, see Wennberg 1999, pp. 77–88. On the puffing in Finland, see "Alkava lentoviikko Oulunkylässä," *Uusi Suometar*, 29 January 1911.

made perfectly exact, and absolutely the best materials have been used in its structure."[31] The machine seemed indeed ready for air.

The "flight artist" was a hero, even on the ground in wintry Finland. Newspaper articles pictured the pilot Thorup in his blue dungarees as a fearless man with nerves of steel. They said he would remain calm when his aeroplane sped wildly across the airfield. In reality nothing like that seemed to happen, but boosted by the romantic characterizations, and by the coverage of the latest aviation news from Europe, the expectations in Helsinki kept increasing. For some days the audience waited patiently in freezing temparatures but as the weather remained unfavourable for two weeks and cancellations followed one another, the crowd grew smaller and smaller. Thorup's *Blériot*-machine was replaced by a *Voisin* owned by another Dane, Robert Svendsen, and the "airfield" was moved closer to town, but this did not bring back the disappointed audience. Finally, on 12 February 1911 when Svendsen made the first aeroplane flight in Finland, only ten people or so witnessed the miracle.[32] One of them described the happening: "The enormous bird trembled. . . The screaming beast was let loose and with a wild speed it rushed forward. The aeroplane rising higher and higher was a tremendous vision."[33] Svendsen had flown six hundred metres and reached the height of twentyfive metres. Everything was over in a minute and a half. The organizers sustained a heavy loss and the public who had seen nothing accused them of cheating. One of the thousands of viewers who had come to see the flights, but was forced to return home frustrated, was sculptor Adolf Aarno.[34]

April Fool's Day

"The greatest invention of our century, the Aeroplane, is on display," said the advertisement in the newspaper and did not lie. Adolf Aarno had bought the light-weight *Demoiselle* from the corpulent Sergei Nikolajeff at one third of its original price, and in order to cover part of the expenses the practically minded sculptor had decided to organize an exhibition.[35] The place was as central as possible. Aarno had rented the so-called "pump room," a disused fire-fighters'

. . . .

31   "Kun katselee konetta, heikkoja, siroja tankoja, ristiin rastiin kulkevia teräslankoja, ajattelee wäkisin, että 'ei tuo tuollainen mitään kestä.' Mutta niin täydellisen tarkasti on siinä joka osa tehty ja niin ehdottomasti parhaita aineita on rakenteessa käytetty, että se kaikista arveluista huolimatta kestää." *Helsingin Sanomat*, 29 January 1911. It has been argued that in reality Thorup's machine, a weak Swedish-made copy of *Blériot XI*, was not in flying order during its stay in Helsinki, see Janarmo 1963, p. 53.
32   Janarmo 1963, p. 52.
33   "Valtava lintu tärisi. . . Ulvova peto päästettiin irti ja hurjalla vauhdilla se syöksyi eteenpäin. Yhä korkeammalle ja korkeammalle nouseva aeroplaani tarjosi valtavan näyn." *ibid.*
34   Ahonius 1961, p. 42.
35   All taxes and transportation included the aeroplane had cost Nikolajeff 9,000 Finnish marks but he eventually sold it to Aarno for a mere 3,000. (Ahonius 1961, p. 28 and p. 43.) Tickets to the exhibition were at first 1 mark for adults and 50 pennies for children, but later Aarno reduced the prices to half so that also workers could afford to come. Around 1,000 visitors saw the aeroplane exhibition in nine days. (*ibid.*, p. 50.)

equipment building at Hämeenkatu, the main street of Tampere, right next to the Town Hall. At the time there were no specific galleries or museums in Tampere, and the empty and undecorated pump room offered possibly the best surroundings for such an extravagant exhibition. As soon as the crate containing the *Demoiselle* had arrived in Tampere and had been moved to the pump room, Aarno and his helpers built a podium for the aeroplane and started to put the machine together. None of the men had any previous knowledge of aeroplanes, but since there were no aeroplane mechanics in the whole country they were compelled to do everything themselves. Aarno knew something about machines and had learned to maintain his motorcycle, but the most qualified technician in the team was Kustaa Tuominen, the owner of a local bicycle shop.[36] Luckily, the construction of the *Demoiselle* was fairly simple and the kit came with illustrated French instructions which Aarno could easily read and translate. This small manual remained his basic education on flying also at a later stage when he tried to launch his plane into the sky from the frozen Lake Pyhäjärvi.[37]

The first news about the aeroplane appeared in the Tampere newspapers *Aamulehti*, *Tampereen Sanomat* and *Kansan Lehti* on 1 April 1911 and many readers mistook it for an April Fool's Day hoax. The workers' daily *Kansan Lehti* commented on the two other papers and announced that unlike its competitors it had confirmed information about the plane's time of arrival. Meanwhile, the local Swedish newspaper, *Tammerfors Nyheter*, having written seriously about the plane already a day before, now decided to make a genuine April Fool's Day hoax about the plane's public test flights, which of course did not take place, and thus encouraged the man on the street in his disbelief. The whole aeroplane business sounded basically fictional since the local restaurant *Hämeen Pohja* also advertised its Great April Masquerade as an "Aviation show" with an opportunity to see a real aeroplane.[38] No wonder that the journalists later had to convince their readers that "*the aeroplane really is in Tampere.*"[39] Aarno himself advertised the show in the city's three Finnish language newspapers with a total of ten advertisements.

The aeroplane was put together and placed in the middle of the room on a purposely-built pedestal approximately fifty centimetres high. The machine and the pedestal were then surrounded with a rope. It is fairly easy for us to imagine

. . . .

36 Tuominen also did the repairs to Aarno's motorcycle. See Ahonius 1961, p. 44. Aeroplanes and bicycles were of course by 1911 a historical combination as the stories of the legendary Wright Brothers were printed over and over again.

37 According to Rainer Ahonius, who came to know Aarno during the exhibition, the only other text on flying Aarno had read was C. H. Hermodsson's small two-part booklet *Flygkonsten* [Art of Flying], published in Stockholm in 1910. Ahonius 1961, p. 50. The flight attempts with the *Demoiselle* do not concern us here, but let us note that the first on Lake Pyhäjärvi (20 April 1911) ended ignominiously and the second on Lake Näsijärvi (8 March 1914) in a crash. A piece of the propeller is all that remains.

38 According to *Kansan Lehti*, the aeroplane arrived at Tampere railwaystation on 1 April at 8.08 p.m. but this is hardly the case since *Tampereen Sanomat* published an original drawing of the assembled aeroplane standing in its showroom in their Sunday number 2 April. According to Ahonius the aeroplane had been presented to some journalists already in the morning of 31 March. The aeroplane then must have arrived to town at least a day before.

39 *Kansan Lehti*, 3 April 1911.

what such a simple exhibition must have looked like, but much harder to feel what it was like to see an aeroplane for the first time. Reading through the contemporary articles the new machine appears to have been difficult to understand – and all the more difficult to be understood within an aesthetic context like that of Soldan-Brofeldt. For beauty and function had a bond. As Benjamin Baker, the British engineer and designer of the *Forth Bridge*, had noted when defending his own work in the 1890s: "It is impossible for anyone to pronounce authoritatively on the beauty of an object without knowing its function."[40] The reporters of the Tampere newspapers write about the aeroplane without really understanding how it works and the lack aesthetic evaluations in their texts seems to prove Baker right. What indeed was the function of this aeroplane standing as an exhibition piece in Tampere? It had never left the ground, and was not famous for anything, unlike the Channel-crossing *Blériot* that attracted masses of people in London two years earlier. How was Aarno's aeroplane to be admired?

Aarno's Demoiselle pictured on the front page of Tampereen Sanomat, 2 April 1911.

The Tampere newspapers *Aamulehti* and *Tammerfors Nyheter* give detailed information about the machine but the texts are clearly based on a technical briefing given by Aarno, who in his turn had gleaned the statistics from the French manual. The firsthand impressions of the reporters are missing because they did not know what exactly to be impressed by. They seem to have understood the historical importance of this technical device as the first of its kind in the country, but not the device itself, nor its form. And naturally the reporters did not make a connection between the sculptor Aarno's profession and the machine standing on the pedestal. An exhibition with nothing but an aeroplane sounds potentially ultra-modern, but there were no Futurists whatsoever in Tampere in 1911, and, as seen in Part One, even the Futurists were not particularly clever with machines at the time. That Aarno's machine represented the

. . . .
40   From an unnotated quotation in Baxandall 1988, p. 24.

latest development in urban technology was, however, duly noted. *Aamulehti* is happy that the citizens of Tampere are finally catching up with modern times; at first the handsome automobiles (*"often two or three in a row"*), then the plans to build a tramway, and now, the ultimate culmination, the aeroplane.[41] But when it comes to writing about the actual flying machine its name, weight, and horsepower seem to suffice. The upper class readers of *Tammerfors Nyheter* are given an equally impersonal technical list but with a touch of continental finesse. According to the reporter's sources the *Demoiselle* is *"le plus joli, le plus vite, le plus léger et le plus petit aeroplane du monde,"* but the fine description goes no further than a Clément-Byard advertisement.[42]

The first, and it seems that also the only, attempt at a description of the aeroplane's visual appearance is by a reporter for the workers' daily *Kansan Lehti*. On 6 April he writes about the show in the "Sports" column: "Yesterday we went to see that wonderful apparatus. It is indeed an aeroplane, similar to those you have seen for example in the images displayed in Kansan Lehti's show case. The frame is made of lightweight tubes, and at the front, over the plane which is made of silk fabric, there is a powerful engine which spins the two-blade propeller made of applewood. In the tail are the three parts forming the elevator plane and the rudder. Right under the front planes is the pilot's seat and the control devices. And underneath the whole thing there are three rubber wheels on which the bird goes and buzzes along the ground before lifting itself into the air. As a whole the machine is quite beautiful, like a giant dragon-fly [...]."[43] Here the writer bases his story on his observation of the materials, and although he compares the beauty of the *Demoiselle* very unsurprisingly to what its French name suggests, a dragon-fly, it is remarkable that he talks about beauty at all. The fact that he is really writing about what he sees is proved by the mistake of taking the propeller material (mahogany) to be applewood. Although the short aesthetic evaluation appears to be a lonely one, it was shared by at least one spectator. Among the audience was a boy of fifteen who came to see the aeroplane every day. Aarno soon noticed him and took him on as his young assistant. Fifty years later he wrote a book on Aarno, describing also his own feelings about the exhibition: "To a person interested in flying, who for the first

. . . .
41 *Aamulehti*, 1 April 1911. Tampere was the industrial centre of Finland and by no means a backward town. Tampere had seen the first knitting machine (1839) and the first paper machine (1842) in Finland, as well as the first electric light in the Nordic countries (1882). The town produced high technology, such as railway engines, but for some reason the automobile did not arrive to Tampere earlier than 1906.

42 *Tammerfors Nyheter*, 31 March 1911. For Clément-Byard's advertisement, see Wykeham 1962.

43 "Eilen käwimme katsomassa tuota ihmeellistä laitetta. Se todellakin on lentokone, sellainen, joita olette nähneet kuwallisina esim. Kansan Lehden kuwakaapissa. Runko kewyistä putkeista, edessä wahwasta stikkikankaasta [?] tehty taso, jonka päällä woimakas moottori pyörittää kaksisiipistä, omenapuusta tehtyä potkuria. Häntäpäässä kolmiosainen korkeus- ja ohjaustaso. Etutasojen alla on ohjaajan istuin ja ohjauswehkeet. Ja koko laitoksen alla kolme kumipyörää, joilla lintu mennä hyrisee maata myöten ennen kuin se nousee ilmaan. Kokonaisuutena on kone warsin kaunis, on kuin jättiläissuuri sudenkorento [...]." *Kansan Lehti*, 6 April 1911.

time saw a real aeroplane, the graceful *Demoiselle* standing on a pedestal made a fabulous impact. The brand-new machine with its beautifully curving wings of brownish yellow was a truly splendid sight. The big and beautiful mahogany propeller in its front strengthened the general impression. The aeroplane made a wonderfully simple, yet in every way appropriate impression. The longer the viewer studied its details, the more convinced he was that the *Demoiselle* was perfect. It felt like – and so it was at the time – that the machine represented the highest peak of progress, something which hardly leaves room for improvement. No-one doubted its excellent ability to fly."[44] The aeroplane on the pedestal left a deep mark on the young boy. When he grew up he would think of only one profession.

Venny Soldan-Brofeldt's lines about the simple beauty of the flying machine were exceptional. For most people it was not easy to grasp the artistic dimension of the machine even when it was displayed on a pedestal. The technical dimension alone seem to have been difficult enough to understand. We do not know if the sculptor Adolf Aarno ever thought about his flying machine in the same way as the painter Venny Soldan-Brofeldt had written about the Wrights' aeroplane, that is, as an artefact analogous to a work of art. But standing on its pedestal, the *Demoiselle* did indeed make some people talk about aesthetic matters. It was, after all, a beautiful machine to look at.

. . . .

44 "Ilmailusta kiinnostuneeseen, joka ensimmäisen kerran näki oikean lentokoneen, teki korokkeella seisova, siro Demoiselle suurenmoisen vaikutuksen. Uutuuttaan hohtava kone kauniisti kaarevine kellanruskeine siipineen oli todella komeata katseltavaa. Sen edessä oleva iso ja kaunis mahonkipotkuri tehosti vielä koneen yleisvaikutelmaa. Lentokone teki ihmeteltävän yksinkertaisen, mutta silti kaikinpuolin tarkoituksenmukaisen vaikutuksen. Mitä enemmän sen moniin yksityiskohtiin syventyi, sitä vakuuttuneemmaksi katselija tuli Demoisellen täydellisyydestä. Tuntui siltä – ja sitähän se silloin olikin – että kone esitti kehityksen ehdotonta huippua, jossa parantamisen varaa tuskin enää oli. Sen verratonta lentokykyäkään ei kukaan epäillyt." Ahonius 1961, p. 49.

■ Helsinki 1921: The Eyes in the Sky

The man who is intelligent, cold and calm has grown wings to himself. Men – intelligent, cold and calm – are needed to build the house and to lay out the town.[1]

Le Corbusier

The bird's-eye view: at the present, from directly overhead, cities look like currycombs, like hairbrushes. Will it be like that in a city of winged inhabitants?[2]

Velimir Khlebnikov

In spring 1921 an article appeared in a small Helsinki journal called *Kerberos*. It was a description of the first aeroplane flight by the twenty-three year old architecture student Alvar Aalto. The article resulted from an exchange of dreams: Aalto's flight seems to have been a payment for the bedroom furniture he had designed for the pilot, his friend Captain Gunnar Holmqvist.[3] To settle the contract the two men had met on a mild winter morning at the military base of Santahamina, five kilometres outside Helsinki:

"It is a sunny morning at the hangars of Santahamina island. Aeroplanes are buzzing outside on the ice, engines are being tested in the hangar, it's all life and the rhythm of engines. A *Caudron* stands ready, Captain af Looping's machine.[4] – The engine starts rumbling. I get my goggles on and climb up. The captain is sitting behind me, the mechanics let go, and we're off, way out onto the ice and then – rising.

. . . .

1   Le Corbusier 1995, p. 100. The English translation here by Frederick Etchells (*Towards a New Architecture*, 1927).
2   Khlebnikov 1987, p. 347.
3   Aalto does not say that that the flight and the drawings for the furniture was a change of favours, but circumstantial evidence supports this view. For captain Holmqvist's furniture, see the list of Aalto's early works, No 21, in Schildt 1984, p. 265. Holmqvist got his wings in 1918. He has been called the "Father of Finnish Aerobatics," which explains why Aalto names him "Captain af Looping" (*af* being a Swedish equivalent for German *von*). On Holmqvist, see Lauri Larjo, *Taitolento ja sen historia* [Aerobatics and its History]. Helsinki: Otava 1947, pp. 52–56, 60–61 and 302–303.
4   In the original text the aeroplane is called "Oudron," in Schildt 1984 "Oudon." Both are misspellings. The machine was *Caudron G.3*, a one-engine French training plane with two seats. For no apparent reason it was nicknamed in Finland as "Tutankhamen." The Finnish Air Force had 19 of these planes in service between 1920 and 1924. See Timo Heinonen, *Thuli-*

The sun is shining and the machine climbs straight up towards it. I have heard people call the sun beautiful. They should see it through a propellor, a motor-wing revolving at dizzying speed – then it is really something. But one thousand four revolutions per minute is also beauty of a high order. There is almost more art in that figure than in all the watercolours and antique furniture in the world, to say nothing of porcelain painting.

And the machine rises, soaring up like the devil himself at an angle whose every degree is poetry, and after a few minutes' manoeuvering my friend the captain has set the whole proud city of Helsinki at our feet. At last we have found our true place in life.

Who has not sometimes looked down on his neighbour and felt himself superior. But the problem always used to be that the environment did not acknowledge this higher level. Things were different here. Now we were actually superior, exactly defined in metres. We were riding high and there was no point in anyone grumbling about it.

We saw the people on the ground, on the Esplanade, and they looked terrifyingly small, just as small as they really are. And they said to us. – "*Die Wirklichkeit kann bisweilen zur Dichtung werden.*" [Reality can sometimes turn into poetry.]

Then we took a look at Helsinki, the city and its architecture. My friend the captain and myself exchanged opinions on the art of town planning. We shouted, but if there was something that had to be said pianissimo, the engine was stopped. A machine is its master's slave.

Senate Square and the city around it really is beautifully arranged. Even the Esplanade runs nicely, but it is short and blunt. All the rest of the town, built by idiots, will be blown up when the captain and I become regents.

I thought of the old men who had looked after this city, of Ehrenström and Engel. They wanted to draw many a beautiful line in their time, and there is still much beautiful in our city, but a flyer can see that apes have been at work and have destroyed quite a lot. I thought of Saarinen's avenue. A lovely idea. We'll see whether anything will come of it.

But to come back to the machine. It spiralled until the city danced beneath us, it glided down in *vol plané*, and rose again. It waved its wings to the larvae and all the poor souls on the ground. Up in the air captain af Looping does what the devil he wants. (I believe he does the same down there among the people, but that is another matter.)

It was windy and cold up there, of course. But we saw a large slice of the republic, shadows cast by clouds and all. It was like a vast seven-league forest with one solitary railway line through it. And beautiful. Our archipelago is really fine.

. . . .

nista Hornetiin. 75 vuotta Suomen ilmavoimien lentokoneita. [From Thulin to Hornet. 75 Years of the Finnish Air Force Aeroplanes] Tikkakoski: Keski-Suomen Ilmailumuseo 1992, pp. 52–53.

MIN VÄN KAPTEN „AF LOOPING."

Helsinki's Esplanade seen from the aeroplane, and a perfect landing. Alvar Aalto's drawings for his article 1921. (Kerberos 2/1921, p. 10.)

Then we start approaching Santahamina again. On the way we take a peek at Kulosaari and look down a chimney to see Armas Lindgren and family, just miss taking a few tiles off the professor's roof and are soon circling a few hundred metres above the hangar.[5] The captain stops the engine, and we come down in the world's finest spiral and land in cotton. Fine – damn fine.

I could go on about flying with my friend the captain or go on about him; he is the first to have looped the loop in Finland. But you can all see him daily above Helsinki. Keep an eye on the machine which carries a white Cerberus with golden wings on its keel, for it is my friend captain af Looping. He who can read man's emotion from the curves which an aeroplane draws in the air should look up. All the others with their down turned eyes should go to the pub.

Tomorrow I will go out and hit a well-dressed man on the head, just to show that flying creates power. This is to honour 'les Hommes-Oiseaux' and above all my friend Captain af Looping."[6]

As Seem from Above

Alvar Aalto's flight over Helsinki on 16 February 1921 was little more than a short circle over the town, but he makes it sound like a larger-than-life experi-

. . . .

5   Architect Armas Lindgren, best known for his collaboration with Eliel Saarinen, was Aalto's teacher at the Technical University.

6   Aalto 1921. The text was written in Swedish. Apart from its first paragraph the text is printed here in full. The English translation follows the one by Timothy Binham in Schildt 1984, pp. 134–135. I have added here the parts omitted by Schildt and made minor corrections. When Aalto's friend and biographer, Göran Schildt, prints the text he leaves out some relevant passages without telling his readers. The "censored" parts are the ones where Aalto talks about his superiority over ordinary people, how from above people look as small as they are in real life, and the end where Aalto promises to go and hit a well-dressed man on the head.

ence – which it probably was.[7] Civil aviation was still in its infancy in Finland, and the architectural layout of the capital, as seen from a military plane, is a rarity. Aalto treats the flying machine with such enthusiasm that in the 1980s his biographer Göran Schildt would write about his "almost Futuristic outpourings."[8] Despite the vivid vocabulary, the reference to Futurism may give the wrong idea. Its advocates were not very well known in Finland and at the time of his flight the young architect – he would receive his degree later in the spring 1921 – was drawing anything but radical architecture.[9] But at the same time his text is certainly different from all the other flight accounts in contemporary Finnish papers. Aalto was an experienced causerie writer with the skill to describe both the aesthetics of flying and the landscape underneath him, whereas the real journalists and writing pilots only usually recorded boring facts.[10] But Aalto's humorous text, appropriate for the light entertainment magazine, also has a darker side. The joke about blowing away the rest of the town, "built by idiots," has unconscious irony. Of course Aalto could not foresee the future mass bombings of World War II, but his approach to his fellow men down below is characterized by a feeling of superiority, a sentiment not untypical of many modernist architects. The aeroplane seems to bring out this side of his personality: to Aalto the people on the streets look small because they actually are small compared to him. The flying architect can see that "apes have been at work" and that grand lines are missing. A telling detail is that the only acceptable part of the town, the area around the Senate Square was built during the autocratic rule of the Russian Tsars. Of the more recent city planning only Eliel Saarinen's 1918 proposal for a grand avenue was to Aalto's liking. It comes as no surprise that Aalto himself would return to these ideas later at the height of his career and propose a masterplan for the centre of Helsinki.[11]

. . . .

7   Aalto talks about morning but according to Holmqvist's flight log, the plane 2A 490 took off from Santahamina at 3.15 pm and returned at 3.30 pm. Aalto is named as a trainee. (Gunnar Holmqvist, Flight Logs, flight N:o 175. Finnish Air Force Museum Archives, Tikkakoski.) The weather during the flight was half cloudy but otherwise fine. The ground temperature at 3.00 pm was –2.3 °C and the wind 6 m/s from WNW. (Ilmatieteelliset havainnot Suomessa vuonna 1921. *Suomen Meteorologinen Vuosikirja XXI – osa 1 – 1921*. Helsinki 1926.)

8   Schildt 1984, p. 134.

9   The reference to Futurism may also overshadow the fact that in Finland some architects had expressed new modernistic ideas well before the first Futurist manifesto of 1909. In their pamphlet *Architecture: a challenge to our opponents* from 1904 Gustav Strengell and Sigurd Frosterus had declared: "[...] the future architect has far more to learn from the the Atlantic steamer and the electric tram, from the racer and the motor car, from American office interiors and English lavatories, than he does from art forms belonging to the past." (See *Abacus*. Yearbook 3. Helsinki: Museum of Finnish Architecture 1983, p. 64.) In the following years Frosterus became the leading theorist of machine aesthetics in Scandinavia, publishing many articles and two collections *Moderna vapen* [Modern Weapons] and *Olikartade skönhetsvärlden* [A Different World of Beauty], both from 1915. Aalto used Swedish fluently and may have read Frosterus' essays. Later in the 1920s Finns had some brief contacts with Futurists. Traveling in Italy in 1923, the sculptor Wäinö Aaltonen met Marinetti in person. See *Wäinö Aaltonen 1894–1966*. Turku: Wäinö Aaltosen museo 1994, p. 318.

10   See for example Kuno W. Chanson, "Vaikutelmani 6000 m. korkeudessa," [My impressions at 6,000 m.] *Suomen Kuvalehti* 24/1920, p. 548. Two years later, however, Chanson came up with a more impressionistic article "Miltä lentäminen tuntuu," [On the feeling of flying] *Finlandia vuosikirja 1922*. Helsinki: Matkatoimisto Finlandia 1922.

11   For Aalto's Helsinki plan of the 1960s, see Schildt, 1991, pp. 288–299, with a picture of Eliel Saarinen's proposed avenue, mentioned in Aalto's text, on page 288.

Judging the city from above. Alvar Aalto's drawing from 1920. (Kerberos 2/1920, p. 12.)

Flying created a feeling of power, especially in this young architect, and made him see his fellow-men in a new light. Aalto's delight in flying was a sign of his enthusiasm for "modern life," but it also became a metaphor of his desired status. Aalto was an upstart and for some time aeroplanes served his flamboyance. Three and half years after his first flight Aalto – still an unknown provincial architect with two commissions – accompanied his wife Aino on a honeymoon in Italy in a *Junkers F 13* passenger plane from Helsinki. A rather extravagant gesture from a man looking "[…] like a little country boy. His hat was much too big and hung down over his ears," "surprisingly countrified," and even "unkempt."[12] But a few years later Aalto's suits were immaculate and his modern self-confidence overwhelming. Returning home from his European study-trip in 1928 he proclaimed: "Flying is now the only acceptable form of travel for a cultured person. Trains and ferries are packed with all sorts of mixed folk, whereas in aeroplanes one only meets selected people in whose company one

· · · · · · · · ·

12   Recollections of Aalto by Swedish contemporaries from 1923 and 1926; see Schildt 1984, p. 124, and 1986, p. 49. The honeymoon took place in October 1924. The Finnish airline AERO had started in March with one aeroplane and a staff of three: director Lucander, pilot Lihr, and errand boy Niinivaara. During the year 1924 the company's "bird," *Junkers F 13*, named at the factory as *Regenpfeifer* (Golden plover) and marked D 335, carried 269 passengers, four at a time. See Esko Laine, "Aero Oy Helsinki 1923–1933," *Suomen Siivet* 5/ 1973, pp. 12–14.

need never feel embarrassed."[13] In reality Aalto could not afford flying as much as he may have liked, and he still had to condescend to third class railway coaches, as he did on his way to the CIAM congress in Athens in 1933. The theme of this famous congress, where Aalto joined the company of Le Corbusier, Sigfried Giedion and others, was the "Functional City." The concept had perhaps more to do with dreams than with existing reality. In those dreams, however, aeroplanes also played a part.

As the poet Velimir Khlebnikov anticipated in the opening lines of this chapter, the bird's-eye view of aviation was going to change the notion of the city. The consequences of this new architectural viewpoint were discussed soon after the aeroplane became a practical reality. Joseph Corn has revealed an early comment published in a magazine called *American Homes and Gardens* in 1911. "The architect of the future may be obliged to lavish the same care upon the roof as he now bestows upon the fasade of a public building," wrote the journalist, and cited an architect who was convinced that architectural style would change simply because flat roofs are needed to handle aircraft landings.[14] It was only a matter of time before the city of "winged inhabitants" emerged on the drawing-boards.

Poet of Rooftops

Velimir Khlebnikov's father was an ornithologist, and as a young man the poet, too, published some articles on birdwatching.[15] Yet in the above comment about "winged inhabitants" he is not talking about a city of birds but a city of flying people. The citation comes from the essay *Ourselves and Our Buildings*, written probably around 1915, where Khlebnikov discusses his architectural vision.[16]

· · · · · · · ·

13 "Lentomatkustus on nykyään ainoa kulttuuri-ihmisen matkustustapa. Junat ja laivat ovat täynnä kaiken maailman sekakansaa, mutta lentokoneissa tapaa vain valittua väkeä, jonka seurassa ei koskaan tunne vaivautuvansa." Aalto's interview "Mitä arkkitehti Aallolle kuuluu." [How is architect Aalto doing?] in the newspaper *Sisä-Suomi*, 18 August 1928. (English translation based on Schildt 1986, p. 55.) Others may have felt embarrased, though. Later in the 1940s, when flying had become more ordinary, Aalto could arrive at Helsinki airport deliberately late and keep the transatlantic plane – and its passengers – waiting for him. See Schildt 1991, p. 304.

14 Walter Kaempffert's article from 1911, quoted in Corn 1983, p. 37. The subject was known in Europe too, as shown by the article entitled "Luftschiffahrt und Architektur" [Airship travel and Architecture] in *Frankfurter Zeitung* on 21 March 1909. Mentioned in Asendorf 1997, p. 1.

15 For information on the poet's family, see Khlebnikov 1987, pp. 1–7; the articles on birds, *ibid.* pp. 199–221.

16 I use here the English title given in the *Collected Works*, other renderings of the title are "Houses and Us" (Lodder, Zhadova) and "We and Houses" (Cooke). The text was published posthumously and we have no exact dating; in the *Collected Works* Charlotte Douglas thinks it could be from 1920–21, but Raymond Cooke believes it was written about 1915. (Raymond Cooke, *Velimir Khlebnikov. A Critical Study*. Cambridge: Cambridge University Press 1987, p. 185.) The earlier dating is supported by Zhadova, who gives the date 1915–1916 also to the sketches "Architecture of the Future," where Khlebnikov has drawn pictures of some of the buildings he discusses in his text. (Zhadova 1988, pictures 224 and 225.) Lodder on the other hand dates the same drawings *c.* 1920, but the manuscript 1914–1915. See Lodder 1983, picture 7.1. and p. 298, n. 17.

He is convinced that flying will bring about a radical change in the way we normally see our cities: "People now look at a city from the side; in the future they will look from directly overhead. The roof will become the main thing, the axis of the standing structure. With swarms of flyers and the face of the street above it, the city will begin to be concerned about its roofs and not its walls. Consider the roof as a thing in itself."[17] Khlebnikov's ideas about a future architecture are based on social rather than formal considerations. Roofs represent a new, cleaner and healthier life: "It basks in the blue, far from the dirty clouds of dust. A roof has no desire to imitate the pavement."[18] The poet also offers a broader picture of this new city, charactrized by light, iron, glass, and order: "We ride high in the saddle and shout: that's the way we want to go, toward those glass sunflowers in the iron shrubbery, toward cities whose patterns are as harmonious as a fisherman's net streched out on the beach, cities of glass, shiny as inkwells, who compete among themselves for sunshine and a scrap of sky as if they were part of the vegetable kingdom. 'Sunward' is written upon them in the terrifying alphabet of iron consonants and vowels of glass!"[19]

According to Khlebnikov, the traditional city with its dusty and noisy streets belongs to the past. In the new city the direction is upwards towards the sky: "People will no longer gather in the vicious streets, whose dirty desire reduces human beings to residue in a washbasin; rather they will throng upon rooftops, beautiful young rooftops, waving their handkerchiefs after a giant levitating air-cloud, sending goodbyes and farewells after their departing friends."[20] Eventually the whole structure of the future city is based on the new invention: "The city crowds will no longer move about on foot or on their four-legged colleagues; they will have learned to fly above the city, raining their glances upon the place below."[21] But at this point Khlebnikov fails to explain what would be the means of flying. The practical aeroplane was of course available, yet it seems that Khlebnikov has something else in mind. His reference to walking and riding suggests a muscle-powered solution, not a motor-driven one. This reminds us very much of the ideas of Khlebnikov's friend and collaborator Vladimir Tatlin, who believed that with his machine the *Letatlin* people could fly in the air in the same way they swim in the water. It has been reported that Tatlin, just like Khlebnikov, believed that the flying machine would be a key to a healthier urban environment: "The air bicycle will relieve

. . . .

17 Khlebnikov 1987, p. 348. Khlebnikov has a great variety of ideas for future houses and not all of them relate to flying. His "poplar-tree-building" is interesting as its central shaft resembles an enormous bell tower and the top of the building serves as a landing platform. *ibid.* p. 353.

18 *Ibid.*, p. 348.

19 *Ibid.*, p. 347.

20 *Ibid.*, p. 348.

21 *Ibid.* This science fictional idea found its most fantastic architectural expression in the "flying city" of Georgi Krutikov. He envisioned that the buildings would also fly in the air. On Krutikov, see O. S. Han-Magomedov, "Georgij Krutikov. Projet de ville volante." *Cahiers du musée national d'art moderne* (Centre Georges Pompidou, Paris) 2/1979, pp. 241–247.

the town of transport, of noise, and overcrowding, and will cleanse the air of petrol fumes."[22]

Young rooftops and buildings of iron and glass were more than day-dreams of one peculiar poet. They were ideas that came to interest also Le Corbusier, the self-proclaimed leader of the new architecture. "Why is it that the pretty suburban villas have these immense useless roofs?" he asked in 1923 in his book *Vers une architecture*.[23] He also tested the idea of making use of the roof in his buildings, most famously in *Villa Savoye* (1928–1931) with separate levels for automobiles and people, and the roof opening to the sky.[24] Le Corbusier did not suggest that rooftops should be decorated for the pleasure of aviators, but it is not without meaning that in the book his main slogans for the new kind of architecture – *Le problème de la maison n'est pas posé* – *La maison est une machine à habiter* – appeared under the heading *Les Avions*. For some reason Le Corbusier saw the structure of aeroplanes as analogous to his rational principles of building. He argued that the functional aeroplane was the result of a well stated question. As an example of the opposite served a familiar machine: Clément Ader's "Bat," the *Avion III*, which, said Le Corbusier, never left the ground because it was not based on pure mechanics but on the wish to fly like a bird.[25]

In *Vers une architecture* Le Corbusier did not analyze the flying machines further than this, but he decorated its pages with many pictures of aeroplanes. The most popular selection, appearing on seven pages, was *Goliath*, a large passenger plane built in 1919 by the Farman company.[26] Another aeroplane attractive to Le Corbusier was the gigantic triple-three-winged flying boat *Caproni Ca.60 Transaero*, also known as the *Capronissimo*. Its elaborate system of nine wings was indeed an architectonic sight and reminiscent of the box-like system of floors and *pilotis* in functionalist houses. But instead of saying this, Le Corbusier wrote that the *hydrotricellulaire* aeroplane was capable of carrying one hundred passengers.[27] In reality it did not carry a single one. The badly overweight machine was destroyed in 1921 in an accident during its first flight attempts.[28] The *Capronissimo* case shows that Le Corbusier's conception of pure mechanics and machine aesthetics was rather flimsy. Contrary to his claims, the spirit that built the *Parthenon* and the one that made aeroplanes like the *Caproni Ca.60* was not the same.[29] And if the constructive-

. . . .

22 According to the undated memoirs of Hanna Begicheva, quoted in Lodder 1983, p. 214. I will return to Tatlin's plans and discuss them in detail right after this chapter.
23 Le Corbusier 1995, p. 90.
24 See Curtis 1986, p. 98. Curtis writes about "the urgent expression of a utopian dream," and points out that the famous free-standing washing basin in the ground level hall "invites ablutions before the ascent." *ibid.*, p. 96.
25 Le Corbusier 1995, p. 89
26 *Ibid.*, pages 86, 91, 93, 94, 95, 97, 99.
27 *Ibid.*, p. 89.
28 See for example Dollfus & Bouché 1938, p. 535, and Abate, Alegi & Apostolo 1992, p. 100.
29 "On peut donc affirmer que l'avion a mobilisé l'invention, l'intelligence et la hardiesse: l'*imagination* et la *raison froide*. Le même esprit a construit le Parthénon." Le Corbusier 1995, p. 85.

looking Italian aeroplane that captured his imagination did not perform any better than Ader's much earlier bio-technical apparatus, then what was the point of the *problème bien posé* arguments about the design of aeroplanes? What was it that he wanted to prove with the aeroplane images? Le Corbusier obviously thought that the *Capronissimo* would do what its designers had promised, and did not bother about it. But was this all he knew about aeroplanes and other modern machines?

In his article "The Machine Aesthetic" from 1955, Reyner Banham discussed Le Corbusier's superficiality in technical matters, as well as his crooked, partly verbal and partly visual argumentation in *Vers une architecture*.[30] According to Banham, Le Corbusier was not even a provincial, but a complete backwoods-man in the world of engineering. Banham saw that Le Corbusier's view of machinery was a form of self-deception, but admitted that the falsity of this Machine Aesthetic was not visible at the time, for automotive, aeronautical and naval design were currently going through a phase when their products did literally resemble those of Functionalist architecture.[31] If it was the resemblance that mattered most, we might presume that aeroplanes did not attract Le Corbusier so much because they flew but because their construction looked interesting. They looked functional, and that sufficed. Perhaps this passive admiration was all he meant when he wrote that there is a mechanical side in every modern man.[32] Other, more organic sides may have been predominant and active. It is not surprising that judging by his notebooks, Le Corbusier did not find aeroplanes a subject worth drawing. Automobiles, ocean liners, and aeroplanes were part of the *L'Esprit Nouveau* rhetoric, but it seems that in private Le Corbusier remained more interested in organic forms than in machines. The notebook from his visit to South America in 1929 has some views drawn from an aeroplane, and one of these depicts an engine and part of the landing gear, but that is all. In the same notebook Brazilian ladies are treated much more passionately, as Françoise de Franclieu remarks: "Portraits of women (busts and silhouettes) are massive and powerful, drawn with a vigorous pencil line that reflects the artist's emotion."[33] The aeroplane may well have been a symbol of the new age but big women were always more alive.

Bomber

Although Le Corbusier studied the details of machines, his way of using them is just as rhetorical as it had been in the manifesto of the Futurists and in the text of Guillame Apollinaire from the early 1910s. Alongside the photographs, however, we can find another, more important link between the flying machines and

. . . .

30   Banham 1981, p. 44.
31   *Ibid.*, p. 45.
32   "Dans tout homme moderne, il y a une mécanique." Le Corbusier 1995, p. 100.
33   Le Corbusier 1981, p. 13. The aeroplane engine appears in pic. 252.

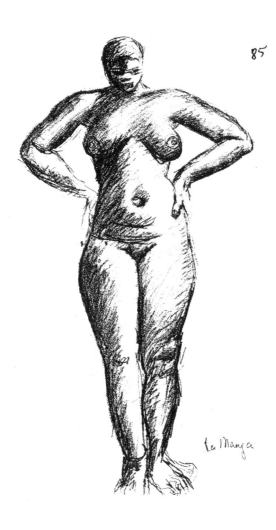

From Le Corbusier's Brasilian notebook. (Le Corbusier 1981, pic. 276.)

85

the architectural ideas of Le Corbusier. In the Salon d'Automne of 1922, Le Corbusier introduced his plan *Une ville contemporaine,* a functionalist city for three million inhabitants. One of the main characteristics of this plan was the central station. On the lowest level underground would be the railway stations, over them on ground level the motorway, and on top the aerodrome.[34] All the

. . . .

34 The idea of building an airport on top of a railway station had appeared earlier in Antonio Sant'Elia's plan for a *Stazione Aeroplani* in 1912. Le Corbusier's idea gave wings to even more daring proposals. In 1924–1925, Naum Gabo drew plans for towers with an aircraft platform on their top. (See Martin Hammer & Christina Lodder, *Constructing Modernity. The Art & Career of Naum Gabo.* New Haven & London: Yale University Press 2000, pp. 144–145.) The architects' airport proposals were, however, rather general compared with the vision of H. G. Wells in his *When the Sleeper Wakes* (1899). Wells describes Flying Stages where passengers are waiting for their flights in theatres, restaurants, newsrooms, and shops. There are also devotional chapels and medical establishments, as well as a complex system of special passages and lifts and slides for the convenient interchange of people and luggage between stage and stage.

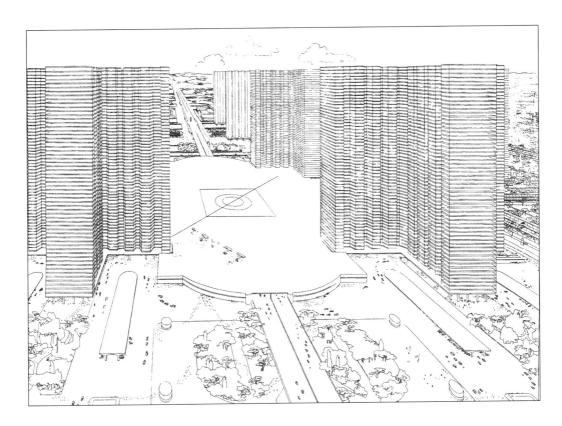

A city for aeroplanes. Le Corbusier's Plan Voisin. (Le Corbusier et Pierre Jeanneret 1967, p. 109.)

main panoramas of this "Contemporary city" show aeroplanes circling low amidst the skyscrapers. Le Corbusier writes that these are *aéro-taxis*, but once again his knowledge about technical realities proves very limited.[35]

The original plan for a contemporary city was not designed for any particular place, but in 1925 Le Corbusier developed it into a novel version for the centre of Paris. For financial help to display his idea he went to see the automobile manufacturers Peugeot and Citroën, but both turned him down. It was then the Voisin factory, the former maker of aeroplanes turned into automobile business, which immediately supported his idea.[36] The scheme, named now *Plan Voisin*, was introduced to the public in the same year in the L'Esprit Nouveau Pavilion at the *Exposition des Arts Décoratifs*. In the new plan aeroplanes no longer hovered over the town, but the aeronautical view had found an even more radical expression.

. . . .

35 See Le Corbusier 1994, p. 162. He returned to the subject in 1929, explaining that in 1922 he was fully aware that it was impossible to have such an airport in the middle of the city. However, he says that in 1929 a representative of French aviation from a specialist commission declared to him: "L'aéroport doit être au centre de Paris, car, dans deux ans, les avions atterriront verticalement sans aucun danger." Le Corbusier 1967, pp. 110–111.

36 Le Corbusier 1994, pp. 263, n. 1.

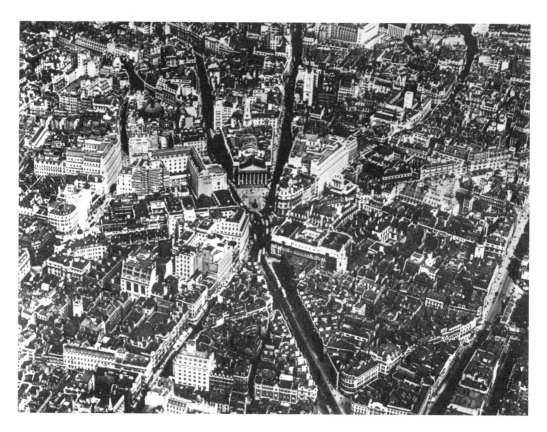

According to this plan, printed in his 1925 book *Urbanisme*, Le Corbusier wanted to demolish what he calls "a particularly antiquated and unhealthy part of Paris," or "terrible districts," and build a business city on their site.[37] Like Khlebnikov, who said that seen from a distance the present day cities look like scrap heaps, Le Corbusier claims that the city is flattened-out, jumbled, and terrifying in its confusion. Moreover, he says, it is the aeroplane that reveals these things to us for the first time.[38] Just as Aalto, who on his first flight felt like bombing the parts of the city he did not like from above – the Helsinki built by idiots and apes – Le Corbusier wanted his plan to "attack the most diseased quarters of the city."[39] He does not explain the disease, nor the means of this attack, but he continues with military terminology and talks about "opening up the strategic point of Paris." The photograph of the allegedly infected parts of the town is taken from directly above, as if through a bomber's sight. Underneath the picture Le Corbusier's text "Is this a view of the seventh circle of Dante's Inferno?"[40] acquires a double meaning, depending on how we

"The eye of the airplane is pitiless. This time we have the actual record of reality. What an appalling thing!" Picture of Paris in the book Aircraft shows the Place de l'Opera, through which Blériot's aeroplane was paraded in 1909. (Le Corbusier 1988, p. 102.)

37   *Ibid.*, pp. 263–264 and p. 267.
38   "The so-called 'beautiful' cities of the present day, seen from a certain distance, look like scrap piles." Khlebnikov 1987, p. 348. Corbusier's comment in Le Corbusier 1994, p. 266.
39   "Ce plan s'attaque aux quartiers les plus infects [...]." *ibid.*
40   *Ibid.*, p. 268.

suppose the attack to happen. Perhaps with firebombs and without warning? Certainly the destruction of the quarters would not be a democratic decision but an act of absolute power. After all, Le Corbusier compares his own plan to the openings in the city made by Louis XIV, Louis XV and Napoleon. Their works, he says, are a signal example of *creation*, of that spirit which is able to dominate and compel the mob.[41]

Alvar Aalto's article and Le Corbusier's *Plan Voisin* prove that the aeroplane elevates the architect's spirit to a whole new perspective. From above it is easy to see that the ordinary people are terribly small and that "grand lines" are missing. The problem is that someone inferior has already filled in all the gaps. The difference to radical demolition, such as Haussmann directed in Paris, is that the aeroplane offers the architect the chance to see all this from directly above. I suggest the eye of the architect who wants to create something new out of an old city thus becomes of necessity the eye of the bomber. This does not mean that killing people was in Aalto's or Le Corbusier's intentions. In their minds the destruction of the infected old town was an investment in the future. Even if it meant relocating thousands of people, everything served a beautiful end – the best of people – as seen from above. And, let us not forget, if one is an admirer of aeroplanes, even bombing missions can have their aesthetic side. A report of the air raids in London during the First World War described the appearance of the German *Gotha* bombers – enormous by the standards of their day – in an almost poetic way: "[...] enemy aeroplanes journeyed through the clouds like little silver birds and their passage was watched by thousands of men and women. . . It was amazing because it was so beautiful."[42] The devastation and suffering are removed from the new beauty. When Le Corbusier talks about his plan he does not make it sound like destroying a place where people are living rather than clearing up the ruins of an already bombed city: "Imagine all this junk, which till now has lain spread out over the soil like a dry crust, cleaned off and carted away and replaced by immense clear crystals of glass [...]."[43] This could be a proposal twenty years ahead of its time – for the rebuilding of Dresden.

In public the *Plan Voisin* was half-heartedly received. One critic even called it a city for the dead. This did not, however, dim Le Corbusier's spirit, and in his 1933 book *La ville radieuse*, he wondered if the fear of the air war would be the providential key which would start the necessary action to rebuild cities, and came up with a comment from a military authority, favouring his architectural vision: "Given the present state of city planning, only those cities which are conceived along the lines of the Radiant City are capable of emerging victoriuosly from an air war."[44] Le Corbusier also drew pictures, showing how

. . . .

41 "[...] l'esprit qui a dominé, qui a maté la cohue." *ibid.*, p. 267. The English translation here by Frederick Etchells.
42 A report on 13 June 1917. Quoted in Stephen Kern, *The Culture of Time and Space 1880–1918*. Cambridge, Mass.: Harvard University Press 1983, p. 311.
43 Le Corbusier 1994, p. 268.
44 "Seules, dans l'état actuel de l'urbanisme, les villes conçues selon le type 'Ville Radieuse' sont capables de resister victorieusement à la querre aérienne." Le Corbusier 1933, p. 60.

An ordinary city under aerial attack. (Le Corbusier 1933, p. 60.)

under attack an ordinary city is a death-trap while in the Radiant City bombs cause hardly any damage and the poisonous gas will not gather between the houses. Thus Le Corbusier had found a new argument for the demolition of the old town: his architecture will survive the future bombings better. At the time, he was so taken with the idea that he ended *La ville radieuse* with a exposition of the means of building the new city: "Equipment: high command and army, machines and transportation, discipline – ALL EXACTLY THE SAME AS FOR WAGING WAR!"[45]

In order to see how the new city would appear, we can take a look at an article from 1929. In his text *La Rue* Le Corbusier had returned once more to his masterplan of replacing the centre of Paris with a business city. Gone were the aeroplanes of the earlier versions and the view from above. Now the viewpoint was on the ground level. Everything was described as if it was already built. The place sounded like a paradise – or a version of the dreams of Velimir Khlebnikov and Vladimir Tatlin: "The air is clear and pure; there is hardly any noise. What, you cannot see where the buildings are? Look through the charmingly diapered arabesques of branches out into the sky towards those widely-spaced crystal towers which soar higher than any pinnacle on earth. These translucent prisms that seem to float in the air without anchorage to the ground [...]."[46] Le Corbusier described his sky-scraping office blocks in a way that also brings to mind the discussions about the architecture of the *Crystal Palace*, introduced in the first part of this study; "[...] from top to bottom the facades of

. . . .

45 "Outillage: commandement et armée, machines et circulation, discipline? EXACTEMENT LE MÊME QUE POUR FAIRE LA QUERRE!" *ibid.*, p. 345. English translation as in *The Radiant City*, New York: The Orion Press 1967.

46 Le Corbusier 1967, p. 118. (Quotations are from the English version *The Street*, the French text is on pages 112–115.) The article first appeared in *L'Intransigeant* in May 1929.

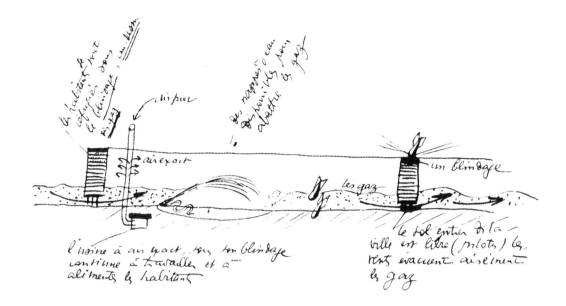

The Radiant City under aerial attack. (Le Corbusier 1933, p. 61.)

the new city's office-buildings form unbroken expanses of glass. These colossal structures evince no vestige of masonry. All that remains visible is glass. . . and proportion. The architect has discarded brick and stone."[47] The environment was green, full of diverse parks and artificial hills, but visible everywhere were the new buildings of impeccable order; "[...] to right and left, over there, and further away still, those gigantic and majestic prisms of purest transparency rear their heads upon another in a dazzling spectacle of grandeur, serenity and gladness."[48] This bright new world was not very far from the visions of Khlebnikov, whose interest in design was after all an expression of a search for unifying principles of organization.[49] Approaching the future in their own ways, both Khlebnikov and Le Corbusier saw that the street as we know it will cease to exist.[50] But whereas the poet's architectural dreams were part of search for the "general principle" that determined every force in the world, the architect's poetic dreams were based on cold knowledge of another principle: "The idea of realizing it [the business city] in the heart of Paris is no Utopian flight of fancy. There are cold figures to substantiate this thesis. The enormous increase of land-values that must result would yield *a profit to the state running into milliards of francs* – for to acquire the central part of Paris and redevelop it in accordance with a coordinated plan means the creation of an immense fresh source of wealth."[51] Here was the gap between French business and Russian poetry – a

. . . .

47 *Ibid.*
48 *Ibid.*, p. 119.
49 Charlotte Douglas in Khlebnikov 1987, p. 166. According to Douglas, Khlebnikov's interest in design also embraced words, railroads and the letters of the alphabet.
50 Le Corbusier 1967, p. 119.
51 *Ibid.*

city for 400,000 clerks. No cries of joy, no families gathering on the rooftops, as in Khlebnikov's world where sounds and smells existed. Here only the clerks scanned the landscape from above, and, noted Le Corbusier with satisfaction, "The stillness is absolute, for whence can noise proceed?"[52]

Married to the Mob

In 1935 Studio Publications in London published *Aircraft*, a work Le Corbusier had made specially for them. The book is a classic picture essay with a short introduction titled "Frontispiece to Pictures of the Epic of the Air." It is a rather curious text. Le Corbusier opens up with a personal, somewhat inaccurate, yet highly interesting recollection from the years of early aviation.[53] In it he describes himself as a happy hooligan, who, during a cramped and frustratingly slow train journey to an aeroplane meeting in Juvisy, starts smashing the train coaches for fun: "Along the track, where we were camped like nomads, were returning coaches. We conscientiously demolished them with stones. We had broken everything breakable in our own train. The trains that followed, hastily pressed into service and waiting behind us in a straggling queue, were inspired by our methods. We also demolished the signals."[54] The innocent daytrip to see the flying machines had then turned into something else. As the crowded and broken train finally reached Juvisy, the flights had already ceased and masses of people – Le Corbusier exaggerates and talks about 300,000 – were heading for trains to get back to Paris. Le Corbusier happily recalls what happened next: "There was then a beautiful manifestation of the human intelligence, human solidarity and the collective spirit. The mob, one knows, generally becomes inspired when it is necessary to take action (this the great poets of the great epics have celebrated in song). As our train did not leave and other trains arrived in the night, filled with would-be spectators for the 'aviation meeting,' we set to work to demolish the station. The station at Juvisy was a big one. The waiting-rooms went first, then the staff offices, then the stationmaster's office."[55] Thinking of this occasion in connection with his later *Plan Voisin*, it seems that in Le Corbusier's mind the prospects of flying somehow relate to breaking things and demolishing houses – an epic manifestation of the human intelligence.

. . . .

52 *Ibid.*
53 Le Corbusier says that his memories have no historical precision and he is right. He recalls the Comte de Lambert flying around the Eiffel Tower in spring 1909. In reality this first ever aeroplane flight over a city took place on 18 October, that is, one day after the first *Salon de l'Aviation*, discussed above, closed at the *Grand Palais*. See Le Corbusier 1988, pp. 6–7. For the flight, see Gibbs-Smith 1985, p. 150.
54 Le Corbusier 1988, p. 7. Le Corbusier does not mention the time of the incident, but it was 10 October 1909. See Dollfus & Bouché 1938, pp. 216–217.
55 Le Corbusier 1988, p. 7. For a contemporary newspaper photograph of the broken railway coaches, see Wohl 1994, p. 254. In his book Robert Wohl quotes Le Corbusier's description as an example of the enthusiasm and the powerful emotions the flights of 1909 inspired, but does not discuss the matter further than that.

Kindred structures. Count de Lambert flying around the Eiffel Tower in October 1909. (Aviation. The Early Years 1997, p. 103.)

As the text unfolds, Le Corbusier turns to more familiar rhetoric and talks impersonally about the war as "the hellish laboratory in which aviation became adult, and was shaped to flawless perfection." Indeed, it was the kind of perfection that allowed more possibilities for demolition: "What an unexpected gift to be able to set off at night under cover of darkness, and away to sow death with bombs upon sleeping towns."[56] In the time of peace, with nothing more to destroy, aviation then became unemployed. But luckily, and thanks to Le Corbusier, the aeroplane now looks at the city "with its eagle eye."[57] The eye of the aeroplane and the eye of the architect have become one, and the solution to the problems of the city is then same as it was ten years earlier in the *Plan Voisin*: "The aeroplane instils, above all, a new conscience, the modern conscience. Cities, with their misery, must be torn down. They must be largely destroyed and fresh cities built."[58] Le Corbusier's ideals may have been humanistic but

. . . .

56 *Ibid.*, pp. 8–9. For the grim cultural history of bombing, see Sven Lindqvist, *Nu dog du – Bombernas århundrade* [Now You Died – The Century of Bombs]. Stockholm: Bonniers 1999.
57 Le Corbusier 1988, p. 11.
58 *Ibid.*, p. 12.

taken as such his rhetoric and the megalomania of his plans were not far from the contemporary architectural ideas nurtured by Hitler and Stalin. They believed, too, in their own wicked way, that they were the heirs to the spirit that built the *Parthenon*.[59] Despite their stylistic differences, the plans for Paris, Berlin, and Moscow were based on the idea of demolishing much of the old capital from their way. We can even imagine some of Le Corbusier's words read aloud with a thick German or Russian accent: "It is the moment when the conditions which have plunged persons and society into apathy, misery, and misfortune, must be revolutionized. The brief and rapid history of aviation, so close to us, explains to us the hostile elements surrounding us, and provides us with the certainty that soon the very laws of life will justify us."[60]

Clearly the type of rhetoric used by Le Corbusier could have served many masters and furthered aims other than good city planning and purity of air. It is, however, the personal memory of smashing the train coaches and the Juvisy station that I find more intriguing and complex. In the *Plan Voisin* Le Corbusier openly likened himself to the autocratic rulers who had the power to dominate and coerce the mob, while in his memory he relives the joy of being part of the mob, the manifestation of collective spirit, the "we" that finishes off the old station architecture. This is the dark side of things on which Le Corbusier remains silent in his *Plan Voisin*: the unexplainable pleasure of demolishing houses. In his work on mass psychology, *Crowds and Power*, Elias Canetti pointed out that the crowd particularly likes destroying houses and objects like window panes, mirrors, pictures and crockery. According to Canetti, the noise of destruction adds to its satisfaction; "the banging of windows and the crashing of glass are the robust sound of fresh life, the cries of something new-born."[61] This kind of destruction has also a symbolic dimension: "Windows and doors belong to houses; they are the most vulnerable part of their exterior and, once they are smashed, the house has lost its individuality; anyone may enter it and nothing and no one is protected any more. In these houses live the supposed enemies of the crowd, those people who try to keep away from it. What separated them has now been destroyed and nothing stands between them and the crowd. They can come out and join in; or they can be fetched."[62] It would be of course possible to intepret Le Corbusier's texts in greater detail: the contem-

. . . .

59 On the classical reference; Eero Kuparinen, "Tavoitteena loistava menneisyys – klassismi Hitlerin Saksassa" [Aspiration to a Glorious Past – Classicism in Hitler's Germany] and Timo Vihavainen, "Stalinistinen klassismi" [Stalinistic Classicism] in M. Härmänmaa & T. Vihavainen (eds.) *Kivettyneet ihanteet? Klassismin nousu maailmansotien välisessä Euroopassa.* Jyväskylä: Atena 2000, pp. 177–252.
60 Le Corbusier 1988, p. 11. It is not surprising that in Germany – the land of *Zeppelins* as well as *Stuka* divebombers – many of Albert Speer's major plans were represented in "aerial photographs" taken of the scale models. See *Albert Speer. Architecture 1932–1942.* Bruxelles: Archives d'Architecture Moderne 1985. For Speer's Berlin-plan and Le Corbusier's ideas, see the final chapter in Lars Olof Larsson, *Die Neugestaltung der Reichshauptstadt. Albert Speers Generalbauungsplan für Berlin.* Stockholm: Almqvist & Wiksell 1978.
61 Canetti 1981, p. 20.
62 *Ibid.*, p. 21.

porary political uses of the vocabulary of disease, sanitation, and surgery for example. However, our context of flying takes us only as far as this.

In *Vers une architecture* Le Corbusier declared: "Architecture or revolution."[63] Exactly what sort of revolution he had in mind, I do not know. Perhaps the battleground was not the centre of Paris after all, but the heaven and hell in his own mind: the ordered New Spirit of architecture and the spontaneous collective spirit of the mob. It was to be either or, and Le Corbusier chose to dominate and compel the darker side in him. His words in the *Aircraft* of 1935 tell us about it: "The true heroes are trim and smart, masters of themselves. They are not hirsute, dishevelled, covered with blood. The gods smile. Such is strength of character."[64]

. . . .

63   Le Corbusier 1995, xxi.
64   Le Corbusier 1988, p. 11.

3.
End
. . . .

■ The Dream

Lucid, fluttering like the upper wing of an insect, the name Lilienthal since my childhood years has sounded marvellous to me. . . Flying, as if streched on light bamboo laths, this name is connected in my memory with the beginning of aviation. The flying man Otto Lilienthal was killed. Flying machines have stopped resembling birds. The light wings transilluminated with yellow have been replaced by flippers. You can see for yourself that they beat against the ground on take-off. In any case, dust rises on take-off. Now flying machine resembles a heavy fish. How quickly aviation has become an industry.[1]

Yuri Olesha

Which artists did my father admire? He had a great respect for Vladimir Tatlin – he very much liked his Letatlin flying machine.[2]

Andrei Leonidov

Suddenly, rain falls on Moscow.[3] All over the town people are looking for shelter. Only soldiers on guard and civilians queueing for bread or kerosine will not leave their place. The Muscovites who run along Volhonka street, where the Cathedral of Christ the Saviour used to take people under its wing, find nothing but an empty building site with a big hole in the ground, now slowly filling with water.[4] Perhaps some of them cross the street instead, and decide to escape the rain in the Art Museum. There they can wait for the sky to clear up under the eyes *David*, by Michelangelo (a plaster copy of course), in the spacious Italian Hall. Decorated with the portal of a medieval church, friezes, and statues, the

· · · · · · · · ·

1   Yury Olesha, *Envy*. Ann Arbor: Ardis 1975, p. 30.
2   Gozak & Leonidov 1988, p. 24.
3   The Moscow weather in May 1932 was not particularly bad. The average temperature was 14 °C and the monthly rainfall 30 mm. I have here imagined all that water coming down at once. For the weather, see *World Weather Records 1931–1940*. Smithsonian Miscellaneous Collections, Vol. 105. City of Washington: The Smithsonian Institution 1947, p. 246.
4   The church (built 1837–1883) was the largest in Moscow. It was demolished in 1931 to make way for the Palace of Soviets. An architectural competition for the palace was held between 1931 and 1933 (see Chan-Magomedow 1983, pp. 403–404 and 414–423.) Walter Gropius and Le Corbusier took part, but the winner was finally Boris Iofan, whose proposal was developed into an enormous neoclassical wedding-cake with a giant Lenin on top. The 420 metres high building was meant to be the largest in the world; the great hall alone would stand 100 metres high, with seating for 15,000 people. (The building never proceeded further than its foundation, which in turn was made into an open-air swimming-pool. Today the church has been rebuilt on its site, housing a large car park underneath it.) Later Boris Iofan designed the Soviet pavilion for the Paris World Fair of 1937.

hall has a peculiar atmosphere of old Europe, alien to the spirit of the proletariat and the achievements of the Five Year Plan. On the last days of May the hall looks even more anachronistic with an exhibition of three, apparently ancient flyers hanging from its ceiling.[5] It may come as a surprise to many viewers that they are not Leonardo's fabrications but something utterly new and proletarian. They are air bicycles of the future, the latest works of the Soviet artist Vladimir Tatlin.

It is not uncommon to tell the story of Vladimir Tatlin's *Letatlin* with a reference to Leonardo da Vinci's studies of birdflight and his plans for an ornithopter.[6] At first glance, this link seems to be a natural one; after all, in both cases an artist planned to build a muscle-powered flying machine. But sometimes this remains all that the commentators have to say about Tatlin's project in relation to the history of aviation. They portray him standing more or less alone with his

Aerial photograph from the Palace of Soviets competition program 1931. The Cathedral of Christ the Saviour is left of centre and the State Museum of Fine Arts, where Tatlin exhibited his Letatlins, in the middle of the upper edge of the picture. (Naum Gabo and the Competition for the Palace of Soviets, Moscow 1931-1933. Berlin: Berlinische Galerie 1993, p. 204.)

. . . .

5   The exhibition at the National Museum of Fine Arts in Moscow (now known as the Pushkin Fine Arts Museum) was open from 15 May to 30 May 1932.

6   For instance, Andersen 1968, p. 9; Galanov 1977, printed in Zhadova 1988, p. 441; Körner 1985, p. 83; Milner 1983, p. 217; Stern 1993, p. 60; Zhadova 1988, p. 149. Leonardo's name was mentioned in connection with Tatlin's project already in 1932 by Zelinsky, as was Lilienthal's.

artistic genius and see his *Letatlin* as a unique, if not tragic, example of an utopian artwork during the waning of the Soviet avant-garde. If names like Lilienthal and Tsiolkovsky are mentioned, their work is usually left unstudied. This picture may suffice for purely art historical purposes, but from an aeronautical point of view it leaves too many questions unanswered. Where did Tatlin get the idea to build this sort of machine? What kind of knowledge did he have about contemporary aviation? Was he really as alone with his project as has been supposed?

When it comes to ornithopters and art Leonardo da Vinci may stand out as a figure that no-one would dare to be uninfluenced by, and certainly Tatlin did not ignore him. It is reported that he even had a copy of Leonardo's death mask in his studio.[7] There were, however, other people much closer to Tatlin's own time who had pondered upon the problem of man-powered flight, often with more inspiring results than Leonardo.[8] In the following text I will first examine the modern history of muscle-powered aviation and discuss its links to the famous work of Vladimir Tatlin. After that I will discuss reactions to the *Letatlin*, study the reasons behind the project's cancellation, and finally examine the concept of this machine in relation to the ideas expressed in contemporary Soviet architecture. This also involves taking a look at the social utopias they represented.

Art of Flying

It is one of the paradoxes of the twentieth-century Western mind that a failed machine has become known as an outstanding work of art. Today Vladimir Tatlin has a place in the history of art, but should his *Letatlin* have flown, he would be perhaps better remembered as one of the most amazing aviators of all times. This is not, however, a common way of thinking about the *Letatlin*, as Éva Körner's story illustrates. While working as a consulting editor for Larissa Zhadova's massive *Tatlin*, she asked the authors why the *Letatlin* never took off: "The first reaction to my question was shock. This cantankerous, 'Western' technocratic question had obviously not occurred to any of them. As a result of consultations the book provided an answer, something like that: if the Letatlin had really functioned it would have got lost in the mass of technical achievements and would never have attained its significance as an art object."[9]

. . . .
7   Begicheva 1968, p. 160. Zhadova 1988, p. 149. Whether there exists a genuine death mask of Leonardo is unknown to me. Hanna Begicheva's memoirs, only part of which is published, seem to contain information on Tatlin unknown from any other sources. She tells, for example, that Tatlin once made plans for an artist's "automobile-studio." (Begicheva 1968, p. 166.)

8   Ornithopters and other muscle-powered aircraft will be discussed here only from 1890s onward. For the earlier history of such machines, see Hart 1985 and Gibbs-Smith 1985. On Leonardo's contribution, see for example Ivor B. Hart, *The Mechanical Investigations of Leonardo da Vinci*. Berkeley – Los Angeles: University of California Press 1963 (1925) and Charles Gibbs-Smith, *The Inventions of Leonardo da Vinci*. London: Peerage Books 1985 (1978).

9   Körner 1985, p. 84. Anatoli Strigalev deals with the question in Zhadova 1988, p. 38. He takes the view that Tatlin consciously took an enormous risk, knowing of the failure of numerous previous attempts to fly with muscle-power. According to Strigalev, it is good that the project was a romantic utopia; unlike a succesful invention, a work of art will always preserve its uniqueness.

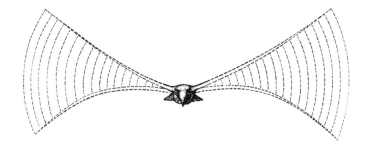

Lilienthal's drawing of bird's wing movements. (Lilienthal 1889, p. 138.)

It is difficult to believe that the beauty of the invention would have been lost, even if the *Letatlin* had fulfilled the seemingly impracticable dream of flying like a bird. But what interests us here is that there was a reason for the permanence of this dream. The situation appeared parodoxical: on the one hand the theoretical possibility of such a machine had been denied many times, on the other birdflight still served as an inspiration for serious researchers.[10] All depended on the kind of birdflight people were talking about: flapping or soaring. The most important nineteenth-century work on aviation was written by Otto Lilienthal, a German engineer who made over two thousand flights in his gliders before the fatal accident in 1896. Lilienthal's calculations in his book *Der Vogelflug als Grundlage der Fliegekunst* (1889) were an important source of information for the Wright Brothers in their search for laws for a practical, motorized aeroplane. For them, the real problem solvers, Leonardo's speculative sketches would have offered little, whereas pictures of Lilienthal's gliders and his words about birdflight had true value and meaning, based on empirical experiments. The evidence suggests that Vladimir Tatlin also studied Lilienthal's book, the Russian translation having been published in 1905 in St Petersburg. According to Daniil Danin, who came to know the artist in the 1930s, Tatlin always had a book on Lilienthal's studies at hand.[11]

Tatlin was not among the first to read Lilienthal in Russia. The pioneers of Russian aviation, such as Professor Nikolai Zhukovsky, had studied Lilienthal's

. . . .

10 A famous refutation of human muscle-powered flying appeared already in Giovanni Borelli's *De Motu Animalium* in 1680 (see Borelli 1911, pp. 36–40.) Closer to Tatlin's time, Hermann von Helmholtz had studied the ratio between the size of the flying body and the work required for flying. In 1872 he concluded: "Under these circumstances it can scarcely be considered probable that man, even with the help of the most ingenious wing-like mechanism, depending on his own muscular force as the driving power, will be placed in a position to be able to raise his own weight in the air, and to retain it there." Quoted in Moedebeck 1907, pp. 284–285.

11 Otto Lilienthal, *Polet ptits, kak osnova iskusstva letat.* St Peterburg 1905. Danin says that the book was either a German or a Russian edition. (See Danin 1984, p. 596. Danin's memoir of Tatlin, titled *Uletavl*, first appeared in *Druzba narodov* 2/1979) I would assume the Russian edition to be the more likely one, also the easier one for Tatlin to come across. He had some knowledge of German language, though. Alfred H. Barr met him in 1927 and wrote: "Tatlin, who spoke as bad German as I did, was very modest and kindly." (Barr 1986, p. 124.) How bad Barr's German was remains unknown.

work already in 1890, and five years later Zhukovsky and two of his colleagues travelled to Germany to meet the engineer in person. Lilienthal's historical work was introduced to the Russian public in December 1909 when his standard glider was one of the central exhibits in the aviation exhibition at the Technical University of Moscow.[12] That year Tatlin was in Moscow too, finishing his rather unsystematic studies in art, but whether he saw the exhibition or was already inspired by aviation at this time we do not know. Although Tatlin may have read about aviation already ten years before the exhibition, documents of his life suggest that his aeronautical ideas started to take shape much later.[13] Whatever the date was, the basic ideas that Tatlin began with were presented in Lilienthal's book. Although Lilienthal would not have encouraged anyone to build a muscle-powered plane – he had tested the concept and already given it up by the age of sixteen – he laid great emphasis on the observation of big birds, such as storks.[14] Tatlin's research into the anatomy of birds is, in my opinion, much easier to understand as a direct influence from Lilienthal and his con- temporaries than as an important historical link with Leonardo's work.[15]

Forgotten History

In the art-historical literature a passing reference to Leonardo's drawings and plans easily makes muscle-powered flight seem like a long forgotten possibility that Tatlin somehow revived. This presupposes that, apart from the often suicidal attempts to jump in the air with poorly home-made wings, no serious efforts were made. Here aviation history proves the opposite.[16] When Troels Andersen discussed the *Letatlin* he rightly pointed to the popularity of gliding in the 1920s

. . . .

12 On early Russian aviation and Lilienthal, see articles Sobolew 1992 and Bytschkow 1992.
13 Strigalev (*Vladimir Tatlin – Retrospektive* 1993, p. 40.) believes that Tatlin (b. 1885) had read a Russian book on the subject around 1899. This may well be the case; many boys read about flying machines at the age of fourteen. However, the subject does not become manifest in his works until thirty years later.
14 Gustav Lilienthal's introduction in the second edition of his brother's book. See *Birdflight as the Basis of Aviation*, London: Longmans, Green, and Co. 1911, xii–xviii. In the first German edition, storks appear opposite the title page in a coloured lithograph executed after Lilienthal's own painting and in a poem describing their flight (Lilienthal 1889, p. 148–149). Both these aesthetic elements are missing from the English translation. At one time Tatlin kept birds. Whether they were cranes (Zelinsky 1968, p. 78.) or storks (Zhadova 1988, p. 149.), or both, is unclear. According to Begicheva, Tatlin kept a stork and frogs to feed it in his flat in Kiev. (Begicheva 1968, p. 161.)
15 This is not to say that Tatlin had not heard about Leonardo's technical inventions. The *Codice Atlantico,* which contains most of Leonardo's drawings of ornithopters was published in 1894–1904 (*Il Codice Atlantico di Leonardo da Vinci nelle Biblioteca Ambrossiana di Milano.* Reale Accademia dei Linsei), and after that in numerous books around the world. Danin tells that alongside Lilienthal's calculations and observations Tatlin mentioned Leonardo's drawings, and studies done by ornithologists. Danin 1984, p. 596.
16 For an attempt to list all heavier-than-air flying machines from 850 B.C. to A.D. 1783, see Hart 1985, pp. 195–208. For little known examples of early Russian aviation, see D. A. Sobolev, *Roshdenie samoleta. Pervyie proektyi i konstryktsii.* Moskva: Mashinostroenie 1988 (for example S. I. Baranovsky's "Letun" project from 1882, p. 56.), and Sobolev 1992. Brief information also in B. N. Vorybyev's preface in Tsiolkovsky 1960, pp. 1–3.

and mentioned the German plane *Bavaria*, but from the byways of aviation we can find machines with an even closer similarity.[17] Using muscles for flying, although popular only among a marginal group of people, was a concept alive well before, during, and after the *Letatlin* project. In order to understand fully the idea of the *Letatlin*, it is essential to take a closer look at these contemporary attempts at man-powered flying.

We do not even need to go very far to get started. In late nineteenth-century Russia, several scientists and aviators were making experiments with birds, often using such cruel methods as glueing together their feathers or deep-freezing them with their wings in various positions and seeing then how they glided when dropped from fifty metres. Many of these experiments – some of them were inspired directly by Lilienthal's studies and by the works of E. J. Marey and J. Bell Pettigrew – were only of theoretical interest, but some of them were done as preliminary tests for ornithopters. One such flapping-wing machine was built and tested by the aviator Shiukov in 1908 at Tblisi.[18] The obscure Shiukov was not alone with his dream, however. During the early years of the twentieth century, prototypes of muscle-powered machines were built in different parts of Europe, Britain, and the United States, but usually these attempts aroused no general interest. The public had already seen too many poorly-equipped birdmen learning the basics of gravity the hard way and was now more interested in aeroplanes that really flew. It was not until 1912 that the more experimental aspect of flying activity appeared in the headlines and public attention was drawn to the strange event of winged bicycles.[19]

In February 1912, the French motorcar and bicycle company Peugeot donated 10,000 francs towards a competition involving man-powered flight, the so-called *Prix Peugeot*. The competition attracted a great deal of interest and brought together all kinds of contestants from sportsmen to eccentric inventors.[20] According to a contemporary article in *Scientific American*, however, "the ignorance displayed by many of the designers of the machines entered is simply amazing."[21] It is not necessary for us here to go into the detailed rules for the competition, suffice it to say that when twenty-three contestants gathered for the first trial none was capable of leaving the ground. Peugeot agreed to donate another smaller sum for a "flight" of one metre at an altitude of ten centimetres. This was eventually won by the racing cyclist Gabriel Poulain who later made something of a career of entering similar competitions.

Despite the poor results of the aviation bicycles, or more likely because of them, bigger prizes were offered, such as the 100,000 francs by the Paris newspaper

. . . .

17 Andersen 1968, p. 10. The *Bavaria* was a normal glider, not a muscle-powered flying machine.
18 Reay 1977, pp. 57–59.
19 For pre-1912 projects, see Reay 1977, pp. 59–64.
20 News about the competition were also published in Russia. See for example "Priz Pezho. 10.000 frankov za polet bez motora," *Vjestnik Vozdukhoplavaiia* 5/1912.
21 Quoted in Reay 1977, p. 65.

*An aviette
photographed in
November 1912 by
Jacques-Henri
Lartique. (Burhan &
D'Astier 1989, p. 62.)*

La Justice for a non-stop flight from Paris to Versailles and back using muscle-power. The tyre manufacturers Michelin were more down to earth and promised to give two thousand francs for a flight of five metres, which they eventually had to pay in December 1912. Five metres seemed, however, to remain very much the maximum range for these *aviettes*.[22] The poor results are easy to understand when considering the general format of the constructions. Half of them were simply bicycles with wings, and the pilot had to pedal hard to generate enough speed to leave the ground. The more "sophisticated" vehicles had either a propeller or flapping wings, or both, so that in theory they had the means to sustain flight once they were airborne. Needless to say, theory and practice remained mostly far apart, and if the constructions were admired it was for their appearance rather than their function.[23] Yet the Peugeot prize did not cease to interest the aviation vanguard, and in June 1913 around fifty machines were tested, once

. . . .

22   According to Stubelius the word *aviette* (a short form derived from *avion-bicyclette*?) was not used before 1912. (Stubelius 1960, pp. 88–89.) When Mr. J. Gaunt exhibited his construction in a London exhibition in 1909 it was described only as: "A peculiar-shaped aëroplane fitted to a bicycle." *The Aëronautical Journal*, April 1909, p. 65.

23   The audience certainly enjoyed watching these apparatuses. One eye-witness was young Jacques-Henri Lartique who photographed the *aviettes* and described them in his diary: "Dimanche, à Paris. Je suis à Buffalo, où se trouve la piste de course de bicyclettes, pour voir les courses d'aviettes. . . . Une aviette est une bicyclette ailée. Les coureurs espèrent voler, voler comme des oiseaux sans moteur, sans vent, sans être tirés par une automobile. . . . Même si elles échouent toujours, elles sont bien amusantes à regarder, ces aviettes. Il y en a de toutes les formes et certaines sont étrangement belles." Quoted in Carter 1992, p. 58.

again with rather disappointing results: not one of them left the ground. The constructions had by now grown more complicated, many were equipped with propellers and several designs consisted of ornithopters with flapping wings.

It may seem logical that the First World War and the rapid progress it had encouraged in aeroplane construction would have led to the total extinction of all man-powered flying apparatuses, but this was not the case. In 1920 the *Prix Peugeot* was launched again, with revised rules, and this time it attracted not only the usual eccentrics but also a number of well-known manufacturers of aeroplanes, among them Farman and Nieuport. The latter company had build a new aero-cycle for Gabriel Poulain, the hero of the first *Prix Peugeot* contest and now also a qualified aeroplane pilot. During the second competition week in June 1921, he managed to break the magical ten-metre line and at his best flew almost twelve metres at a height of approximately one and a half metres. Poulain's remarkable jumps left no room for speculation about the winner of the 10,000 francs. But Poulain's successful *aviette* was still nothing but a bicycle with wings, and he realised that without a propeller the prospects for making longer flights were limited. There were plans to arrange another Peugeot competition in 1922, this time with a 20,000 francs prize for two flights of fifty metres, but for some unknown reason this never happened. Gabriel Poulain and his fellow "pilots" suddenly disappeared from the public limelight.

From Muscle-Flight to *Muskulet*

Judged in terms of metres flown, the results of the Peugeot competitions may have been very small, but the publicity achieved was certainly worth every franc the company paid out. The most interesting result, however, was a glider contest organized in Germany in the 1920s. This "Rhön Contest" was not a publicity stunt like the *Prix Peugeot*, but – despite the equally poor results – it was the starting point for a more serious study of man-powered flight during the 1930s.[24] Since we are now approaching the time when Tatlin was building his *Letatlin*, let us take a look at the German achievements and the Soviet response to them.

Many of the proposals for the Rhön Contest were based on highly hypothetical inventions like rotating airfoils and moving wingtips, but a more calculating mentality started to show itself in the late 1920s when research on human energy output was understood to be an essential part of the project. The progress made in Germany reached its highest point in 1935 when a special "Muskelflug-Institut" was established by the Polytechnical Society at Frankfurt. From then on man-powered flight was, at least for a moment, a scientific project and as such also in the interests of the German Ministry of Aviation.[25] Germany was

. . . .

24 The Rhön Mountains, east of Frankfurt am Main, were a well-known place for gliding, a sport very popular in Germany in the 1920s. See Adaridi 1925, pp. 25–42. The glider competition was started in 1920 and the muscle-powered gliders were a side show.
25 On the head of the Muskelflug-Institut Oskar Ursinus and other German researchers in the 1930s, see Reay 1977, pp. 88–102.

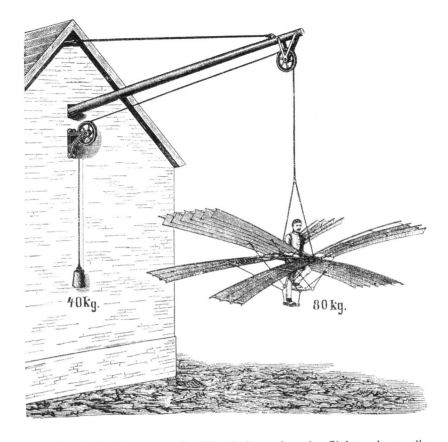

Lilienthal's machine for testing flapping wings. (Lilienthal 1889, p. 43.)

at the time the leading country in glider design and soaring flight, and naturally the news of their muscle-power projects attracted attention abroad. In Italy the Government announced a prize for a flight of one kilometre, and in the following years some progress was indeed made: the aeroplane-like *Pedaliante*, designed by Enea Bossi and built by the sailplane manufacturer Benoni, allegedly flew 90 metres in 1936. Even if the results were disappointing, it is clear that man-powered flight was seen as a realistic possibility by many members of the aviation community in Europe. If the original *aviettes* built by Parisian eccentrics were nothing but objects of public entertainment, the new ideas of the 1920s and 1930s came from trained engineers and experienced aeroplane designers with no intention of looking ridiculous in the eyes of their colleagues. One of these serious designers was Boris Ivanovich Cheranovsky.[26]

Boris Cheranovsky became interested in man-powered flight in 1921, a date that coincides with Poulain's victory in the *Prix Peugeot*. The news of the ten metre flight in Paris had travelled to Russia and caught the imagination of

. . . .

26   For information on Cheranovsky´s work I have relied on Nemecek 1986, pp. 365–368 and Shavrov 1994, pp. 430–432, 482–483, 567–568, and 658. See also Guston 2000, pp. 69–70.

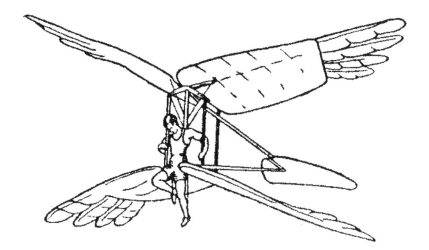

Boris Cheranovsky's drawing of his 1921 ornithopter. (Tikhonravov 1949, p. 183.)

young aviation enthusiasts like Cheranovsky.[27] What he proposed, however, was not an *aviette* but a four-winged ornithopter, meant to be powered by the pilot's legs in a fashion similar to that in the illustration in Otto Lilienthal's book. The upright position of the pilot made the machine aerodynamically unfavourable and impossible to operate during takeoff and landing. After brief testing the concept was abandoned. In the following years Cheranovsky studied basic aeroplane design, but chose not to follow the mainstream.[28] In 1934 his interest in muscle-powered aviation was reawakened, and he returned to work, now building a flapping-wing plane *BICh-16*. The inspiration for the new project, as well as for those of the less well known constructors Gribovsky and Smirnov, who were both working on their own muscle-powered planes at that time, may have been the first conference of "rowing flying" (*grebnoi polet*) in April 1934.[29] The reason behind this sudden scientific interest was most likely the news of the *Muskelflug* experiments and the official interest shown towards them in Italy and Germany.[30] Cheranovsky's *BICh-16* was tested without success

· · · · · · · · ·

27 That Poulain's record was known in Moscow is confirmed by the glider pilot K. K. Artseulov, who wrote about the *Letatlin* in 1932: "To date all attemps to rise into air using only human effort have been limited to 10m long jumps at the most." Zhadova 1988, p. 408. According to Andersen, photographs and reports from different kinds experimental flying machines were presented at regular intervals in Russian publications. Andersen 1968, p. 10.

28 On the ornithopter, see Tikhonravov 1949, pp. 182–183. Cheranovsky's next planes were constructed during the time he was at the Military Aviation Academy. The earliest ones from 1923 and 1924 were tailless gliders, followed by a motorised version in 1926. Cheranovsky was attracted to the tailless design almost to the point of obsession and in some of his planes this created serious problems with stability. See Nemecek 1986, pp. 365–366.

29 The conference was organized by the Society for the Promotion of Defence and Aero-Chemical Development (OSOAVIAKhIM). Around the same time Professors V. P. Vechinkin, M. K. Tikhonravov, B. S. Pyschnov, and V. V. Golubev were studying the theoretical aspects of ornithopters. Nemecek 1986, p. 366, and Tikhonravov 1949, p. 185. According to Bill Guston, OSOAVIAKhIM gave Cheranovsky financial support for the building of *BICh-16*. Guston 2000, p. 70.

30 Let us note that Germany had given aeronautical aid to the Soviet Union 1925–1933, but withdrew it after Hitler's accession to power. (Bailes 1978, p. 385.) In the eyes of the Russians this may have made the German muscle-flight projects seem more secretive and remarkable than they really were.

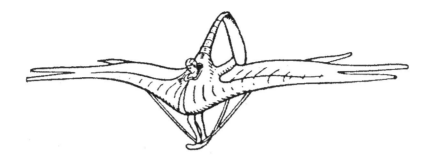

Boris Cheranovsky's drawing of his ornithopter BICh-16. (Tikhonravov 1949, p. 186.)

between 1934 and 1938, partly in parallel with another, more glider-like construction called the *BICh-18* or *Muskulet*, short for "Muscle-Powered Aircraft." This strange biplane, built between 1935 and 1937, had two pairs of flapping wings arranged in a X-like shape, so that the upper left and lower right wings were joined together and the same was done with the upper right and lower left wings. The pilot of Cheranovsky's plane was supposed to use pedals to flap the symmetrically moving wings, and on a promising test flight in August 1937 the wing movements extended the flight of the plane by several hundreds of meters compared to a flight with fixed wings. It is interesting that the concept of *Muskulet* is again a distant reminder of the machine young Otto Lilienthal had built and later discussed and illustrated in his book.[31]

Lonely Tatlin?

So far we have established that, parallel to the more popular motorized aviation, man-powered flight was being widely tested in Europe from the 1910s until the outbreak of the Second World War, and that in the 1930s in the Soviet Union there were several experiments with and academic studies of man-powered flying machines. However, the difference between the official studies and those of Tatlin was a matter of scientific status rather than results. While Tatlin's machine was open to criticism (for being neither the right kind of art nor the right kind of technology), the ornithopter projects in the technological institutes were allowed to continue even under Stalin's dictatorship and during the armament programme. The subject was not something to be discussed in secret, for we can find at least two Soviet books dealing with ornithopters. In 1929, when Tatlin started to build his machine, an author named Aleksandr Rodnykh wrote a booklet titled *Mechanical birds; Ornithopters and orthopters; their description, history and utilization*. The booklet is mostly a historical survey, beginning with Leonardo, but it introduces two projects from the late 1890s, and two from 1920s. The recent German interest in the subject is also men-

. . . .

31   On *Muskulet*'s tests, see Tikhonravov 1949, pp. 187–192, and Nemecek 1986, p. 369. In Guston 2000, p. 70, the plane's name is transcripted *Muskulyet*. On Otto Lilienthal's machine Lilienthal 1889, pp. 43–46.

tioned.[32] In 1937 the Soviet professor Mikhail Tikhonravov published a substantial book on birdflight and flapping-wing machines. Moreover, the book was reprinted in 1949, when advanced aviation research was focusing on rockets and jet-engines. In his book Tikhonravov first takes a look at 157 different species of birds, comparing their weight and wing area, and discusses the different shapes of birds' wings and their aerodynamical properties. The second part of the book deals with the mechanics of the beating wing, while the third takes a look at the quills, their shapes and structure. In the fourth part thermals are explained, the fifth part deals with insects, and the sixth with prehistoric animals. Part seven introduces some mechanical ornithopters, while part eight finally deals with our subject, the muscle-powered ornithopters. Tikhonravov mostly explains Boris Cheranovsky's machines, and mentions in passing the German attempts to solve the problem. Tikhonravov also provides basic numerical information about the *Letatlin*, and says that the machine was based on "artistic imitation of bird." The results of this machine, says the professor, were not positive.[33]

In the last part of his book Tikhonravov takes a look at suggestions for motorized ornithopters. In Soviet technical circles this idea lived on, and in 1951 Tikhanravov's colleague, Vladimir Golubev, published two papers on the theory of the beating wing.[34] Even after that the Soviet interest in flapping-wing projects has been so great that the aviation historian Bill Guston has concluded: "More than any other country the Soviet Union has tried to build orni-thopters."[35] In the light of his estimation it is worth recalling what Camilla Gray wrote in 1962, in her book *The Great Experiment*: "It is reported that new experiments are being done in Russia on the basis on that design of Tatlin's."[36] What these reports were, and whether the comment on Tatlin's role was only wishful thinking, remains unclear. It is known that Tatlin took part in a scientific and technical conference at the Zhukovsky Aeroclub of the Soviet Air Force Academy in January 1953, giving a talk on the *Letatlin*. This talk has remained

. . . .

32 Rodnykh 1929, pp. 40–46. An orthopter is a small flapping-wing model plane.
33 Tikhonravov 1949, p. 184. In the literature dealing with the *Letatlin* Tikhonravov's book is mentioned only once in Kovalev 1990, p. 34, n. 4., but he does not discuss its contents. It is interesting to think Cheranovsky's work and Tikhonravov's book in connection to the fact that in 1935–1937, when Soviet pilots broke several world records in aviation, many of the best aeroplane designers – the great A. N. Tupolev among them – were arrested, imprisoned, and replaced with "proletarian" engineers. Correspondingly, development of new military aeroplanes met a serious halt, and in 1938 special prison research centres had to be established. See Zhores A. Medvedev, *Soviet Science*. Oxford – Melbourne: Oxford University Press 1979, pp. 34–37.
34 For Golubev's articles, see *Aeronautical Sciences and Aviation in the Soviet Union* 1955, Nos. 479 and 488. In Germany at least thirteen articles and one book were published on the theory of muscle-powered flying between 1933 and 1936 (see bibliography in Reay 1977, p. 329.), and the experiments were still discussed in an aviation yearbook 1938 ("Muskelkraftflug," in *Fortschritte in Flugfahrt und Flugtechnik. Ein Jahrbuch für 1938*. München: Curt Pechstein Verlag 1938, pp. 452–458.) This German activity at least partly explains the motive behind Tikhonravov's and Golubev's work.
35 Guston 1983, pp. 78–79.
36 See the revised and enlarged edition: Camilla Gray, *The Russian Experiment in Art 1863–1922*. London: Thames & Hudson 1993 (1986; first edition 1962), p. 183.

Tatlin's last documented activity as he died only four months later.[37] Seen now against the background sketched in above, it is clear that Tatlin's *Letatlin* was not so much a unique creation as a member of a large family of flapping-wing machines. The information concerning other Soviet ornithopters, no matter how poor the documentation, means that in the future the *Letatlin* deserves to be studied in a new light.

Calculations

Vladimir Tatlin never gave a clear-cut answer to the question where the idea for the *Letatlin* came from. He simply referred to mankind's age old dream to fly, and felt that the aeroplane has robbed us of the bodily feeling of flight.[38] This suggests that the human physical element played a very important role in the concept of the *Letatlin*. Could not then the efforts of other muscle pilots have inspired him? Although it may be impossible to pinpoint the year Tatlin conceived the idea of his *Letatlin*, different writers have mentioned that he was talking about it in the early 1920s.[39] As was the case with Cheranovsky's awakened interest in man-powered flying, it seems as though the beginnings of Tatlin's project too coincide with the successful *Prix Peugeot* flights of Poulain in 1921. We should also take note of the artist Petr Miturich who, although interested in the problem of flying already earlier, also started to construct his first ornithopter in 1921.[40] In the following years Tatlin explained his ideas about flying to trusted friends, such as the art critic Nikolai Punin. In March 1923 Tatlin visited Punin and spoke with him about the culture of the future and deurbanization. According to Tatlin, the contemporary city was the unstable type produced by a dying era. Punin remarked in his diary: "Once space has been conquered people would not need to live in them [cities]. Instead of having their private life there, they would fly in, say, from Crimea, to work or for business. In this way, our countryside would preserve its human meaning."[41] Punin found Tatlin a wonderful speaker, but completely unconveyable in writing. In July 1924, Punin wrote: "He speaks with a wonderful, childlike, and passionate intonation, sincere and always with some kind of great thought – a wonder-child – a man of immense stature."[42] This time Tatlin discussed his flying machine, on which, wrote Punin, it seemed he was now working. Tatlin criticized the existing aeroplanes, and saw their evolution as extraordinarily misguided and not organic. He stated his disbelief in flying by means of science, and held that the aeroplane designers did not know or did not want to know how birds fly; "I

. . . .

37   Kovalev 1990, p. 28; *Vladimir Tatlin – Retrospektive* 1993, p. 397.
38   Zelinsky 1968, pp. 78–79, also Lodder 1983, p. 213.
39   See Lodder 1983, p. 300, n. 59; Zhadova 1988, p. 149; *Vladimir Tatlin – Retrospektive* 1993, p. 391. Tatlin's time in Kiev in 1925 has been mentioned as an important period in the development of the idea, see Zhadova 1988, p. 149 and Kovalev 1990, p. 28.
40   Lodder 1983, p. 218. More widely on the art of Miturich, pp. 217–223.
41   Punin's diary, 23 March 1923. Punin 1999, p. 107.
42   Punin's diary, 5 July 1924. *ibid.*, p. 127.

don't believe in them as a source of instruction. I will fly in my own way, no matter what, as I breathe, as I swim. My means of flying will always be more perfect than their apparatuses that rely on air suction," quoted Punin and wrote: "I had the impression that T. really had the impulse to fly with his arms."[43]

Tatlin was not the only one in the Soviet Union to yearn to build an ornithopher, but further studies are needed to establish how much these different people knew about each other's projects. Tatlin and Miturich are known to have been friends and to have discussed the subject of aviation in the 1920s, but according to Lodder they were no longer on speaking terms during the early 1930s when the *Letatlin* was being constructed.[44] In a letter to Miturich on 1 April 1927 Tatlin wrote that his bird was almost completely thought out. He underlined the difference between his project and that of Miturich, and considered that willow-wood used by Lilienthal would not work in the construction he had in mind. Tatlin also mentioned that he had made some model parts and some on a natural scale. Finally, he noted that although Miturich had been studying the subject of aviation longer, he had been able to make rapid progress thanks to his Leningrad friend, the aviator A. V. Losev.[45] Tatlin's friend Losev and his status as a pilot are now lost in obscurity, but it seems that the contact remained unofficial. In Soviet aviation circles of the late 1920s the names of Miturich and Tatlin were most likely unfamiliar. Members of the artistic and technical establishments may have remained unknown to each other even later on, but since Tikhonravov, who worked on theoretical calculations for man-powered aeroplanes, knew about the *Letatlin*, it is possible that engineers like Cheranovsky had knowledge of it, too. News about the machine was certainly circulating in 1932, when a superior officer sent the pilot Konstantin Artseulov to the Novodevichy Monastery "where an artist called Tatlin is patching together a bird-shaped flying structure. If what he is doing is really interesting, we must help him."[46] Tatlin exhibited the *Letatlin* the same year, and Artseulov wrote a text for his catalogue.[47] Given the press coverage and the thousands of people who were reported to have visited the show, it seems reasonable to conclude that the local aviation community heard about the machine.[48] Some pilots also had a chance to see its tests at the Meeting of Glider Pilots of Moscow in 1933.[49]

. . . .

43 *Ibid.*, p. 128. What Tatlin meant by air suction is unclear. Punin mentions to "the new English jet airplanes," but in 1924 such things did not exist. The first practical proposals and experiments were made in 1926–1928 by A. A. Griffith, but the project was shelved until the mid-1930s. (Gibbs-Smith 1985, p. 193.) Tatlin's comment may have based on some science-fictional rumour.

44 Lodder 1983, p. 301, n. 114.

45 Tatlin's letter was written while he was still in Kiev. The letter is in Nikolai Khardzhrev's archive at the Stedlijk Museum, Amsterdam, and is printed in Russian in *Experiment* (Los Angeles) No 5, 1999, pp. 193–194.

46 Körner 1985, p.83; Zhadova 1988, p. 440.

47 Translated in *Vladimir Tatlin* 1968, p. 76; Zhadova 1988, p. 408.

48 According to Milner: "When Letatlin in its various versions was exhibited in 1932, it aroused considerable interest." (Milner 1983, p. 220.), and Danin: "In the beginning of 1930s thousands of Muscovites, especially boys, walked into the Museum of Fine Arts to look at Tatlin's bird." (Danin 1984, p. 595.)

49 Zhadova 1988, p. 148.

*Konstantin Tsiolkovsky
with his models of a
metal airship. (Our
Gagarin. Moscow:
Progress 1978, p. 70.)*

One interesting aspect of the written history of the *Letatlin* is Troels Andersen's suggestion that Tatlin was inspired by the calculations of the famous
Russian scientist and space-flight theorist Konstantin Tsiolkovsky. According
to one Soviet source, Tatlin even contacted him. Regarding the evidence,
however, this looks like a romantic addition to the tale.[50] Tsiolkovsky had no

. . . .

50 The information concerning the possible contact with Tsiolkovsky is exceedingly scarce.
    Andersen simply thought that Tatlin may have known about Tsiolkovsky's articles.
    (Andersen 1968, p. 9.) Milner says that Tatlin is known to have admired Tsiolkovsky.
    (Milner 1983, p. 178.) Zhadova does not mention Tsiolkovsky at all. The only standard work
    saying that Tatlin actually contacted Tsiolkovsky is Lodder 1983, p. 215. The view is based
    on an unpublished manuscript by Hanna Begicheva who came to know Tatlin in Kiev in
    1925–1927. Unfortunately Begicheva's text is not available and it is difficult to say anything
    about its reliability. Some parts of her memoirs have been printed in Ukrainian; see
    Begicheva 1968. (In Zhadova 1988, p. 154 and p. 439 the year is misprinted as 1969.)

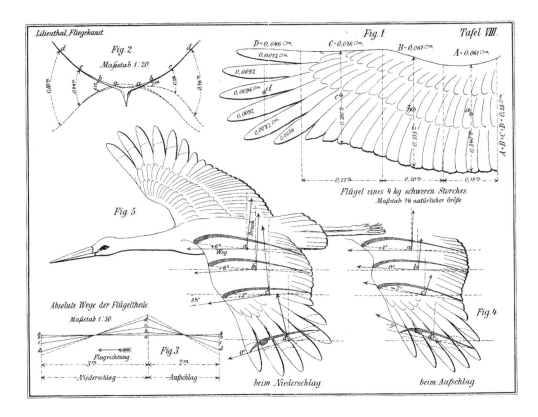

interest in human-powered flying other than proving with calculations that man's muscles are not strong enough for the job. Andersen's main point is that the proportions of the *Letatlin* correspond with "striking exactness" to those used in Tsiolkovsky's calculations. In my opinion, this does not suggest that Tatlin was inspired by Tsiolkovsky. The exact ratio between the total flight weight and the wing surface used in the *Letatlin* (8 kg /m²) can be easily found in Otto Lilienthal's book, a source well known to Tatlin.[51] Tsiolkovsky, for his part, was not even interested in gliding, but had in mind a totally different kind of flying. In his article of 1895 "The Aeroplane or Bird-like Flying Machine" Tsiolkovsky suggested a very advanced design for a powered monoplane.[52] In 1903 he published his paper "The probing of space by means of jet devices," and a year later "A simple study of the airship and its construction." In 1929, the

The aerodynamics of a stork, according to Lilienthal. Note the calculation of the wing surface A+B+C+D=0.25 m². (Lilienthal 1889, Tafel VIII.)

. . . .

51 Andersen 1968, p. 10; Lodder 1983, p. 215. From Lilienthal 1889 see the Tafel VIII with drawings and measurements of a four kilogram stork and its wings (0.25 m² / wing). In the case of the *Letatlin* this ratio meant that the pilot should not weigh more than 60 kg. It is interesting that when Boris Cheranovsky's BICh-18 *Muskulet* was tested in 1935, the pilot was R. A. Pishchuchev whose weight was only 58 kg. See Tikhonravov 1949, pp. 189–191, and Nemecek 1986, p. 366.

52 The article appeared in the journal *Nauka i zhizn* in 1895. Gibbs-Smith, however, refers to a German version from 1894 but without giving any bibliographical notes. See Gibbs-Smith 1985, p. 71.

same year as the building of the *Letatlin* began, Tsiolkovsky wrote about a new aeroplane with a pressurized cabin, and published his famous book *Space Rocket Trains*. In it the seventy-two-year-old scientist laid the theoretical basis for modern multi-stage rockets. A year later he published a paper on jet planes.[53] These publications are highly specialized, full of mathematical formulas, and simply lightyears away from the handmade and artistic world of Tatlin.[54]

Making of the Machine

Most of the world around Tatlin was handmade, too. At the end of the 1920s Russia was largely a backward, agrarian society. Moscow, although different from the rest of the country, was not a modern capital. The NEP period (New Economic Policy, 1921–1928) had helped the city to recover from the first, difficult post-revolutionary years and conditions caused by the breakdown of water supply and sanitation, yet it was still crippled by many of the problems of a growing metropolis. A city with accommodation for a million, already had a population of over three millions. Thousands more poured into Moscow every day. The American newspaper correspondent Eugene Lyons, who arrived in Moscow in January 1928, described the situation: "Flats that formerly housed one family now contained half a dozen, with an overflow of 'house workers' (servants) sleeping on boxes in the corridor, on the kitchen floor, on the common oven. On most apartment doors there was a card listing the inmates, with complicated instructions for ringing:

> Alexandrov...........ring 1
> Stepanov..............ring 2
> Lazarovsky...........ring 2 short, 1 long
> Kagan.................ring 4 short, 3 long; etc."[55]

Not only doorbells had intricate rules; the city itself appeared to Lyons, a New York communist, as a straggling, meandering place with an utterly Eastern character. Despite the broad avenues, boulevards, and several "skyscrapers," the tallest of them twelve stories, Moscow was Asiatic rather than European in its sprawling chaos, its squat houses, its quaint old churches, and profusion of

· · · · · · · · · ·

53 See K. E. Tsiolkovsky, *Selected works*. Moscow: Mir Publishers 1968, especially "A New Aeroplane" (pp. 219–236), and "Reactive Aeroplane" (pp. 237–247). For a short discussion of Tsiolkovsky's work, see B. N. Vorobyev, "Konstantin Tsiolkovsky and his work on interplanetary travel" in Tsiolkovsky 1960.

54 John Milner has written about Tsiolkovsky's science fiction novel *Beyond the Planet Earth* (1920) in connection with Tatlin's Tower. (Milner 1983, pp. 178–179.) I will return to that novel later in this text. For a discussion of Tsiolkovsky's influence on Russian art, see Michael Holquist, "Tsiolkovsky as a Moment in the Prehistory of the Avant-Garde" in *Laboratory of Dreams* 1996, pp. 100–117. Holquist mentions Tatlin's Tower but says nothing about the *Letatlin*.

55 Lyons 1938, p. 87. I will use Lyons' book as a source when describing the general atmosphere of Moscow in the late 1920s and early 1930s. Lyons' account of his years in Moscow, although an outsider's view, is an interesting and critical document.

coloured cupolas.[56] And indeed, it was not in a skyscraper but in an old church, under one of its golden cupolas, that Vladimir Tatlin would start working on his flying machine.

The Novodevichy Monastery was founded in the sixteenth century on a prominent bend of the Moskva River, five kilometres southwest from the Kremlin. After the Revolution, the beautiful place survived as a museum. The Baroque belfry where Tatlin created the three versions of his *Letatlin* was cramped and had no heating. In Daniil Danin's memory, the smell of the studio was a mixture of dry wood and the dampness of a musty casemate. The artist's appearance at this time was rather sad too: "His pallor was not white but blue from the cold."[57] Tatlin simply could not use his studio during the winter months, but at the end of the 1920s any heated belfry-studio would have been an unimaginable luxury. There certainly were much bigger problems all around the country. The economic growth of the NEP years seemed like a distant memory, and shortage of goods resumed. Food rationing was introduced from the end of March 1929 onwards. Every manual worker under the new dispensation was entitled to two pounds of bread daily; white collar or brain workers were only allowed one pound. From spring 1929 until autumn of 1933, the food situation grew steadily worse.[58] The financial depression of the Western economies also affected the USSR. It now received less income from its exports, and the value of the rouble suffered dramatic inflation. In late 1930 popular faith in the currency collapsed, and people in vast quantities started to change their money into coins, simply hoping that the minute value of the metal would survive.[59] A year later *Torgsin* shops were introduced, selling their goods such as butter, cheese, meat, and, above all, white bread to everyone – but only with Western currency or in exchange for gold, silver, and jewels.[60] The forced collectivization of agriculture brought death rather than bread, and the real results of industrialization were lagging far behind the arbitrary plans and the euphoric propaganda. At the end of 1932, when the first Five Year Plan ended, an internal passport system was introduced, restricting the right of Soviet citizens to travel inside their country.[61] These were the times when the *Letatlin* was made.

According to Aleksandr Kovalev, Tatlin's contemporaries described him as being angry and impatient during the years of building the machine.[62] Not only

. . . .

56   *Ibid.*, p. 59. See also pp. 413–414. This was Moscow before the Stalinistic architecture, or "socialist classicism," so characteristic of the city later on. Even the Lenin Mausoleum seen by Lyons was still a temporary construction made of wood – according to Alfred H. Barr's contemporary analysis: "a well-designed wooden structure in the Assyrian style." (Barr 1986, p. 109.) The stone mausoleum was built in 1930.
57   Danin 1984, p. 597 and p. 586.
58   Lyons 1938, pp. 176–179.
59   *Ibid.*, pp. 364–365.
60   *Ibid.*, pp. 447–450.
61   *Ibid.*, pp. 514–518.
62   Kovalev 1990, p. 30. Danin's recollection indirectly supports this. For instance, he remembers meeting Tatlin in the house of Misha Litvinov's family, where Tatlin would "melt" and become more talkative and open. Danin 1984, pp. 597–598.

food but materials, too, were scarce. In an autobiographical sketch from 1929 Tatlin wrote: "Working with materials, I have felt the whole time a considerable lack of means, since this area demands greater material expenditure than paints and canvas."[63] In view of the circumstances, it is a miracle that he managed to find all the things he needed for his flying machine, from whale-whiskers to Duralumin. The parachute silk for the wings proved to be especially difficult to get. The artist had to face material problems but he did have assistants helping him. Tatlin himself mentioned the VKhUTEIN students Georgi Pavilionov and Aleksei Sotnikov as his colleagues. When the *Letatlins* were exhibited in 1932, he also named his deceased ex-wife, the surgeon Maria Geyntse and the flying-instructor A. V. Losev as assisting comrades.[64] Later commentators have also listed the painter Aleksandr Shchipitsyn and sculptor Aleksei Zelensky as members of the team; it has been claimed that Tatlin's helpers were his only friends at the time.[65] This is understandable, since as a rule, according to Sotnikov, Tatlin never let any artist step inside his studio.[66] The banner above the entrance called it a *laboratoriia*, but for a "laboratory" there was not much to see. In the nine known photographs taken in the studio we can sense a bare room with simple materials lying around, mostly wood.[67] John Milner has called Tatlin's team "a small group of researchers" but this too sounds rather high-flown when compared to the picture of Pavilionov and Sotnikov posing with some simple carpentry tools, the latter dressed like a traditional Russian peasant.[68] The added ethnic element was an aspect of the project. After all, Tatlin's aim at the time was to create "an object which is original and radically different from objects in the West or in America."[69] One of his designs before the *Letatlin* was a wooden sleigh, a means of wintertime conveyance commonly used in Moscow streets still in the 1930s.[70] His unwillingness to imitate the West – partly a forced decision because of the obvious lack of resources – underlined the primitive and mystical aspects in Tatlin's work. It has been said that it also

. . . .

63   Printed in Zhadova 1988, p. 265.
64   Tatlin, "Art into Technology" (1932), printed in Zhadova 1988, p. 311. (Another translation in *Vladimir Tatlin* 1968, pp. 75–76.) On Geyntse († 1927), see Zhadova 1988, p. 149. VKhUTEIN is the abbreviation of the Higher State Artistic and Technical Institute, Moscow.
65   "Die Helfer werden Tatlins engste Freunde," *Vladimir Tatlin – Retrospektive* 1993, p. 393. According to Danin, Sotnikov and Zelensky were still with Tatlin in 1937 when he had to leave the studio. (Danin 1984, p. 598.) Pavilonov died in 1937. (Zhadova 1988, p. 312.)
66   Zhadova 1988, p. 439.
67   Three pictures in Kovalev 1990, p. 31, and six in Zhadova 1988, pics. 325, 328, 329, 330, 331, and 338. The use of the term *laboratoriia* was typical to Russian Constructivists, (see Lodder 1983, p. 7.) but also Clément Ader named his workshop as *Laboratoire d'Aviation*.
68   Milner 1983, p. 217. Milner seems to be unaware that Geyntse was Tatlin's former wife and that they met for the last time in 1924 or 1925 (according to Zhadova 1988, p. 149). For the photograph of Pavilonov and Sotnikov, see Zhadova 1988, pic. 317, and Kovalev 1990, p. 31.
69   Tatlin, "The Problem of the Relationship between Man and Object. Let us Declare War on Chests of Drawers and Sideboards" (1930), printed in Zhadova 1988, pp. 267–268.
70   See Tatlin's comment on the sleigh in 1929, printed in Zhadova 1988, pp. 266–267; also pic. 254. For ordinary sleighs, see for example Rodchenko's photograph of Konstantin Melnikov's Svoboda factory club, in Starr 1978, p. 145.

One of the Letatlins in the belfry, early 1930s. (Kovalev 1990, p. 31.)

gave it a special nationalistic colouring.[71] When the pilot Artseulov arrived at the studio in 1932, the place did not remind him of a modern laboratory but of something out of the Renaissance: "Not only was it ancient in itself but it was also crowded with all kinds of archaic contraptions [...]."[72] Electric light was by far the most modern element in Tatlin's laboratory.

. . . .

71 See Groys 1993, pp. 255–256. Perhaps Tatlin's point could be read in connection to the strong Slavic element in young Khlebnikov's writings. See for example Khlebnikov 1987, pp. 225–264. Tatlin also contrasted Russia and China with Europe and America, and believed that Russians had entered a primitive stratum of culture, like the archaic. Punin 1999, p. 128.

72 Printed in Zhadova 1988, p. 440. It is a rather amusing co-incidence that in 1934 when the Soviet Writers' Congress discussed Socialist Realism, a contemporary article declared: "A tremendous cultural revolution is going on in the Soviet Union. This Soviet era is sometimes compared with antiquity or with the Renaissance period [...]." See *Soviet Writers' Congress 1934*. London: Lawrence and Wishart 1977, p. 8.

Three Birds in a Row

With limited resources, Tatlin and his team nevertheless managed to produce three versions of the flying machine. All were made of a variety of materials: wood (ash, linden, willow), cork, silk, Duralumin, leather, steel wire, and whale's whisker.[73] Twenty years after they had been built Tatlin explained that all the *Letatlins* had had different wing surfaces and had been of different weights:

> No 1: wingspan 8 m, weight 32 kg, wing surface 8 m²
> No 2: wingspan 8 m, weight 34 kg, wing surface 10m²
> No 3: wingspan 9–10 m, weight 36 kg, wing surface 12 m²
> The total weight of the wings did not exceed six kilograms.[74]

The information is scarce, yet it may help us to understand the logic of building three separate *Letatlins*.[75] The interesting thing with these numbers is that Tatlin would have reached the optimal "birdlike" ratio between the total flying weight and the wing surface (8 kg/m²) only with his third machine.[76] The same holds true for the ratio between the weight of the wings and the total weight (1:6 without pilot), mentioned, somewhat misleadingly, by Artseulov.[77] This suggests that in the first two constructions Tatlin's problem was the weight of the fuselage, and, because it proved difficult to reduce this, he was forced to give his third machine longer wings. As the wingspan of the first two versions is the same, the larger wing surface of No 2 may be explained in terms of the addition of the so-called "wing-stiffening struts," filling the gaps between the fuselage and the inner side of the wings.

. . . .

73   The list given by Artseulov in his text "On Letatlin" (in the exhibition catalogue 1932), printed in *Vladimir Tatlin* 1968, p. 76, and in a slightly different form in Zhadova 1988, p. 408.

74   The talk given in 1953, according to Kovalev 1990, p. 28. Unfortunately Kovalev does not state where the information comes from. Is there possibly a transcription of the talk? The numbers given are slightly different from those in Artseulov's article of 1932. Artseulov gave only one set of numbers: "weight 32 kg, wing surface 12m², load/m² 8 kg." This of course sounds like an ideal combination of the No 1 and No 3, and would allow the pilot to weigh 64 kg. (Or if he was thinking about No 3, the 32 kg could simply be a misprint for 36 kg). Let us note that Tikhanravov gives the values as listed for No 3. (Tikhanravov 1949, p. 184.) Therefore I am inclined also to accept the other figures given by Kovalev. They seem to make sense and explain why Tatlin had to build three versions instead of one or two.

75   Comparing the information with the photographs we have of the three different machines, it is possible to discern differences in their structure. Although the *Letatlin* is generally accepted as a work of art, relatively little has been done to analyze it as such. There have, for example, been no attempts so far to identify the three different versions of the *Letatlin* in art history literature. Similar situation would not be possible with, say, the different versions of Brancusi's *Bird in Flight*.

76   Assuming again, as in note 51 above, that the pilot's weight was 60 kilograms. In the first plane the ratio would then be 11.5 kg/m² and in the second 9.4 kg/m².

77   Artseulov says that the 1:6 corresponds to the ratio of wings' weight and total weight in most birds. This has been accepted and repeated by many later commentators (Lodder, Milner, Zhadova). However, there seems to be a flaw in this logic. In the *Letatlin* the ratio holds good only for the *empty* structure, that is, before the pilot gets in, whereas birds do not have extra pilots. If Artseulov talked only about birds' skeletons, then what is the point of this calculation? How to separate from each other the essential parts (bones?) and non-essential parts (muscles, feathers?) of a flying creature? In any case, the 1:6 ratio was reached only with *Letatlins* No 2 and 3, while the first version would have allowed the wings to weigh a maximum of 5.3 kg.

During the years 1929–1932 Tatlin improved the shape of his construction in order to meet the measurements chosen by Nature.[78] He sincerely thought that man had enough strength to fly and steer his *Letatlin*; man only needed to come to a correct understanding of the flying technique. Flying itself would take no more energy than ordinary swimming. Tatlin's assistant Sotnikov later expressed the same idea: "Flying is a perfect phenomenon, yet at the same time a simple one. It cannot be copied but must be perceived."[79] To explain the that way he saw flying, Tatlin combined two different metaphors. On the one hand, flying was going to be organic like swimming in the air, on the other, the flying apparatus was going to be as simple to handle as a bicycle. Even children were going to learn how to do it.[80] But "swimming in the air," no matter how beautiful it sounds, was not on a par with the reality of aviation in the early 1930s. Richard Stites has described the atmosphere: "Pilots and aviators played a special role in the mythology of the 1930s – and not only in the USSR. They embodied the leading edge of applied science and technology, the frontier spirit, bravery and

One of the Letatlins in Tatlin's exhibition 1932. (Kovalev 1990, p. 33.)

. . . .

78 Zhadova was not after the technical details of the *Letatlin*, and thought that the reason why Tatlin built three planes was because he "foresaw eventual mishaps during experiments." Zhadova 1988, p. 148.
79 See Zhadova 1988, p. 310 and Kovalev 1990, p. 34, n. 4.
80 "We have to learn to fly with it in the air, just as we learn to swim in the water, ride a bicycle and so on." (Zelinsky 1968, p. 78.) "A man in 'Letatlin' will lie in the position of a swimmer. And do the flying. He will work with his arms and legs as he already works when he's swimming."; "[…] children will have to learn to fly from about the age of eight." (Tatlin at the Moscow Writers' Club on 5 April 1932, printed in Zhadova 1988, p. 310. See also Rakhtanov 1980, pp. 324–325.)

Під прапором партії більшовиків, під керівництвом Ленінського ЦК і вождя світового пролетаріату тов. Сталіна—

Stalinistic aviation. Tupolev TB-3 bombers with the Palace of Soviets on the background. A poster from 1935. (Tyrannei des Schönen. Architektur der Stalin-Zeit. München – New York: Prestel 1994, p. 247.)

adventure in distant and forbidding locales, and spirited youth tempered by fatherly mentors. Record flyers and the heroes who soared over arctic waste-lands became overnight media personalities. Stalin adopted them as his 'falcons'; and writers, actors, singers, and comedians feted them at their clubs and made radio shows and films about them."[81] The achievements of brave Soviet pilots certainly made good propaganda both at home and abroad, but Stalin's real emphasis was on military aviation. In one of the most impressive shows of the era, the First of May parade in 1933, more than fifty *Tupolev TB-3* heavy bombers flew over Red Square, taking Western observers by surprise. During these years of heroic flying and full scale armament, Tatlin's ideas were not the most practical kind. It looks as if only two official bodies were interested in his eccentric work between 1929–1932: the secret police and the OSOAVIAKhIM.[82]

It is not as surprising as it first appears that the secret police would have taken an interest in the *Letatlin*; Kovalev claims that Tatlin had from his youth been a

. . . .

81 Stites 1992, p. 69. Much of this propaganda underlined the great technological progress made in the USSR but in reality the aviation technology was still based on buying Western expertise and products. For example, between 1932 and 1940 more than twenty American companies supplied their aircraft or accessories. See Antony C. Sutton, *Western Technology and Soviet Technical Development 1930 to 1945*. Stanford: Hoover Institution Press 1971, pp. 219–235.

82 Rakhtanov recounts in his memoirs that there were men who came to see Tatlin, wearing imported overcoats and thick-soled shoes, but they were always given an answer in German: "Nein, Herr Professor, Tatlin ist nicht zu Hause. Er spaziert." [No, Professor, sir, Tatlin is not in. He is on a walk.] Rakhtanov 1980, p. 325. (Rakhtanov's memoir "Spiral khudozhnika" was also printed in the catalogue *V. E. Tatlin. Zasluzhennyi deiatel iskusstve RSFSR. 1885–1953*. Moskva: Sovetskii khudozhnik 1977.)

non-conformist, and was constantly under police surveillance.[83] The interest shown by OSOAVIAKhIM, however, had more to do with aviation. OSOAVIA-KhIM (Society for the Promotion of Defence and Aero-Chemical Development, 1927–1948) was basically a civilian organization, yet its members wore military uniforms and had their own insignia. They also had their own flying and technical central school at Tuschino airport, westward of Moscow. Staff and students followed military forms and were entitled to rationed provisions, although smaller to those in the Air Force.[84] Most of the OSOAVIAKhIM pilots were capable of flying only rather old and slow aeroplanes, but the organization also employed dare-devil pilots expelled from the Air Force for doing aerobatics.[85] The pilot Konstantin Artseulov, whom OSOAVIAKhIM eventually sent to see Tatlin in 1932, was one of the most experienced aviators in the country. He had started flying in 1911 and had after that made a career both in the Tsar's Air Force and in the Red Army. In the 1920s and 1930s he was attracted to gliding, and acted in his spare time as the head of the gliding section of OSOAVIAKhIM.[86]

Artseulov knew very well that Tatlin's construction was not something that one could swim with in the air. He expressed his reservations in the text he wrote for the catalogue of the 1932 exhibition: "A calculation of the physical effort involved in flight also points to the almost insurmountable difficulty of solving this problem."[87] Yet at the same time he was fascinated by Tatlin's character: "I was struck by the charm that man possessed, by his sturdy appearance which was also reminiscent of the Renaissance."[88] Artseulov also admired the well-modelled structure of the machine and the inventive use of materials. Tatlin's ideas about birdflight and nature's flexible forms seemed to interest him too. Compared with any successful flying apparatus, the *Letatlin* was an illogical construction, yet as an idea it captured something uniquely beautiful. Artseulov wrote that he awaited the coming tests of the *Letatlin* with great interest.[89] Artseulov must have seen that as an invention Tatlin's machine was hardly going to be dangerous, unlike some other contemporary devices. In the winter of 1930–1931 newspapers had published reports about a Soviet engineer–inventor and his "aero-sledge," a push-propeller machine on skis. The inventor died in his apparatus right after its first public demonstration.[90]

. . . .

83   Kovalev 1990, p. 28 and p. 30. (Unfortunately Kovalev does not explain where the information comes from.) In Kiev in the 1920s Tatlin is said to have answered the question whether he is a leftist by saying: "Not leftist, not rightist – aboriginal." Begicheva 1968, p. 162.

84   Krawetz 1936, pp. 45–46. The OSOAVIAKhIM logo contained a propellor, a rifle, and a gas mask on top of a red star. To raise funds OSOAVIAKhIM organized an annual lottery. In 1930 the first prize was a two-week holiday or 5,000 roubles. See advertisement in *Krasnaya Niva* 3/1930.

85   *Ibid*, p. 47. One of the renegade Air Force pilots who suffered the fate of ending as a passenger plane pilot in OSOAVIAKhIM 1929–1930 was Valeri Chkalov. Later he made a new career as a test-pilot. With a non-stop flight from Moscow to Vancouver (Washington, USA) across the North Pole in 1937, he became one of the most famous of Stalin's long-distance aviators.

86   Zhadova 1988, p. 409.

87   Artseulov's text is printed in full in Zhadova 1988, p. 408.

88   Artseulov in the 1970s, *ibid.*, p. 440.

89   *Ibid.*, p. 408.

90   Lyons 1938, pp. 445–446. Such machines were continuously re-invented in Russia both before and after the Revolution. See *Ogonek* 7/1911 and 12/1911, and *Krasnaya Niva* 7/1929, 10/1929, 14/1929.

Earthbound

In an interview in 1932, Tatlin promised that tests of his *Letatlin* would start soon: "Now, in the spring, we are going out with tents and we're going to start trying it out on slopes."[91] It seems, however, that there was not much time to do the testing in spring 1932. The interview came out in April, when the skeleton of the *Letatlin* was displayed at the Moscow Writers' Club. It has been suggested that lack of resources was the reason behind this first display of the *Letatlin*. Kovalev quotes Tatlin's assistant Sotnikov, explaining that because the silk fabric for the wings arrived late the tests were made in autumn 1932.[92] By May, when all three versions of the machine and the two loop-ended wing supports were on display in Tatlin's exhibition at the National Museum of Fine Arts, two of the three *Letatlins* had got their uniform silk covering.[93] One machine never advanced beyond the skeleton-like frame, but it is apparent that several tests were made with the two covered planes. Reconstructing the chronology of events may prove to be difficult, but everything indicates that the beginning at least was not easy. According to Rakhtanov, one wing got broken already when the *Letatlin* was moved to the testing ground.[94] Sotnikov recalled that some tests were made in Zvenigorod by the Moskva River, but the rainy weather made it difficult. Other problems may have occured too, as Sotnikov ends: "And then there was not much sense in doing it any more."[95]

Being too tall and heavy to try out his own invention, Tatlin himself could only give orders. However, we know the names of some young and slim men who were eager to fly the *Letatlin*.[96] A pilot named Chuhnovsky is said to have volunteered.[97] Then there are claims that Misha Litvinov, son of the Foreign Minister, flew the plane a few yards in the autumn of 1933, when it was again brought to Zvenigorod.[98] Another known pilot, whether on the same occasion or at the Glider Pilots Meeting in the summer 1933, was V. V. Nefedov, whose test ended before the take-off when a sudden gust of wind turned the plane over. According to Vladimir Khapov, who had also been preparing for a flight, the *Letatlin* was then badly damaged.[99] The few existing photographs show the

. . . .

91   Zelinsky 1968, p. 79.
92   Kovalev 1990, p. 32 and p. 34. It is entirely possible that Tatlin was still short of silk. If the evening at the Writers Union was a fund-raising occasion, Tatlin certainly was in a hurry as the opening of the exhibition at the Museum of Fine Arts was only forty days away.
93   See an interesting view of the exhibition in *Vladimir Tatlin* 1968, p. 83; also in Milner 1983, p. 220. To the best of my knowledge it is the only photograph showing all the three versions at the same time. For the wing supports, see Zhadova 1988, pic. 335 and *Vladimir Tatlin* 1968, p. 81.
94   Rakhtanov 1980, p. 325.
95   Kovalev 1990, p. 34.
96   Danin 1984, p. 596.
97   Rakhtanov 1980, p. 325.
98   Lodder 1983, p. 300, n. 63.
99   It is of course possible that this is the same incident Rakhtanov wrote about. See the pilot meeting mentioned in Zhadova 1988, p. 148, and Khapov's reminiscence printed in Zhadova 1988, p. 441. According to *Vladimir Tatlin – Retrospektive* 1993 (p. 393), one of the *Letatlins* was broken at the bottom in a test in 1932. If the years are right and these really are

Letatlin being tested in summer 1932(?). (Vladimir Tatlin – Retrospektive 1993, p. 38.)

Letatlin on the ground, being moved by pilots with leather helmets, or being explained to the surrounding folk. Unfortunately none of these pictures show any attempted flight, not even a pilot inside the machine. From the photographs it is even difficult to tell which of the two covered *Letatlins* is being tested. What shows clearly, however, is that the so called "wing-stiffening struts," still intact in both versions during the exhibition, have been removed.[100]

The failed tests were certainly discouraging, but Tatlin did not give up immediately. During 1933 one *Letatlin* – probably the uncovered one – was shown in various clubs, and a year later exhibited at the Moscow Polytechnical Museum.[101] But after that the news becomes scant, and the later history of the three *Letatlins* is mostly shrouded in obscurity. Tatlin stayed on in the belfry studio for some years longer. Apparently the damaged machines and their parts were kept there, and Tatlin may have done some modifications and repairs. Daniil Danin related that around 1936 Tatlin's assistant, Pavilionov, spoke about another unlucky flight attempt, claming that his own mistakes had caused the

. . . .

two different incidents, and if the damage was serious, then we have at least a possible way of explaining what happened to the two silk-covered *Letatlins*. Two broken machines leaves only one left, the partly surviving skeleton No 1. When Danin tells about the moving of the machine's wings from the studio in 1937, he speaks only about one *Letatlin*. See below.

100 The six known photographs are reproduced in *Vladimir Tatlin – Retrospektive* 1993 (pp. 36–39); Zhadova 1988 (pics. 341–343); Milner 1983 (p. 233). Either they are from two different occasions or there is a disagreement about their date: in the *Retrospektive* 1932 is given, in Zhadova 1933. The sailplanes in the background of one of the photos (Zhadova 1988, pic. 343) suggest the later date. The name "wing-stiffening struts," given for the parts best seen in Zhadova 1988, pic. 328, may well be misleading as we do not know their exact meaning.

101 There is no information saying which of the three versions was displayed in 1934. If the two covered versions were already broken (see above note 99), then it may have been the skeleton. It is also possible that after the Polytechnical Museum's exhibition the machine never actually returned to Tatlin's studio.

failure.[102] This is the last time we hear about the machine being tested. Tatlin had to leave the studio in 1937, and as he could not house the *Letatlin* in his small flat he took it to bits and gave the pair of wings to Danin and his friend Misha Litvinov, who took them on two bicycles to the latter's family house. The silk covered wings acted like sails when the two students drove, almost flying along the crowded streets of Moscow.[103] What remains today is one of the two beautifully bent wing supports shown in 1932 and a "reconstruction" of the skeletal *Letatlin*.[104] Although it has been said that Tatlin worked on the *Letatlin* until his death, there is nothing to support the view that he was rebuilding the machine after 1937.[105] The atmosphere of the following years – the growth of Stalin's terror and the hardships of the Great Patriotic War (World War II) during which Tatlin lost his son – was not exactly inspiring.[106] People who knew him in the

. . . .

102 Danin 1984, p. 596.
103 *Ibid.*, 597–598.
104 The separate wing support survived with the sculptor Zelinsky's widow and is now in the Costakis Collection. According to Rakhtanov, the *Letatlin* ended to the museum of DOSAAF (a voluntary co-operation organization of the Army, the Navy, and the Air Force), see Rakhtanov 1980, p. 325–326. However, it has been claimed that the *Letatlin* was also exhibited in the USA, and that it has been displayed at the Soviet Air Force Museum in Monino since 1958. (B. Korolkov & V. Kazashvili, *A Guide to the Russian Federation Air Force Museum at Monino*. Atglen, PA: Schiffer Military History 1996, p. 9.) The machine was restored in the 1960s by Artseulov and three others. (Zhadova 1988, p. 508.) Judging by the photographs, the result is not altogether satisfactory. The body seems to be the authentic "skeleton" made by Tatlin, but the tail is a later fabrication and clearly different from the original. At least part of the wings is authentic but the position of the shafts is incorrect and therefore the partly covered left wing gives a totally wrong idea about the original shape of the wings. The landing gear, i.e. the three leather balloons visible in the photographs of 1932 have gone missing. What happened to the wings Tatlin handed over to Danin and his friend in 1937 is unclear.
105 Lodder 1983, p. 264 and p. 300, n. 59. It is safe to say that the idea never left him. After all, he came to public and spoke about his planes in 1953.
106 According to Milner, Tatlin was himself evacuated to Sverdlovsk 1941–1943. See John Milner, *A Dictionary of Russian and Soviet Artists 1420–1970*. Woodbridge: Antique Collectors Club 1993, p. 424.

1950s have talked about a bitter man whose life was very hard. He was critical towards most of the former avant-garde artists, Rodchenko being the only one whom he respected. Only seven or eight people attended Tatlin's funeral in 1953.[107] His ashes rest in the Novodevichy graveyard, only a short flight from the belfry where the *Letatlin* was born.[108]

Artwork or Machine?

It has been argued that for the most part the *Letatlin* actually was not meant to be a functional machine.[109] Christina Lodder, for example, believes that "the fact that the Letatlin never really flew does not detract from the significance of the project [...]."[110] This view stresses the artistic value of the *Letatlin*, something that most art historians today would not deny, but it is clearly in contradiction with Tatlin's own words, according to which he was building something that really worked. Even if the *Letatlin* is today seen merely as a work of art that was not successful as a machine, this kind of transfiguration through non-functionality was not in Tatlin's original intentions. His efforts to keep the weight of the construction as low as possible clearly suggest functional aims. The problem was that his idea about the functional *form* was different from the others'. In the 1920s, when Tatlin conceived his first plans for the *Letatlin*, the modern aeroplane, its light weight and its structural strength, was a fashionable topic among the avant-garde. Following Le Corbusier's example, Soviet architectural theorists idealized the high functionality of the flying machine. In 1926 the journal *Sovremennaia arkhitektura* published the article "The form of the aeroplane and the methods of designing it" by the engineer K. Akashev.[111] One of Akashev's key arguments was naturally the elimination of all superfluous weight. He also held that the "present type of aeroplane" – the main picture showed the old 1919 *Farman* also favoured by Le Corbusier – was aesthetically superior to the machines of 1909–1910. According to Akashev, the heroism and the romantic ideas of the medieval inventors produced no real results, whereas

. . . .

107 See V. B. Elkonin as printed in Zhadova 1988, pp. 438–439, and George Costakis' recollection of Tatlin, in *Art of the Avant-Garde in Russia: Selections from the George Costakis Collection.* New York: The Solomon R. Guggenheim Museum 1981, p. 12.

108 Milner says that "An urn with his ashes was taken to the cemetary of the monastery where he had studied the flight of cranes," (Milner 1983, p. 234.) but this seems to be a misunderstanding. Tatlin did not study birds in Novodevichy but much earlier in the 1920s when his wife, Geyntse, also did the dissections mentioned by Milner (*ibid.*, p. 224.). Tatlin also kept a stork in Kiev around 1926. (Begicheva 1968, p. 161.)

109 Christina Lodder takes the view that Tatlin's approach had been pre-eminently artistic. (Lodder 1983, 215.) Radu Stern suggests that the *Letatlin* should be analysed not only as an original flying device but also as a "flying sculpture." (Stern 1993, p. 59.) According to Aleksandr Kovalev it is "a unique work of art" (Kovalev 1990, p. 28.), while Larissa Zhadova sees it as "an etheral kinetic sculpture." (Zhadova 1988, p. 148.) Anatoli Strigalev thinks that Tatlin believed in advocating beautiful things which might never be realized. (in Zhadova 1988, p. 38.)

110 Lodder, 1983 p. 223 and p. 215.

111 *Sovremennaia arkhitektura* 3/1926, pp. 65–66.

now the new aesthetic forms were founded on scientific thinking.[112] Six years later the critique on the *Letatlin* would also contrast "scientific" with "medieval."

When the former Constructivist Kornely Zelinsky interviewed Tatlin for the newspaper *Vechernaya Moskva* in the spring 1932, he asked if the *Letatlin* was a work of art or a technological product, a demonstration of attractive forms or whether one can really fly with it.[113] On the one hand, Tatlin's answer gives support to the aesthetic emphasis chosen by Lodder and many others; he does not want the *Letatlin* to be taken purely as something utilitarian, he has made it as an artist. On the other, however, Tatlin expresses himself loud and clear, leaving no room for misunderstandings: "I count on my apparatus being able to keep a person in the air. I have taken into account the mathematical side, the resistance of the material, the surface of the wings."[114] In short, it is evident that the *Letatlin* was designed and built as a functional technical machine with aesthetic values. Above all it was meant to fly.[115] The question of technological and artistic forms was in itself nothing new. The subject had been discussed in Constructivist texts, such as an article from 1921 by A. Toporkov.[116] Whether Tatlin was familiar with his text remains unknown, but clearly some of its points come close to the *Letatlin* project.

According to Toporkov, a machine can be a work of art when technological form is inadequate and requires a supplement: "[…] art here, as indeed everywhere, is the leader. Calculation is possible only on the grounds of wide-awake intuition, and one can construct only when one possesses great creative imagination."[117] The most interesting point in Toporkov's text is, however, his claim that the machine is more like an animate organism than is generally thought, and that we must learn to regard the machine as something animated, organic, alive.[118] Understanding this is essential. In working with a machine, a man merges with it in a general rhythm with his breath, his heartbeat, and his blood. Only this way, says Toporkov, can he come to love his work. In these feelings, in this love, lies the key to the understanding of the machine as an

· · · · · · · ·

112 *Ibid.*, p. 66. Arguments favouring the new aeroplanes were the same in Germany, for example. A fighter with 300 h.p. had "wunderbarer Schönheit." Kollman 1928, p. 17.

113 Zelinsky 1968, p. 78. Zelinsky was a literary critic and the leading theoretician of the literary group of Constructivists. In 1930 he turned his coat and wrote an article *The End of Constructivism*, criticizing it as "bourgeois" and "imitating the West." See Zhadova 1988, p. 309.

114 Zelinsky 1968, p. 78.

115 V. B. Elkonin takes the same view in his remembrance of Tatlin. He was struck by the beauty of the *Letatlin* but adds: "[…] somehow it did not even occur to one to wonder whether the machine would fly or not. But actually all the calculations were correct and it could be used for flying." Printed in Zhadova 1988, p. 438. According to Danin, Tatlin did not have doubts about being on the right track, and he firmly held that there are scientific arguments for his machine. See Danin 1984, p. 596. We can find a similar attitude in Gabriel Poulain's texts from the 1920s: "I firmly believe that whatever may be said to the contrary, the aerocycle is destined for a great future." Quoted in Reay 1977, p. 71.

116 "Technological and Artistic Form" in *Iskusstvo v proizvodstve*, published in Moscow by Narkompros. Toporkov 1974, pp. 26–32.

117 *Ibid.*, p. 27.

118 *Ibid.*, p. 30.

artistic product; "The man who does not understand the machine's ultimate purpose with his inner being, for whom the machine is merely a dead thing, will never grow to love it, will never give it artistic shape."[119] As a one-time Constructivist Kornely Zelinsky may have known Toporkov's text, but his article certainly showed no feelings of love. Instead it appeared to be the first text to question the real functionality of the *Letatlin*, and with it Tatlin's words about art and technology in general. Zelinsky's journalistic style has (what we now would call) an unpleasant Stalinistic flavour, but it should be admitted that Zelinsky also had a good critical eye for the obvious paradoxes in Tatlin's explanation, often overlooked by later commentators.[120] Boris Groys's article (1993), where he largely follows Zelinsky's criticism, seems to be the first attempt in sixty years to disregard the feelings of love and ask unkind questions about Tatlin's *Letatlin* project.

The main point of Zelinsky, if we leave the political accusations aside for a moment, is in the following: "A new technological creation can give an artistic impression, but it must also serve its direct technical purpose, it must subordinate itself to the iron laws of technology. If 'Letatlin' is a technical apparatus designed for flight, then it must fly – and if it cannot, then it is a mere toy, neither more nor less."[121] Claiming that *Letatlin* would be able to fly, or at least able to support a human in the air as a glider does, Tatlin put himself in a difficult situation. As Groys points out, Tatlin is forced to make excuses and return back to traditional aesthetics when talking about his plane.[122] He could of course have answered Zelinsky's inquiry by admitting that the *Letatlin* was only an artwork, but he did not say so. The question remains, if we accept that Tatlin sincerely believed that his *Letatlin* would fly, what was it that made him so confident about its functionality? Groys, who writes about Tatlin's "*ingenieur-technischer Diletanttismus*" and the non-functionality of his machines, does not believe in Tatlin's technical knowledge and points out that if Tatlin really knew the rocket theorist Konstantin Tsiolkovsky's calculations, as has been suggested, then he must have known that his *Letatlin* was not going to fly.[123] Was, then,

. . . .

119 *Ibid.*, p. 31.
120 The critical dimension has not always been the strongest point in the art historical literature on the Russian and Soviet avant-garde, often treating its subject with an almost romantic admiration. It is amazing that Zelinsky's article, one of the most important eye-witness texts about the *Letatlin*, is omitted – apart from a short fragment – from Zhadova 1988.
121 Zelinsky 1968, p. 80. Zelinsky is right of course, but it may be worth recalling that, contrary to Stalistic propaganda, Russia had not developed independent technology by the early 1930s but was relying on imported Western technology. After the Revolution the manufacturing of both automobiles and aeroplanes had come to a halt and the leading aeroplane designed Igor Sikorsky had left for America. Production of aeroplanes in Russia was restarted by the German company Junkers in 1923 (the Versailles treaty prevented aeroplane manufacturing in Germany), while the first "homemade" aeroplane was patched together in 1924. The first – and for a long time only – bus was "produced" in 1925. Aeroplanes with wooden frames proved much easier to make than automobiles, but it was typical that the Russian aeroplane designs of the 1920s and early 1930s were copies of Western machines and that their engines were usually imported. For the role of Western technology 1917 to 1930, see Sutton 1968; on automobiles pp. 243–249, on aeroplanes pp. 256–264.
122 Groys 1993, p. 255.
123 *Ibid.*, p. 255.

Tatlin's answer to Zelinsky's question a sign of mere technical naïveté or was he perhaps trying to avoid the rising accusations about formalism? The Soviet constructivists were targeted with such claims in the 1930s and it is not difficult to hear a certain tone in Zelinsky's question about some attractive forms versus a functional machine.[124] Tatlin had to watch his words, but I believe that at the same time he was genuinely confident about the possibilities of his machine, and that this confidence was not grounded on technical diletantism only, as Groys suggests, but also on information about other similar flight projects undertaken in Europe and in Russia since the beginning of the 1920s. When it comes to European muscle-powered aviation, Tatlin's knowledge may have been far from detailed. Probably he only had read some illustrated newspaper articles, like the one found in his archive and dating from 1932, a few weeks after the *Letatlin* was finished.[125]

Silencing the Solo Inventor

Technical credibility was only one of Tatlin's problems. The political accusations in Zelinsky's article were serious, not least because in backward Russia the question of the role of technology had been widely discussed by the leading politicians since the Revolution. For Lenin one of the important lessons of the First World War had been the value of modern technology. In 1918 he wrote: "It is essential to learn that without machines, without discipline, it is impossible to live in modern society. It is necessary to master the highest technology or be crushed."[126] What Lenin had in mind was obviously very different from the organic forms that Tatlin experimented with in the late 1920s and early 1930s. Tatlin for his part thought that his field was not technology as such but "material culture." It was indeed under this rubric that Tatlin was given the belfry of the Novodevichy Monastery as a studio in 1929, during the last year of Anatoli Lunacharsky's period as the Commissar of Enlightenment.[127]

· · · · · · · · ·

124 The official ideological campaign against Formalism in literature, architecture, and art was launched in *Pravda* in March 1936, but grave accusations against Tatlin had been raised already in 1933. See *Vladimir Tatlin – Retrospektive* 1993, pp. 393–394.

125 The article titled "Mensch als Vogel" [Man as a Bird] was published in *Münchner Illustrierte Presse*, Nr. 16 / 1932. It explains the man-powered flying experiments of a German inventor called Fritz Ellison. See *Vladimir Tatlin – Retrospektive* 1993, p. 52, n. 36. In his history of man-powered flying Reay 1977 does not mention Ellison.

126 Quotation in Bailes 1978, p. 49.

127 According to Lodder, Tatlin headed the Narkompros' Scientific Laboratory for Investigating the Plastic Arts either from 1931 until 1932 or from 1930 until 1933. (Lodder 1983, p. 213 and p. 264.) However, the biographical data both in Zhadova and in *Retrospektive* tells that Tatlin started to work in the belfry in 1929. (Zhadova 1988, p. 448; *Vladimir Tatlin – Retrospektive* 1993, p. 392.) A study of Narkompros' papers may be necessary, but with the information available I see no reason to doubt that Tatlin got the studio in early 1929, while Lunacharsky was still the head of Narkompros. This view is further supported by Danin's memoirs, where he says that Lunacharsky had arranged the studio for Tatlin. Danin 1984, p. 597.

Lunacharsky had held the post since the October Revolution and had been tolerant of many of the experiments of avant-garde artists. He also knew Tatlin well from the late 1910s when Tatlin started working for Narkompros (People's Commissariat of Enlightenment).[128] And it was precisely for Narkompros that Tatlin's studio, the Experimental Laboratory for Material Culture, now worked.[129] This was not necessarily the best possible context as the political atmosphere was rapidly changing. In his ideas about education Lunacharsky had always leaned more toward the arts and the humanities than towards the sciences and technology.[130] He had not only co-operated with avant-garde artists like Tatlin and Mayakovsky, but he also had been, with his middle-class background and his European education, a spokesman for the old literary and humanistic culture, now regarded as bourgeois.[131] Lunacharsky's approach to education was increasingly questioned after 1928, and by the time Zelinsky interviewed Tatlin all attachment to the "old culture" had become even less esteemed. Meanwhile abstract art was fighting a losing battle. In 1928 the entire Politburo made an official visit to the exhibition of the Association of Artists of Revolutionary Russia (AKhRR), the advocates of "heroic realism."[132]

During 1928, demands for a more technical and more proletarian culture were growing stronger. This did not mean only the arts but something much bigger. According to a contemporary agitator, children of the proletariat were best suited to careers in technology, since they possessed a more concrete form of thinking than bourgeois intellectuals with two ancient languages.[133] When Stalin criticized Narkompros in 1928 as inert and conservative, even most of his political opponents agreed.[134] Lunacharsky answered that Narkompros's budget

. . . .

128 "Tatlin must be regarded as one of Lunacharsky's most active collaborators during the year 1918." Zhadova 1988, p. 23. See also p. 446. This does not mean that Lunacharsky agreed with everything that Tatlin proposed. He did not like the Monument for the III International, for example: "Guy de Maupassant wrote that he was prepared to flee from Paris to avoid seeing the iron monster known as the Eiffel Tower, but in my opinion the Eiffel Tower is a thing of beauty compared with Tatlin's slanting building. I believe it would be a matter of great exasperation, not only to myself, if Moscow or Petersburg were to be adorned with such a product from the creative imagination of one our most important modern artists." *Vladimir Tatlin* 1968, p. 59.

129 "The tower is that of the Novodevichy monastery, placed by Narkompros at the disposal of Vladimir Tatlin for his attempts to create an air bicycle." Zelinsky 1968, p. 77. The connection to Narkompros is mentioned also by Lodder 1983, p. 213 and Zhadova 1988, p. 448, but overlooked for instance by Milner who says only that the Laboratory was "housed in the beautiful and extensive Novodevichy Monastery" Milner 1983, p. 217.

130 Bailes 1978, p. 160.

131 Lunacharsky wrote extensively on world literature and art and wrote plays. For his background and his career till 1921, see Sheila Fitzpatrick, *The Commissariat of Enlightenment*, Cambridge: Cambridge University Press 1970.

132 Lodder 1983, p. 184. In the mid-1920s Lunacharsky often supported the AKhRR. See Brandon Taylor, "On AKhRR" in *Art of the Soviets* 1993, pp. 51–72.

133 O. Y. Shmidt in 1928, quoted in Bailes 1978, p. 166. Lunacharsky reacted against such comments and in February 1929 he wrote to Stalin complaining about the social discrimation against students of the intelligentsia in higher education. O'Connor 1983, p. 98.

134 It was not difficult to find support for this criticism. The aim of the USSR was, after all, to reach quickly the technical level of the capitalistic countries. In a speech in November 1928 Stalin was deeply concerned about the terrible backwardness of the country's technical equipment, as can be seen from the quotation in Bliznakov 1990, p. 166. For the technological progress in USSR to 1930 and the crucial role of Western expertise in different projects from Dniepr power station to Kamchatka fish canneries, see Sutton 1968.

was inadequate to meet the country's educational needs, and argued that the cultural sector should receive more money. However, the result of the debate was clear from the beginning, and Lunacharsky resigned in spring 1929.[135] Another veteran of the Revolution, Nikolai Bukharin, who led the opposition against Stalin 1928–1929 and was subsequently dismissed, summed up the final outcome in 1932: "We have got to understand that the whole of our culture must be less 'literary and humanistic' in the old sense of the term, and in a certain sense become much more 'technical'."[136] The public failure of Narkompros and Lunacharsky to serve the proletariat cast a shadow over Tatlin's project too. When Zelinsky asked whether the *Letatlin* was a technical invention or not he was not simply curious. He already had an answer.

Zelinsky opened his attack by saying that he will try to see the apparatus *Letatlin* "in the light of the practical technology of the working class, to which all the mystification is alien."; he described the Monastery tower as an exotic prop and the studio as a "medieval laboratory." He then reminded his readers of the days of the October Revolution: while the proletariat was flexing its muscle at the fronts, in the ice-cold factories, the petit-bourgeois intelligentsia's Romantic artists behind the front made nothing but a noise with their Constructivist and Futurist manifestations. Zelinsky regarded Tatlin and other Russian Constructivists (Rodchenko among others) as being united with "bourgeois capitalism's fitters," such as Léger, Lipchitz, Severini, Corbusier, Ozenfant, and van Doesburg.[137]

Zelinsky's further accusations are based on the idea of how a proper technical project of the proletariat is to be realized: "Can we really allow the performances of solo inventors to develop?" The question was now placed on the ideological plane. Tatlin was adapting technology to the feelings of the individual, something which Zelinsky saw as an escape from the industrial world. He called it Tatlin's own "*technological Khlebnikovism*," and stated: "There is nothing strange in this, since their class roots are the same."[138] This is strong language and reminds us of the contemporary attitude in the Soviet technological schools where students with wrong (i.e. non-proletarian) class roots were not accepted or were expelled.[139] Zelinsky ended his article with a word of advice. He said that the *Letatlin* should be purged of its rotten ideological supports, and hinted that Soviet scientific institutes should be able to reap the harvests of Tatlin's work. In this way, Tatlin would get the help of the Soviet public he needed.[140]

. . . .

135 O'Connor 1983, p. 97 & 99.

136 Quotation in Bailes 1978, p. 161.

137 Zelinsky 1968, p. 78.

138 Zelinsky 1968, p. 80. Tatlin's father was a transport engineer who had made a study trip to America and wrote a book on American railway technology. Khlebnikov's father was an admistrator and an ornithologist.

139 See Bailes 1978, p. 178, n. 57. Before he was forced to leave Narkompros, Lunacharsky had tried to argue that there was no reason to expel students strictly on the basis of their social origin.

140 Whether the comment was noticed in the scientific institutes is not known to me. Boris Cheranovsky at least was building his flapping-wing machines after this time, possibly with

Tatlin was quick to learn which way the wind was blowing. Zelinsky's article came out in April, and only five weeks later in mid-June, when Tatlin's exhibition opened, his own catalogue text "Art into technology" shows signs of caution. In the text, Tatlin explained the background of the *Letatlin*, but he added a comment criticizing the "Constructivists," in inverted commas, and took his motto from Stalin ("During the epoch of reconstruction technology determines everything.")[141] But even if Tatlin learned the right ideological rhetoric, one difficulty remained intact and on it everything depended: he could not silence his critics by demonstrating that the *Letatlin* could really fly. In another newspaper article less than a year after the Zelinsky interview, Tatlin already sounded like a different, if not broken man. "After boldly challenging our ideas on engineering with his *Letatlin*, the artist now wants to return to painting, with which he began his artistic career," writes the journalist.[142] The end result of this all is that when Tatlin in 1952–1953 wrote his *curriculum vitae* he did not even mention the *Letatlin*. Instead he referred to his early 1930s projects as a scenographer and stated: "I began this work as a realist artist in 1933."[143] This rapid and dramatic turn away from "material culture" and its flying apparatuses to less offending forms of art may have saved Tatlin from trouble, but the clipping of his wings must have been painful. After all, he had not been constructing simply a machine, but a new man: the Flying Tatlin.

Writing the New World

In the early 1980s, Christina Lodder argued that the poet Velimir Khlebnikov had an immense influence on Russian avant-garde artists, especially on Miturich and Tatlin, but that there is no direct evidence to suggest that Tatlin was specifically influenced by Khlebnikov when it comes to flying machines and buildings of the future town.[144] We are still lacking the evidence, but the emphasis on Khlebnikov's role has certainly grown.[145] The evidence may be missing also because we do not know exactly what we would like it to prove. When Khlebnikov died in 1922, his most important essay on architecture *Ourselves and Our Buildings* was still unpublished. It seems, however, that it was written around 1915 when Khlebnikov and Tatlin were working together in Petrograd.[146] It is then not without grounds to assume that Tatlin was familiar

. . . .

OSOAVIAKhIM money, but whether he did it on his own initiative or not remains to be established.

141 Zelinsky's article was published on 6 April 1932, Tatlin's exhibition opened on 15 May 1932. Tatlin's text "Art into Technology" appears (in two different translations) in *Vladimir Tatlin* 1968, pp. 75–76, and in Zhadova 1988, pp. 310–311.

142 The article was published in January 1933. See Zhadova 1988, p. 312.

143 *Ibid.*, pp. 320–325; the comment on page 323.

144 Lodder 1983, p. 245 and p. 208.

145 See Zhadova 1988, p. 149–150. Khlebnikov has been named as the godfather of the *Letatlin*, Kovalev 1990, p. 29.

146 On the dating of the text, see above page 104, n. 16. The city of St Petersburg was renamed Petrograd in 1914, ten years later Leningrad.

with the ideas expressed in Khlebnikov's text. Their visions about "skywriting," for example, are strikingly similar; Tatlin's *Monument to the Third International* was meant to be equipped with a projecter station that could write letters in light in the sky, very much reminding of the words of Khlebnikov: "In cloudy weather the clouds themselves were used as screens, the latest news projected directly onto them."[147] It is also well known that Khlebnikov's habit of playing with words and the name of Tatlin's machine have a link. *Letat'* (to fly) and Tatlin put together makes *Letatlin*, the Flying Tatlin.[148] But perhaps Khlebnikov's influence is best understood if we ask *where* would Tatlin fly to? What sort of liberty would his machine give him? Let us recall that in his essay Khlebnikov had imagined a future city where the inhabitants had learned to fly and would no longer gather on dusty streets. It appears that Tatlin saw the practical value of his machine in a similar context: the town of flying inhabitants would be relieved of transport, of noise, of petrol fumes, and overcrowding.[149] The idea of escaping the dust by flying was in itself nothing new; in the 1860s the famous balloonist Nadar had written about the hardships of normal travel, the dirt and congestion of railway journeys, and the terrible accidents and injuries that occurred. Finally he concluded: "How different from our aerial voyages, without shocks, without concussions, and free from noise, dust, fatigue, and danger." The truth was slightly more complex, of course. The passengers of Nadar's balloon *Géant* did enjoy sailing in the air, but the landings proved to be anything but smooth, often resulting in fractured bones.[150] Khlebnikov and Tatlin, too, were very well aware of the dangers of flying. They knew how the Futurist poet Vasili Kamensky had survived a severe crash with his aeroplane in 1912 and had then decided to give up flying.[151] The physical world was hard, but Khlebnikov had found a softer way into the air: he flew only in his mind and in his writings. In his letter in March 1922, Khlebnikov sympathized with Petr Miturich's plans to build a flying machine, but wrote that he understood nothing about the configuration of force and mass along the axes of the flying body.[152] Instead of focusing on the technical aspects of flying, Khlebnikov had sketched out a whole future landscape for the new form of living. His 1915 essay is a fantasy, not an architectural plan, and because of this it has much in common with other utopian texts. I am positive that from those texts we find something which also illustrates Tatlin's idea of a future world.

· · · · · · · · ·

147 See the text "On the Tower" by Nikolai Punin (1919), as printed in *Vladimir Tatlin* 1968, p. 56, and Khlebnikov's "Skybooks" (1918), in Khlebnikov 1987, p. 344.

148 Khlebnikov had special meanings for consonants L and T, see for example "Let us consider two words," in Khlebnikov 1987, pp. 266–271; "A Checklist: The Alphabet of the mind," *ibid*, pp. 314–317; "Artists of the World," *ibid*. pp. 364–369.

149 *Ibid.*, p. 348; Tatlin as quoted by Begicheva in Lodder 1983, p. 214. (On Begicheva's text, see above p. 123, n. 7.)

150 Nadar 1866, p. 88. On the mishaps of *Géant's* voyages, see for example de Fonvielle 1907, pp. 51–58.

151 On Kamensky, see Wohl 1994, pp. 145–153.

152 Khlebnikov 1987, p. 137.

Return of the Palace

In search for the imaginary landscape behind Tatlin's flying machine, there is one particularly influential book we will have to start from: *What Is To Be Done?* by Nikolai Chernyshevsky. The novel, written in prison and published in 1863, was perhaps the most important social utopia produced in pre-Revolutionary Russia. And after the Revolution its value only rose. It was known to be one of Lenin's favourite books, and when a passage from it was carved on the walls of the Bolshoi Theatre in 1928, Lunacharsky read out the lines at the unveiling.[153] The part of the text that interests me here is towards the end of the novel. It comprises a dream sequence in which the protagonist Vera Pavlovna is shown the future of her land, socialist Russia. Vera and her guide see the landscape from above as if they are flying, and at times they come down to study the new place more closely. The people of the future work in a farming society, but the buildings where they live and gather for eating and dancing are described as huge palaces of iron and glass. "But this building, what is it? What sort of architecture is this? There is nothing like it now," writes Chernyshevsky, and continues: "No, there is just a hint of it in the palace which stands on Sydenham Hill, and which is built of glass and wrought iron, nothing but glass and wrought iron."[154] So, here we meet the building from where we started our journey: the *Crystal Palace*. Chernyshevsky had seen the construction when visiting London in 1859, and a few years later in his novel he epitomized its vastness, its transparency, its materials, and its mechanical construction methods as emblems of the future which will be not only happy but also more healthy. The latter idea is closely connected with purity of air. On her visit to one of the houses, Vera Pavlona admires the voices of a workers' choir and is told that the quality of the choir is a result of the changed way of life: "But the way of life here is so different from the old days – it is a healthy and cultured life, so that the chest expands and the voice is better."[155]

Chernyshevsky, of course, was not the only nineteenth-century author to believe that the idea of a happy future society and the image of the *Crystal Palace* belonged together. In Jules Verne's novel *Les Cinq Cents millions de la Bégum* (1879) we meet two future cities set on the west coast of America. The first, designed by a German professor, is a dark labyrinth of heavy industry, covered with pollution and filled with suffering. The second, designed by a French doctor, is a green and pleasurable town, full of sunshine and joy. The smoky German town, *Stahlstadt*, produces gigantic cannons and other war machines, while the clean French town, *France-Ville*, produces nothing but organizes international conferences and attracts artists.[156] The industrial hell and

. . . .

153 On the novel, see Stites 1989, pp. 26–27. It remained a hugely popular piece of official literature all through the history of the Soviet Union. There were at least 65 editions between 1917 and 1975.
154 Chernyshevsky 1982, p. 319.
155 *Ibid.*, p. 326.
156 "A cette époque, France-Ville avait atteint le plus haut degré de prospérité, non seulement ma-

its aggressive German dictator are gross caricatures, while the unproblematic life in the democratic and art-loving French town is a whitewashed Utopia. Therefore it is hardly surprising that the municipal hall of *France-Ville* is an immense glass-covered nave where the air freely circulates.[157] If the original *Crystal Palace* was a beautiful by-product of the smoky reality of the industrial revolution – partly for this reason the building was considered in its own time as "dreamlike" – it is worth noticing how its image was afterwards separated from the context of industrial production and was set in a green future where both the social and the environmental problems caused by technology can be made, or have been made, to disappear. At the beginning of the twentieth century we find this transformed image of the *Crystal Palace* dominating the vision of utopian London by H. G. Wells: "One will come into this place as one comes into a noble mansion. They will have flung great arches and domes of glass above the wider spaces of the town, the slender beauty of the perfect metal-work far over-head will be softened to a fairy-like unsubstantiality by the mild London air. It will be the London air we know, clear of filth and all impurity, the same air that gives our October days their unspeakable clarity and makes every London twilight mysteriously beautiful."[158]

The books of Verne and Wells were very well known in Russia, and remained in print after the Revolution. When the collected fantasy novels of Wells were published in the USSR (six volumes in 1930), Lunacharsky wrote the preface saying that he is waiting for a "Russian Wells" to appear.[159] Lunacharsky had perhaps deliberately forgotten Alexandr Bogdanov, the Bolshevik revolutionary, science-fiction author, and founder of Proletkult, whose novel *Red Star* he had praised when it first came out in 1908. In Bogdanov's story about the socialist planet Mars, reissued after author's death in 1928, we find again the image of the *Crystal Palace*, this time as a factory covered with "transparent glass vaults."[160] And it comes as no surprise that on the socialist planet – on it even the vegetation is red – the factories do not need decorations because the machines themselves are considered beautiful, very much in the same way as on nineteenth-century Earth: "Powerful machines and their precise movements are aesthetically pleasing to us in and of themselves, and there are very few works of art which would fully harmonize with them without somehow weakening or dissipating their impact."[161]

· · · · · · · · ·

térielle, mais intellectuelle. Là, dans des congrès, se réunissaient les plus illustres savants des deux mondes. Des artistes, peintres, sculpteurs, musiciens, attirés par la réputation de cette cité, y affluaient." Verne 1966, p. 165.

157 "La halle municipale était une immense nef à toit de verre, où l'air circulait librement [...]." *ibid.*, p. 172.

158 Wells 1994, p. 145.

159 According to Lunacharsky, such an author could play a great role in Soviet social-pedagogical literature, but only if he were free from the major mistake of Wells. In Lunacharsky's view this is Wells's petty-bourgeois habit of believing in steady progress instead of promoting change and actively taking part in the creation of the new society, as is done in the USSR. See Anatoli Lunatšarski, "Herbert Wells," in *Kirjallisuudesta ja taiteesta* [On Literature and Art]. Moskova: Edistys 1974, pp. 256–261.

160 Bogdanov 1984, p. 63.

161 *Ibid*, p. 74. In Bogdanov's novel the art museums of Mars are "scientific research institutes,

Returning to the realities of planet Earth, I will next take a look at the ways the change from the dirty, industrial environments to the clean world of glass-covered buildings was believed to happen in the 1920s Russia, and see how those ideas relate to the concept of the *Letatlin*.

Flying with Architecture

After the Revolution there were indeed more Russian counterparts to Verne and Wells than just Bogdanov, although not quite as talented in a literary way as Lunacharsky may have hoped. Visions of the future were mostly discussed in works of popular culture, and their influence is not to be underestimated. As Richard Stites has remarked, utopianism accompanied every phase of Soviet history up to the early 1930s when Stalin came to power.[162] It is interesting to note that in many Soviet science fiction novels of the late 1920s and early 1930s personal flight is a central theme.[163] But a particularly vivid description of flying appears in Konstantin Tsiolkovsky's novel *Beyond the Planet Earth* of 1920. In it, the inhabitants of a future space colony fly in zero-gravity with the help of small wings, which "with very slight effort gave considerable speed and grace of movement." Children especially were eager to learn: "'Mummy! Mummy! Look – I'm flying!' yelled little Oleg. 'Look – see – I'm flying towards the wall – look! I'm coming back...'"[164] Tsiolkovsky then imagines people of all ages joining in, like insects flying over a summer meadow: "Here comes a group of young men, flapping their wings like a swarm of bees, accompanied by their leader, who is adorned with a large flower. Here is a charming flock of little children with their elder; here some young girls, headed by their deputy, who is distinguished by a lovely garland. There go some old people of both sexes, with their representatives; there the family men, and there some women with their children."[165] What separates these stories from similar ones published in the West, is that their blue-eyed optimism was, if not part of the official liturgy of the young USSR, very much like it.[166] In all these dreams the aim was to create a new man and a new society in a positive atmosphere. As in fiction, so in real life the new revolutionary architecture was – at least for some time – one of the tools to attain this end. The most visionary Soviet architecture has a permanent

. . . .

schools at which we study the development of art or, more precisely, the development of mankind through artistic activity." *ibid.*

162 Stites 1989, p. 41. See also Stites 1992.
163 See Stites 1989 for the science fiction in Russia (pp. 30–36) and in the USSR (pp. 167–189). Of the novels mentioned by Stites: V. D. Nikolsky, *In Thousand Years* (1927) "personal flight is used by all citizens"; I. Zhukov, *Voyage into the Wonderland of the Pioneer Detachment "Red Star'* (1924) "personal flight – practically central in this children's tale"; Y. Larri, *The Land of the Happy* (1931) "aeropters (strap-on flying sets)."
164 Tsiolkovsky 1960, pp. 161–162.
165 *Ibid.*, pp. 163–164.
166 We know that dystopias were written too, thanks to Zamyatin's famous *We* (1920), in which all buildings of the future world are also made of glass, "as if woven of air."

place in the history of the international avant-garde, but it also has links to the literature of socialist utopias and to Soviet science fiction. The story of the *Letatlin* can be understood in connection with the same literature. The fictional proletarian gadgets for everyone, such as personal flying apparatuses, were a standard motif and not very far removed from the idea of the *Letatlin*. But the comrades of the future would not only have the new technology, they would themselves be different. Writing on the Soviet architecture of the late 1920s, Anatole Kopp noted: "The object of architecture, its 'goal' as Moses Ginzburg called it, had become the creation of the structures needed to transform the nation's way of life, while the intention of the architects was to erect no longer mere buildings, but 'new social condensers' capable of producing a mutation of man."[167] Likewise, Tatlin's idea implies that with the widespread use of the *Letatlin* future citizens will think differently, live differently, and move differently. Above all, flying people will be, of necessity, healthy and physically strong.[168]

Tatlin started building his *Letatlin* when the First Five Year Plan was announced (1929, retroactive to October 1928), and by the time of the Second Five Year Plan in 1933, he had finished his work. The period between these years was also the time of the Cultural Revolution when the old intelligentsia was first being challenged and then overthrown by militant Communist youth.[169] But, somewhat paradoxically, the years of building the *Letatlin* were also golden years of new Soviet architecture. "The great period of modern architecture in the USSR that followed the early years of confusion and anticipation lasted only from 1925 to 1932. [...] And yet the history of the most important contemporary movement in architecture, constructivism, coincided almost exactly with the seven-year interval," writes Kopp.[170] A look at the works of innovative architects proves him right. Two of these architects are of special interest to us: Ivan Leonidov and Konstantin Melnikov. But instead of discussing what they built – it would difficult with Leonidov who built almost nothing – I will study what kind of projects they proposed and what sort of future world they had in mind.

It has been remarked how "airplanes and dirigibles zoom freely over architectural renderings by Ivan Leonidov and Konstantin Melnikov."[171] However, the images of flying machines, popular among architects ever since Le Corbusier's plans, were used both for decoration and for saying something. In Melnikov's case I would argue that the few airships and aeroplanes in the drawings are unimportant, while in Leonidov's work they constitute an essential

· · · · · · · · ·

167 Kopp 1970, p. 101.
168 Zhadova 1988, p. 147. On the subject, see Toby Clark, "The 'new man's' body: a motif in early Soviet Culture" in *Art of the Soviets* 1993, pp. 33–50.
169 For an overall view of the Cultural Revolution, see *The Cultural Revolution in Russia, 1928–1931.* 1978. The period was especially difficult for technical specialists. 1928 saw the Shakhty affair, a staged trial against a group of engineers and technicians accused of sabotage. O'Connor 1983, pp. 89–91; Sutton 1968, pp. 325–326. For a chilling eye-witness report of the trial, see Lyons 1938, pp. 114–133.
170 Kopp 1970, p. 67.

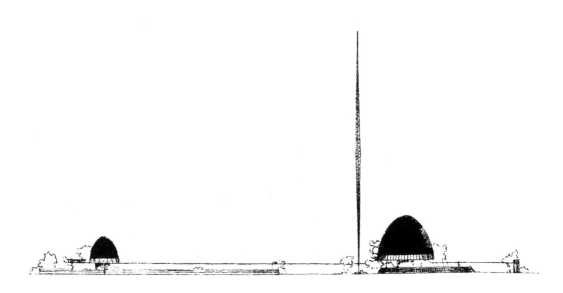

part of the whole. Thinking of the importance of aviation in the architectural ideas of Leonidov, it comes as no surprise that he thought highly of Tatlin; "Which artists did my father admire? He had a great respect for Vladimir Tatlin – he very much liked his Letatlin flying machine," recalls the architect's son Andrei Leonidov.[172]

Leonidov's plan for a Club of New Social Type, 1928. (Gozac & Leonidov 1988, p. 64.)

Clean and Green

Ivan Leonidov became famous in 1927 with his graduation work, a proposal for the Lenin Institute of Librarianship. Although all that remains of it are some drawings and photographs of the original model, the work is still considered a masterpiece. In the words of Andrei Gozak: "Alongside Tatlin's tower of 1919 and Melnikov's Paris Pavilion of 1925, the Lenin Institute has remained to this day one of the great symbols of the revolutionary, innovative spirit of the first decade of Soviet Architecture."[173] It is also the first of Leonidov's works to suggest flying. The most striking detail in the Lenin Institute plan is the spherical auditorium with a huge glazed ceiling and a system of supporting

· · · · · · · · ·
171 Starr 1984, p. 213.
172 Gozak & Leonidov 1988, p. 24.
173 *Ibid.*, p. 8.

wires, evoking, as Gozak points out, "direct associations with the ropes of a balloon, playing on our desire to master the forces of gravity and to conquer the architectural air-space."[174] Leonidov was neither the first nor the only architect to be inspired by these aspirations, but his talent and his personal curiosity about flying – he collected books on aeronautics and was particularly interested in dirigibles – made the Lenin Institute, as well as the subsequent works, exceptional.

If Konstantin Melnikov added the images of dirigibles in his drawings merely as decorations, in Leonidov's plans they always were part of the idea. The usual concept in his pioneering works – the Lenin Institute was followed by the project for A Club of New Social Type (1928), and entries to competions for a Monument to Christopher Columbus (1929) and for a Palace of Culture (1930) – is a vast plain where the buildings are set in geometrical order. All the works mentioned imply an airport or airfield of some sort, glass-clad buildings, and a powerful radio station. For Leonidov, these were symbols of the technical achievements of the era, and accordingly his Monument to Columbus was meant to celebrate not only the ancient sailor but also the *Graf Zeppelin* and "Lindberg's flight from Europe to America."(sic)[175] But Leonidov did not simply draw new buildings. By using the latest technical solutions he proposed a new way of life. In his mind, the old pastimes would give way to new ones; A Club of New Social Type would not have a theatre but instead an open place for gliding and flying. And, not surprisingly, in accordance with the utopian dreams of a clean future, the whole area would be "a large site well protected from dirt and dust."[176]

Melnikov, like Leonidov, also took part in the international Columbus Monument competition, with an even more fantastic entry, difficult to describe in words.[177] They were strange dreams of a machine age, but the enthusiasm for technology – which in many architectural visions is hardly more realistic than in Khlebnikov's writings – reveals only part of the picture. The essential element of the dream was always the clean and dustless environment, the farewell to the vicious streets, described by Khlebnikov. This was the world for which Tatlin was building his *Letatlin*. I have already shown this dream in the works of

. . . .

174 *Ibid.*, p. 9–10.
175 *Ibid.*, p. 68. Charles Lindbergh flew from New York to Paris in May 1927. The first transatlantic flight from east to west was made in April 1928.
176 *Ibid.*, pp. 60–67. The arguments about urban noise, dust, lack of light and air etc., already familiar from the writings of Khlebnikov, were to be repeated in the Green City competition two years later, as in Moisei Ginzburg's entry. See Bliznakov 1990, p. 164.
177 S. Frederick Starr has compared Melnikov's unrealistic plan with Tatlin's idea of building a flying machine: "Both Tatlin's machine and Melnikov's monument dramatically posed the problem of the place of the individual in a collectivized world of technology, but neither solved it." (Starr 1978, p. 168; on Melnikov's Columbus Monument pp. 163–167.) This is general enough, but on another occasion when Starr talks about Melnikov and Tatlin (who obviously did not know each other), he is lost in shrubbery. I find it slightly far-fetched to compare the concrete ramps in Melnikov's parking garage plan and "the laminated ribs of Tatlin's experimental glider, the *Letatlin*." (*ibid.*, p. 104.) The Columbus Monument competition was popular, and Alvar Aalto, discussed in the previous part, also took part in it. For his proposal, see Schildt 1986, p. 240–241.

Chernyshevsky, Bogdanov, Verne, and Wells – it also appears in many others – and we meet it again in the 1930s Soviet plans for Green Cities. "Socialist cities, 'green cities', communal residences, palaces of culture are being built. In this construction there arises before us in all its breadth the problem of *man and object*," believed Tatlin.[178]

Konstantin Melnikov's SONnaia SONata, or the "Laboratory of Sleep." (Starr 1978, p. 178.)

The competition for a Green City was held in 1930, and Konstantin Melnikov's entry was judged to be among the best three.[179] In accordance with the official Soviet policy of the time, Melnikov's proposal strongly emphasized the collective life of the new community.[180] But it was not only the public transportation system, the communal kitchens and the large communal areas that Melnikov had in mind; in the Green City the deeper layers of the collective consciousness were also to be addressed. Melnikov took on board the idea of recreation and developed it to produce a fantastic solution.

I will now interpret Melnikov's proposal for a Green City in a way that needs to be explained. My starting point is the fact, already mentioned earlier, that by 1930 the reality of building socialism had turned rather grim.[181] It was the year the poet Vladimir Mayakovsky shot himself, and Stalin gave the signal for the

· · · · · · · · ·

178 Tatlin, "The Problem of the Relationship between Man and Object. Let us Declare War on Chests of Drawers and Sideboards" (1930), printed in Zhadova 1988, pp. 267–268. The *topos* of the clean environment lived on in science fiction. In 1939 an American magazine descbided a future megalopolis: "In this city smoke will be eliminated, noise will be conquered, and impurity will be eliminated from the air. Many persons will live in the healthy atmosphere of the building tops, while others will commute to far distant residential towns, or country homes." *Amazing Stories* August 1939, back cover.

179 For the background of the competition and its results, see for example Bliznakov 1990, pp. 161–168; Kopp 1970, pp. 172–181; Starr 1978, p. 170–172.

180 For Soviet architecture and the ideas of collective life, see S. Frederick Starr, "Visionary Town Planning during the Cultural Revolution" in *Cultural Revolution in Russia, 1928–1931*. 1978, pp. 207–240; and Mikko Ylikangas, "Ihmissielun insinöörit"- kaupunkisuunnittelu uuden ihmisen luomisvälineenä 1920-luvun Neuvostoliitossa [The Engineers of the Human Soul], in M. Härmänmaa & M. Mattila (eds.), *Uusi uljas ihminen*. Jyväskylä: Atena 1998, pp. 41–69.

181 For the change in the cultural politics, see for example the chapter "The War on the Dreamers" in Stites 1989, pp. 225–241.

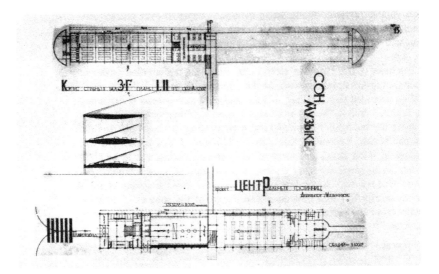

Plan for the SONnaia SONata. Note the curved floors. (Starr 1978, p. 178.)

"liquidation of the kulaks as a class."[182] Even for those saved from bullets, the perverse mathematics of the first Five Year Plan, the famous 2+2=5, meant that workloads were crushing. As if the unrealistic plans, bad management, and poor productivity were not enough, the massive propaganda campaign, the brutal terror, and the continuous food shortages made daily life for many an insane struggle.[183] Melnikov's suggestion was that the most important aspect of rest in the workers' Green City should be sleep. A relief from the nightmare of reality.

Melnikov based his concept on the notion that man spends a great part of his life sleeping: "Today, if I am told that correct food is necessary for health, I reply – 'No, sleep is what is needed.' Everyone says fresh air is necessary but again I command that without Sleep fresh air will do little for our health. Expanding this into Architecture, I was amazed at this arithmetic: Man sleeps one third of his lifetime. Taking that to be sixty years, twenty years are spent in sleep, twenty years of lying down without consciousness, without guidance as one journeys into the sphere of mysterious worlds to touch the unexplored depths of the sources of curative sacraments, and perhaps miracles. Yes, everything is possible, even miracles."[184] The methods of lulling the tired workers to sleep would be first smells and sounds, all in a controlled order with the correct room temperature and humidity. Then gently rocking beds would help the workers to relax. Finally, specially commissioned poems and pieces of

. . . .

182 On Mayakovsky's life, death, and literary afterlife, see Vahan D. Barooshian, *Brik and Mayakovsky.* The Hague: Mouton Publishers 1978. On Stalin and the kulaks, see Lyons 1938, pp. 279–292. Stalin gave the order to kill the kulaks on 27 December 1929 and called a halt on 2 March 1930.

183 Exhaustion was recognized as major problem; one widespread form of mental illness was even called "Soviet exhaustion." As a Stalinistic solution to the problem, no Soviet journals of psychology or neurophysiology were published for twenty years after 1934. On the subject, see David Joravsky, "The Construction of the Stalinist Psyche" in *Cultural Revolution in Russia, 1928–1931.* 1978, pp. 105–128.

184 As quoted and translated in Starr 1978, p. 177.

music would be performed. Free from tensions and anxieties, the workers would then fall into a restorative sleep.[185]

S. Frederick Starr has seen in Melnikov's proposal the means for manipulating the psyche. Certainly they are there, in one form or another. According to Starr, Melnikov had heard of the first scientific experiments with *hypnopedia*, as well as of Hugo Gernsbeck's science fiction story about the subject.[186] Yet I would like to emphasize the other aspects of his plan. In this case Melnikov's architecture, the building where people would sleep, was primarily a healing machine, or, should we re-cycle the slogan of Le Corbusier, *la maison est une machine à soigner*. The idea is in its essence highly critical of the reality of the Soviet state which had turned its citizens into shaken people. In Melnikov's mind, as I propose to read it, they should be freed from the fear of terror and the anguish of work. In daily reality ruled over by Stalin this was of course impossible; the only place of retreat was sleep. On paper, the intention behind the plan was to create a New Soviet Man. But what if Melnikov was not thinking of the cure simply as a week's holiday, after which the workers would return to continue working for the Five Year Plan with renewed energy? What if we read Melnikov's plan as a metaphor for something else – a dream of a different kind of future?

Laboratory of Sleep

Vladimir Mayakovsky's last two plays deal with two timezones, the year of their writing (1929) and the future fifty or a hundred years ahead. Especially the later text, a satire titled *Banya*, shows Soviet reality in a highly critical light.[187] Building communism has failed to proceed, and bureaucracy and slothfulness have won. For those still believing in the ideal the only place left is the future. In Mayakovsky's play the solution, a kind of invisible time-machine, is a dream come true: a door to another time – and an exit from the present one.[188] As the

. . . .

185 *Ibid.*, p. 178. Kopp has written that in his project Melnikov seemed to turn away from reality and indulge in daydreaming, (Kopp 1970, p. 87.) but perhaps that is another way of saying that there was something wrong with the reality.

186 *Ibid.*, p. 181. Unfortunately Starr omits to tell how, when, where, and from whom he got this information.

187 The earlier of the two plays is *Klop* (The Bedbug), where a frozen citizen of 1929 is being defrosted in 1979. The title *Banya* has been often translated literally as The Bath-House, but this does not explain (see the translator's note in Mayakovsky 1987, p. 118.) the meaning of the idiomatic expression *zadat banyu*, familiar to everyone living in a sauna culture.

188 There is an interesting idea behind the time-machine. In the very beginning of *Banya* Mayakovsky introduces the analogy of Volga and Time, an open allusion to Velimir Khlebnikov's text "Excerpt from The Tables of Destiny," published in 1922. (See Mayakovsky 1987, p. 120 and Khlebnikov 1987, p. 417.) Khlebnikov believed he had found a structure in the intervals of important historical events, some sort of universal laws of time, and saw the whole sensation of time melting away. In his letter to Petr Miturich on 14 March 1922 Khlebnikov wrote: "When the future comes clear thanks to these computations, the feeling of time disappears; it is as if you were standing motionless on the deck of fore-knowledge of the future. The feeling of time vanishes, and it begins to resemble a field in front of you and a field behind; it becomes a kind of space." (*ibid.*, p. 137.)

Allegory of "Electricity," the Palais des Machines 1889. (Durant 1994, p. 25.)

machine works it brings forth the delegate of the future, the Phosphorescent Woman, arriving in a flash of Bengal light and shining like the lady of the lightning in the allegory of Electricity in front of the *Palais des Machines*, forty years earlier. The radiant woman has the role of the saviour: the good and truthful builders of socialism are chosen to travel through time with her to the future communist state of the year 2030, while the bureaucrats, opportunists, and sluggards are left behind. Explaining the situation, the Phosphorescent Woman says: "The destination is infinity, the speed – one year per second, and the place – the year 2030, but how many and who, we do not know. We only know the station of destination. Here the value is unclear. The past is stretching out a hand to the future. We will accept those who will remain in a hundred years' time." Later on, at the moment of departure, she gives her final instructions: "Hold fast together, close to one another. Flying time will sweep away the ballast weighed down by trash, the ballast of the sterile and uninspired."[189] With his literary time-machine Mayakovsky expressed an indirect wish to fly away from the Soviet reality. On a more practical level the

. . . .
189 Mayakovsky 1987, p. 149 and p. 161.

Son na aeroplanie [Dream on an aeroplane]. Russian sheet music, early 1910s. (Prendergast 1981, p. 140.)

aeroplane had become the means of escape. After the NEP period in 1929 control on the Soviet borders was thightened and fleeing the country became a difficult task. Consequently, aeroplanes were illegally flown across the border during the 1930s. Two former OSOAVIAKhIM pilots, Georg Krawetz and Vladimir Unichevsky, even published books about their successful escapes.[190] Unfortunately Mayakovsky, who had versed about the flying proletarian, had to content himself with the same method of departing as his colleague Esenin – "as they say, to another world." Mayakovsky's last journey was done on a cata-

. . . . . .

190 See Krawetz 1936 and Vladimir Unichevsky, *Red Pilot. Memoirs of a Soviet Airman.* London: Hurst & Blackett 1939.

falque of Tatlin's design, ending at the Novodevichy graveyard, past the belfry where the *Letatlin* was already under construction.[191]

In his monograph, S. Frederick Starr argued that man's resurrection or rebirth is the *Leitmotiv* of Konstantin Melnikov's architecture. The view has been criticized, perhaps because it is based more on poetic intuition than on explicit historical facts.[192] I find Starr's reading poignant and lyrical, but it is the poetry behind his interpretation of the buildings that I disagree with. Contrary to what Starr suggests, sleep does not need to be "symbolic death."[193] Sleep can be the safe house of dreams, something that death never is. Mayakovsky's decision, no matter how symbolic, ended his dreams once and for all, while Melnikov's dreams survived with him through the difficult times, as did his private house in the centre of Moscow. Both the man and his work slept unknown for decades, but once the professional interest of the outside world was awakened, they awoke too and told their story. One of the most famous details in the architect's own house came to be the way the original, pedestal-like beds rose organically from the floor. Or, perhaps it was the house itself that had grown outwards from the beds: a house built with the dreamwork of the sleeper.

There are, however, two different vistas opening up from Melnikov's bedroom. The one emphasized by Starr shows a way to Lenin's glass coffin, the first of which was designed by Melnikov in 1924, three years before the building of his own house. The poetic dimension behind the glass coffin is undeniable, namely the old fairytale of a sleeping princess, mentioned by the architect himself.[194] Suffice it here to point to the most famous variant of the story, that of Grimms' *Snow-white*; "They said: 'We could not bury her in the dark ground,' and they had a transparent coffin of glass made, so that she could be seen from all sides, and they laid her in it, and wrote her name upon it in golden letters [...]."[195] But unlike the princess, Lenin was actually dead, his brains removed by curious surgeons and kept in a drawer.[196] No, it is the other path that I will follow, the one that leads to the centre of the Green Town, and to the "Laboratory of Sleep."[197] A short discussion of this unique architectural idea will finally bring this study to its closure.

. . . .

191 For the catafalque, see Zhadova, pics. 290–292.
192 See Starr 1978, pp. 240–258. Catherine Cooke has criticized Starr's interpretation (and questioned Melnikov's importance) in her article "Melnikov and his Critics" in *Melnikov. The Muscles of Invention* 1990, pp.125–143.
193 Starr 1978, p. 254.
194 See Starr 1978, pp. 81–84, and pp. 247–249.
195 The Brothers Grimm, *The Complete Fairy Tales*. Ware: Wordsworth Editions 1998, p. 256.
196 For a contemporary article on the subject, see "Issledovanie mozga Lenina," [Examination of Lenin's brain] *Krasnaya Niva* 9/1930, pp. 6–7.
197 Whether the expression "Laboratory of Sleep" was ever used by Melnikov himself is unclear. Starr simply introduces it (Starr 1978, p. 179.) without explaining its origin. At least it does not appear in any of the original drawings reproduced in Starr's book.
Melnikov's Green Town plan included many other elements alongside the "Laboratory of Sleep" (*ibid.*, pp. 172–183.), but I will leave them aside. Needless to say, my interpretation here is limited to the aspects of the metaphor of flying.

Konstantin Melnikov gave his "Laboratory of Sleep" a name that calls to mind the neologisms of Khlebnikov, or the wordplay in the *Letatlin*. Punning on the Russian word *son* (sleep), he called it *SONnaia SONata*, "Sonata of Sleep." If the name with its musical allusions is peculiar, the building itself looks even more extraordinary. Basically it is, as Richard Stites innocently notes, "a double winged structure," but at the same time it gives a feeling that something in its construction has cracked.[198] The symmetrical wings of the building are leaning to the ground. They are of course wings in the architectural sense of the word, but a look at the original drawings reveals something surprising: the floors and ceilings are designed to be curved, almost like the surfaces of aeroplane wings. The beds for the weary workers are then positioned on these curved floors, which in turn are leaning towards the ground at an angle of 3.75 degrees. Why would Melnikov want to do this? Starr's suggestion, that in this way no pillows are needed, is a rather eccentric one.[199] Why does the house for sleeping look as if its wings have collapsed if the only problem were the pillows? I do not propose to know the answer to the mystery of Melnikov's "Laboratory," but it first makes me think about one of the aeroplanes Le Corbusier was attracted to in the early 1920s. I mean the *Caproni Ca.60* flying boat, the *Capronissimo*,

Gianni Caproni with his Caproni Ca.60 Transaereo in the plane's assembly hall. (Abate, Alegi & Apostolo 1992, p. 100.)

. . . .

198 Stites 1989, p. 203. Starr also mentions "two large wings," but both leave it at that. Starr 1978, p. 179. On Melnikov's play with words, see Strigalev 1990, p. 113.

199 "[…] to obviate the need for pillows, the floors sloped gently to the ends of the structure." Starr 1978, p. 179.

The Capronissimo shortly before its destruction in 1921. (Aviation. The Early Years 1997, p. 228.)

illustrated in *Vers une architecture*. In Le Corbusier's visual argument its triple-deck wings came to symbolize one of the structural virtues of the new architecture, namely the floors standing on pilotis. But as an aeroplane it was a total failure. Despite its "modern" looks, it flew no more than did Clément Ader's machine or Tatlin's construction. When the *Caproni Ca.60* faced an accident before its first flight its elaborate wings cracked in the middle.

The *Capronissimo* was known in the USSR, and not solely through Le Corbusier's book, yet its image had only indirect meanings.[200] The idea of mass flying (one hundred people up in the air at the same time) and the new way of building were more important than the question of the real functionality of the *Capronissimo*. I have only the words of the poet to explain, why I see its image, the image of collectivist and constructivist dreams, also in the shape of Melnikov's "Laboratory of Sleep."[201] Not as a celebration of the future prospects, but as an act of mourning for present reality. It was the machine of socialism, the

. . . .

200 For example in 1924, three years after the accident, its image decorated a page in the children's book *Puteshestvie Charli* [Charlie's travel], where Charlie Chaplin travels around the world using different machines: motorbike, ocean-liner, aeroplane, train, submarine, balloon, and finally the *hydroplan*. See Lavrentiev 2000, p. 175. (For the rest of the pages of *Puteshestvie Charli* see the unnumbered colour pages.)

201 Wisława Szymborska ends her poem "Discovery" (1972): "I believe in the refusal to take part. I believe in the ruined career. I believe in the wasted years of work. I believe in the secret taken to the grave. These words soar for me beyond all rules without seeking support from actual examples. My faith is strong, blind and without foundation." Wisława Szymborska. *Poems New and Collected 1957–1997*. Translated by Stanislaw Baranczak and Clare Cavanagh. London: Faber and Faber 1999, p. 124.

И японцы подали ему

ГИДРОПЛАН.

Крикнув японцам „до свиданья“,

Чарли уселся в гидроплане.

— 14 —

machine of dreams, its triple wings broken and leaning to the ground. Unable to leave the earth, its passengers were asked to sleep on its curved wings. With the techniques described above, they would reach a somniferous freedom and turn the crooked building into a collective dream machine. Leaving the ballast of reality behind, the workers might dream their way to another time and place. Perhaps in their sleep they could make the broken machine fly to a land of pure air, as described by Khlebnikov and Tatlin, and envisage the future without fear. For the future is there, waiting. Those who had been up among the clouds had known these dreams too. Travelling with the wind in his balloon, Nadar had seen a new world – not for himself but for those coming after him. Nadar had dreamt about a machine that would give man the real freedom of flight, a machine that would bring with it peace and a new time: "In the meantime, hours disappear, days fly past, and ages accumulate, while indolent Humanity, with eyes upraised towards the regions it contents itself with dreaming about, appears to be waiting for the solution of this great Problem, – the Divine

One hundred men standing on the wings of the Rohrbach-Romar hydroplane, 1928. (Dollfus & Bouché 1938, p. 517.)

solution which will suppress frontiers, render war impossible, and tear up even to the last leaf of the different Codes of our barbarous periods, to dictate another and a last one, the Law of Liberty and of Love."[202] The utopian solution Nadar was dreaming about was the heavier-than-air flying machine. Perhaps it was naïve of him to hope that mere technological progress would further world peace, but that is not to say that we should give up the dream. On 17 December 1903, at approximately 10.35 a.m., the bicycle manufacturer Orville Wright realized one part of Nadar's vision in Kitty Hawk, North Carolina. He did it lying flat on the wing of the first flying machine, as if sleeping.

. . . . . .
202 Nadar 1866, p. 74.

▪ Epilogue

"At the first stage of work on a project there is no a priori law governing the creative process to which one is subject."[1]

Konstantin Melnikov

In accordance with the Corbusian rhetoric, Sigfried Giedion once declared: "We are no longer limited to seeing objects from the distances normal for earth-bound animals. The bird's-eye view has opened up to us whole new aspects of the world. Such new modes of perception carry with them new feelings which the artist must formulate."[2] I see no reason to disagree with Giedion, even if I feel that the formulations by artists like Le Corbusier were at times oversized. Flying did indeed give wings to new feelings. What I have hoped to discuss in this work, however, is a feeling *for* flying rather than *of* flying. The former is something that survives on the ground; a longing for ascent that can materialize in shape of machines and constructions, even if the artist has never been in the air.

In the Introduction I promised to tell a story. Now is the time to see if I have kept that promise. In the third and last part I studied two aspects of the *Letatlin* project. Firstly Vladimir Tatlin's relation to the history of aviation and to the contemporary attempts to build a muscle-powered flying machine, and secondly the worldview behind the *Letatlin*, in connection with the tradition of social utopias and architectural visions from the nineteenth century literature to Velimir Khlebnikov and to examples of Soviet avant-garde architecture. Even if we have only scratched the surface, it seems that both these aspects of Tatlin's project have been overlooked in previous studies.

On a practical level Tatlin's attempt failed in two different ways. Tatlin's technical over-optimism has been admitted in the earlier literature, usually by stressing the artistic value of his machine, but it appears that the political problems were almost as difficult to overcome as the technical ones. According to critics like Kornely Zelinsky, Tatlin's *Letatlin* project was not proletarian but individualistic. The very word epitomized all the wrong tendencies: western influences, eclecticism, anarchism, petit-bourgeois attitudes, and art for art's

. . . .

1   Melnikov in *Arkhitektura SSSR* 5/1933, as quoted and translated in Starr 1978, p. 242. Catherine Cooke's translation of the same sentence sounds entirely different. See Cooke 1991, p. 17. Important here is the idea.
2   Giedion 1947, p. 44.

sake. The architects Ivan Leonidov and Konstantin Melnikov both faced the same accusations, with an added charge of formalism.[3] Zelinsky wrote that Tatlin's work is "technical Khlebnikovism," while Leonidov had to see his own name used in defaming the architectural avant-garde; *Leonidovshchina*, "Leonidovism," became a Soviet catch-phrase in the early 1930s.[4] Melnikov for his part was accused for being too original: "Melnikov's fundamental and sole aim is to produce an architecture which no one has ever before created."[5] In a similar way Tatlin's project of building a muscle-powered flying machine aimed to create something that no one had succeeded in doing before. While in 1930s it was possible to nurse ideas of ornithopters in technical journals and even build actual machines and test them, in art it proved to be a daringly indivualistic attempt and as such neither politically correct nor logically sound. George Gibian has suggested that some things may have even slipped beyond the illogical: "Another distinguishing feature of Russian Modernism is the strength of its lunatic fringe. In fact, perhaps we should call this element the lunatic center rather than a mere fringe. [...] Some of the most important poets and artists displayed very basic irrationalities. Vladimir Tatlin and Kazimir Malevich as well as Velimir Khlebnikov exemplify this."[6] This is certainly an interesting and little discussed point of view, and it would not be overly difficult to find evidence of Tatlin's "lunatic" ideas, say, for example, in his conviction that the human race originates from flying creatures and not from amphibia.[7] Yet we may have to ask which was more lunatic, the Soviet reality of the early 1930s or the artist's dream of swimming in the air. I have argued that the utopian idea behind the *Letatlin* was not haphazard or even unique but came close to the nineteenth-century visions of a clean and happy future, a future where everyone would be able to fly and buildings would be transparent and airy like the *Crystal Palace*.

"The Russian revolution gave wings to earthbound hopes. My problem, the moral and the intellectual problem of millions who know that the revolution has been betrayed and perverted, was to disown the perversions without clipping those wings," wrote the American journalist Eugene Lyons in the 1930s. He, too, had believed in a better future, and even if he did not dare to clip the wings, others did.[8] The dark reality of Stalin's terror is the backdrop against which Éva Körner's claim about Tatlin's work then becomes understandable: "The *Letatlin*

. . . .

3   Melnikov and Leonidov we regarded as the personifications of architectural formalism, the destruction of which was to serve as a lesson to others. Strigalev 1990, p. 109.

4   On the subject, see for instance comrade Mordvinov's lecture from 1930, in Gozak & Leonidov 1988, p. 95.

5   From Karo Albian's article "Against Formalism, Purism, and Eclecticism" (1936), quoted in Starr 1978, p. 219.

6   Gibian in his "Introduction" in *Russian Modernism. Culture and the Avant-Garde, 1900–1930*. Edited by George Gibian and H. W. Tjalsma. Ithaca – London: Cornell University Press 1976, pp. 15–16. Gibian gives examples of the ideas of Malevich and Khlebnikov, but he does not exemplify his comment about Tatlin. It seems, however, as if he was thinking of the *Letatlin*.

7   According to Danin 1984, p. 595.

8   Lyons 1938, p. 606.

was the last monument to the hopeful efforts of the human will."[9] And when the efforts had failed there were only dreams left. Moving on from the utopian world view behind the Letatlin, I have suggested reading Konstantin Melnikov's plan for a "Laboratory of Sleep" as a metaphorical building. Its two cracked triplewings are reminiscent of the failed *Capronissimo*, one of the great emblems of Le Corbusier's architectural new spirit. Sleeping on the wings of this broken aeroplane/house those who were exhausted and injured in building the better future could be healed. Melnikov's plan is at the same time an image of the collapse of functionalistic modernism, with the emblematic pilotis half sunken in the earth, and an almost surrealistic dream machine promoting an escape from the daily reality: "Sleep is the Curative Factor! . . . Anyone Thinking Otherwise is Sick!"[10]

In contrast to the poetic dreams of Tatlin, and to those of his friend the poet Khlebnikov, I set the architectural dreams of the 1920s, as expressed by Alvar Aalto and Le Corbusier. For both architects flying offered a new point of view, one which made them talk about bombing and demolishing the old town. Whether this talk was meant to be taken as something funny (as with Aalto), or as a bold vision of the future (Le Corbusier's *Plan Voisin* in particular), it certainly revealed the darker side of modern dreams. The modern architect firmly believed in the superiority of his individualistic plans and took it as given that the earlier builders were inferior. Such ideas and such egos were nothing new, but the aerial view directly from above, that is, without perspective, gave the architect the possibility to judge the existing town as a sort of abstract chessboard. This view from above was no different from that seen by a bomber pilot ready to release his destructive weapon.

Although in the end the dreams of the architects and those of Tatlin and Khlebnikov have much in common – the glass buildings and emphasis on flying, for example – it is the difference in methods that matters. Both sides were hoping to see a clean and airy future city where many of the problems caused by congestion and traffic had been solved. The architects who had been in the aeroplane and had enjoyed its power were ready to use radical means in building the future, whereas the two Russians who had only flown in their dreams were talking in softer terms. They were not against technology as such – to see the light of the day even the most simple of Khlebnikov's fantastic houses would have needed many new inventions – but what they imagined was a different kind of technology, very much in the same way as the Japanese author Junichiro Tanizaki had written in the early 1930s: "[...] how different everything would be if we in the Orient had developed our own science. Suppose, for instance, that we had developed our own physics and chemistry: would not the techniques and industries based on them have taken a different form, would not

. . . .
9   Körner 1985, p. 84
10   A text in the placard by Melnikov, see Starr 1978, p. 179.

our myriads of everyday gadgets, our medicines, the products of our industrial art – would they not have suited our national temper better than they do? In fact our conception of physics itself, and even the principles of chemistry, would probably differ from that of Westerners; and the facts we are now taught concerning the nature and function of light, electricity, and atoms might well have presented themselves in different form."[11] The soft and organic forms of the *Letatlin* were antithetic to the constructive architectural forms of the aeroplanes admired by Le Corbusier, and the idea of using muscle-power was, of course, as far as possible from the ideals of the architect who was captivated not only the logic of flying machines but that of automobiles and ocean liners as well.[12]

It was not the techinal skills but the concept of the machine which separated Tatlin from his famous Western contemporaries – and from many of his contemporaries in Russia, for that matter. Tatlin did boldly challenge the prevailing ideas on engineering. Although I have shown that there was in those days much more activity towards solving the problem of muscle-powered flying than is usually remembered, the *Letatlin* was entirely original in its organic forms and construction methods. It feels as if Tatlin took the nineteenth-century ideas of "animal machines" much more seriously than others had done before him; the *Letatlin* was intended as an amalgam of man and machine, of organic and handmade. With Tatlin's apparatuses the city of the future would really have become a city of winged inhabitants, a true Cloudcuckooland envisaged by Khlebnikov.

The *Letatlin* never flew but it functioned, and still does, as an exhibition piece. This aspect of the story was studied through earlier examples such as the *Avion III* built by Clément Ader and the *Demoiselle* bought by Adolf Aarno. While these two machines were never treated as works of art, we saw that they did receive some aesthetic acclaim. The aesthetization was not necessarily an easy process as it proved difficult even to understand what these apparatuses actually represented. The words of Léon Delagrange in front of the *Wright A* in 1908 tell us about it: "[…] the machine is already amazing to look at in repose, *especially when one knows it is an aeroplane*."[13] In order to see an aeroplane one needs knowledge of the concept. In the cases of Ader and Aarno such knowledge was not common, while by the early 1930s the concept of aeroplane had become so strong that radical alternatives like the *Letatlin* were becoming rare, more difficult to see, and therefore again rather hard to understand. As a machine of an artist's making the *Letatlin* is, of course, different from the *Avion III* and the

. . . .

11 Junichiro Tanizaki, *In Praise of Shadows*. New Haven, Conn.: Leete's Island Books 1977, p. 7. The essay was originally published in 1933–1934.
12 In city planning Le Corbusier preferred to use straight lines, arguing that the curve is ruinous, difficult, and a paralyzing thing. ("La courbe est ruineuse, difficile et dangereuse; elle paralyse," Le Corbusier 1994, p. 10.) Tatlin disliked modernist architecture and criticized the Soviet "corbusists." He also made his own plans for new cities. Begicheva 1968, p. 166.
13 My emphasis. See above p. 44.

Demoiselle. During the time it has lost almost all of its technical status and has come to be regarded as an exceptional artwork. But we could easily play with the idea of bringing, for example, the *Avion III*, designed by an engineer, to the context of the present artworld. I am sure it would be a roaring success, its surrealistic qualities in particular admired. It is then an unforced irony that Guillame Apollinaire wrote the line about *l'oiseau dans l'espace* in a poem dealing not with a Brancusi sculpture but with the Ader machine.

What the study of the case of Brancusi and his colleagues Duchamp and Léger proved, was that the distance between the inspirational machines on the one hand and the artworks on the other may be longer than it first seems. No matter how much they talked (or remained silent) about the artefacts of aviation, they never felt compelled to use their images in their art. We can safely say that none of them would have begun to build a machine for swimming in the air. I see this difference as important in underlining the special nature of Tatlin's dream. Unlike his colleagues in Paris, who in passing admired the propellers and engines, Tatlin spent years building something that was to challenge the prevailing ideas about technology. It was a lonely project and eventually meant a voluntary isolation from the avant-garde. John Milner has suggested that to interpret Tatlin's removal to the Novodevichy Monastery as a retreat or as a sign of an inward withdrawal would be to construe his circumstances erroneously.[14] Yes and no. We do not know if Tatlin especially asked to work there, but certainly he was not insensitive to the history of the place. Secured within its walls, a monastery like the Novodevichy is always an image of the new heavenly city. Even without spiritual connotations, Tatlin kept aloof. His colleagues in Moscow did not know much about his work between 1929 and 1932, and certainly no-one in the Western artworld was aware of it at the time. His position was also entirely outside the contemporary discussions on machine aesthetics. In France the promoters of *esprit nouveau*, always eager to make references to the *Parthenon*, had begun to see machines as something opposing true art and and true architecture. Le Corbusier did not believe in the artistic skills of the engineers, and his brother in arms Amédée Ozenfant openly discredited the aesthetic value of machines: "But there is no object, or factory, or mechanism, or piece of furniture, capable of inspiring in us emotions comparable with those evoked by Art. Has the most beautiful motor-car or the finest house an effect upon us equal to, parallel with, or equivalent to, some masterpiece of art? [...] Has anyone ever seen a factory or piece of machinery that would move men to tears? The most elegant bicycle would be quite incapable of it."[15] The Americans were more optimistic, though. In the *Machine Art* exhibition of 1934 the organizers had no difficulty in combining the Platonic idea of beauty with the latest industrial products, such as ball bearings and aeroplane propellers.[16]

. . . .

14   Milner 1983, p. 220.
15   Ozenfant 1952, p. 155. Ozenfant's examples of masterpieces are Beethoven's *Fidelio*, and the *Parthenon*, which "takes even the most insensitive by the throat." *ibid*.
16   See the "Foreword" by Alfred H. Barr, Jr. in *Machine Art* 1994, np.

Propeller on the wall. Machine Art exhibition, MoMA, New York 1934. (Machine Art 1994, np.)

Both the rejecting and the approving attitudes towards machine beauty had their roots in the nineteenth century. The *Crystal Palace*, the actual building and its image, was the birthplace for diverse dreams. Fedor Dostoevsky, who visited the *Crystal Palace* in 1862, opposed the ideas expressed in Chernychevsky's utopian novel and wrote that instead of an eternal palace of crystal he would rather choose a hen-house.[17] I have chosen to emphasize the *Crystal Palace*'s link with the utopian ideas. Let us not forget that the promise of the transparent palace lived longer than the full-blown Victorian exhibition. The actual building was still standing in Sydenham when Tatlin made tests with his *Letatlin*. And when fire finally destroyed the *Crystal Palace* in 1936, who else but Le Corbusier payed tribute to the building. He wrote about the spectacle of its triumphant harmony, its grandeur and simplicity. He also remembered it as light within "as fields seen under the open sky."[18] I do not know why the apostle of the functional city was suddenly inclined to fields, but his words bring to mind something that the poet Khlebnikov, a fervent reader of Leibniz, wrote in 1922 when he saw the mysteries of future solved in his own calculations. "When the future becomes clear," he wrote, "the feeling of time vanishes, and it begins to resemble a field in front of you and a field behind; it becomes a kind of space."[19] The interior of the transparent building, the vanishing of time, a kind of space – perhaps this the closest I can get to the possible world of the *Letatlin*, a world where it could fly.

. . . .

17   See the beginning of Chapter X in *Notes from Underground*.
18   Le Corbusier 1937, p. 72.
19   Khlebnikov 1987, p. 137. Also above p. 164, n. 188. On Khlebnikov's interest in Leibniz, see the Introduction by Charlotte Douglas in Khlebnikov 1987, pp. 165–194.

But what is the *Letatlin* today? Is it a failed machine, an example of a new technology which was never born? Is it only an experiment gone wrong? The Russian director Andrei Tarkovsky, in whose films levitation is a repeated theme, had a high ideal about art and he loathed anything half done, anything that had lost the mystery in art and could only be explained away with empty words like "search" or "experiment." He believed that the visual arts especially are almost totally devoid of spirituality.[20] The exceptions, then, are all the more important. I see the *Letatlin* as such an exception. Tatlin's dream certainly failed, but only according to the laws of physics. There is another world in which he was elevated. No matter how we would define that world, we have now reached the limits of this book. Let me draw the last threads together in this study with these words of Andrei Tarkovsky:

The Crystal Palace after the fire in 1936. (Beaver 1977, p. 144.)

> "The only condition of fighting for the right to create is faith in your own vocation, readiness to serve, and refusal to compromise. Artistic creation demands of the artist that he 'perish utterly,' in the full, tragic sense of those words. And so, if art carries within it a hieroglyphic of absolute truth, this will always be an image of the world, made manifest in the work once and for all time. And if cold, positivistic, scientific cognition of the world is like the ascent of an unending staircase, its artistic counterpoint suggests an endless system of spheres, each one perfect and

· · · · · · · ·
20 Tarkovsky 1986, p. 96.

contained within itself. One may complement or contradict another, but in no circumstances can they cancel each other out; on the contrary, they enrich one another, and accumulate to form an all-embracing sphere that grows out into infinity. These poetic revelations, each one valid and eternal, are evidence of man's capacity to recognise in whose image and likeness he is made, and to voice this recognition."[21]

· · · · · · · · · ·
21   *Ibid.*, p. 39.

■ Appendix

The chapter *Paris 1909: The Shiny Propeller* introduced the story of Constantin Brancusi, Marcel Duchamp and Fernand Léger visiting an aviation show in Paris. In what follows I will take a look at the ways this story has been discussed in art historical literature and explain why I have proposed a new timing for this visit.

During the last thirty years at least four different datings have been proposed for the aviation show. Most of these seem to have come from Brancusi scholars, while writers on Léger usually accept his own approximation. The earliest one is by Sidney Geist (Geist 1969, p. 144.) who notes that the visit to *Salon d'Aviation* with Léger and Duchamp happened in December 1908. Radu Varia (Varia 1986, p. 47.) agrees about the date but names the show as the Aeronautical Exhibition at Le Bourget. The year 1908 is also mentioned in *Constantin Brancusi, Plastiken – Zeichnungen.* (Duisburg: Wilhelm-Lehmbruck-Museum der Stadt Duisburg 1976, p. 220.) The second dating comes again from Sidney Geist, but this time (Geist 1975, p. 166.) he believes that the visit was made in 1920. The third dating is by Barbu Brezianu, who writes in his *Brancusi in Romania* (Brezianu 1976, p. 22.) that in 1910 "He visits the *Salon de l'Aviation* with Fernand Léger and Marcel Duchamp." The fourth, and so far most popular dating is given, for example, by Christopher Green (Green 1976, pp. 84–85.) in his book on Léger, and by Dumitresco and Istrati (Hulten, Dumitresco & Istrati 1988, p. 92.), who write that Brancusi visited the Paris Air Show with Léger and Duchamp in 1912.

Unfortunately, none of these chroniclers give any proof to support their dating or, in most cases, even explain how they came up with this particular year. When the story has been repeated in new books and articles from the 1990s its dating – most often 1912 – is commonly taken at face value, especially by some recent commentators on Duchamp. However, the only dating given by any of the three artists appears in Léger's interview, where he says that it was "avant la guerre de 14." (Vallier 1982, p. 63.) The examples where Léger's reminiscence is automatically given the dating of autumn 1912 are numerous and will not be studied here. (See for example Seigel 1995, p. 263, n. 10; Asendorf 1994, p. 209; Sochor 1982, p. 79.) What requires a comment is Christopher Green's suggestion that the visit Léger wrote about in 1923 and the one he mentioned to Vallier were probably the same. (Green 1976, pp. 84–85; also Asendorf 1994, p. 207.) The logic is the following: "Léger did not exhibit at the Salon d'Automne between 1912 and the publication of his essay 'L'Esthétique de la machine' in 1923. This means that the recollection is certainly 1911 or 1912." (*ibid.*, p. 324, n. 52.) I think it only means that the recollection is 1912 or earlier. Moreover, there is nothing in Léger's 1923 essay implying that on his visit he was accompanied by anyone. It is hard to believe that Léger visited an aviation show only once in his life before 1923; actually he talks about his "familiarity with these spectacles." (Léger 1973, p. 60.) I would suggest that we consider the two visits mentioned by Léger as separate occasions. It is entirely possible that the time of the visit mentioned in the 1923 essay was autumn 1912.

Art historians and aviation historians do not often mix. The *Salon de l'Aviation*, for example, has received no more attention from art historians than Duchamp and his friends have been studied by specialists of early aviation. In the case of Duchamp a lack of interest is understandable. His early works often remain unknown to even those who are well read in twentieth-century art. But on the other hand, should an art historian study aeroplanes, s/he would soon find a similar obscurity shrouding many details of early aviation history. There is practically no literature discussing the aviation salons. It is, then, slightly puzzling to see the degree of self-confidence some art historians evince when they write about Duchamp and the aviation show he did not remember visiting – and they themselves know very little about. William Camfield is sure that the visit to the aviation show must have contributed to Duchamp's concept of readymades. (Camfield 1991, p. 149.) André Gervais has expressed a similar view and has linked Duchamp's alleged comments in the Salon with two events from 1912. (Gervais 1991, p. 403.) First, he has pointed to Duchamp's small drawing *Aéroplane*. This was made during his trip to Munich in August-September 1912, that is to say before the presumed visit to the aviation show in October-November 1912. The work itself has been reproduced in only a few books and usually without any attempt to explain its possible meaning. While this rather insignificant scribbling may have visual links with more ground-breaking works from the same period, the subject matter at least remains sufficiently Duchampian: apart from the title the work has no connection whatsoever to aeroplanes or propellers. It seems to me also that Gervais has little to say about the work, other than its title. Jerrold Seigel, writing in the wake of Camfield and Gervais, shows real interpretative zest while looking at the work *Aéroplane*: "an upward-sweeping line seems to suggest a takeoff." (Seigel 1995, p. 263, n. 10.) Jennifer Gough-Cooper and Jacques Caumont, who edited the dates ("Ephemerides on and about Marcel Duchamp and Rose Sélavy") in the big Duchamp book in 1993, go a little bit further and see in the picture "a construction of metallic fuselage." (*Marcel Duchamp* 1993, 19 August 1912.)

The second supporting detail for Gervais's claim that aviation had an impact on Duchamp in 1912, namely Olga Picabia's flying experience, is equally problematic. She recalled her flight and the ensuing conversation with the three Duchamp brothers only sixty-six years later in 1978 and revealed nothing about Marcel Duchamp's possible response, except that "There were discussions about the Machine which, at that time, was considered anti-artistic and an enemy of the mind." (*Marcel Duchamp* 1993, 19 August 1912.) Mrs Picabia probably flew with Henri Farman in 1912. However, the possibility that these memories going back more than half a century may sometimes lead us in the wrong direction is shown clearly in a statement from Mr Duchamp himself. In 1966 he recalled the incident of selling one of his paintings to Isadora Duncan from the *Salon d'Automne* "either in 1910 or 1911." In fact Duchamp did not participate in the *Salon d'Automne* in those years but in 1909, when Duncan bought one of his three works. (*Marcel Duchamp. Entretiens avec Pierre Cabanne*. Paris: Sugomy 1995, p. 31.) With this kind of evidence we cannot draw any conclusions, or even call the *Aéroplane*, Mrs Picabia's flight, and the visit to the aviation show "related events," as Gervais wishes to do.

As was mentioned earlier, there is no proof to support any of the four dates used in the art historical literature: 1908, 1910, 1912, or 1920. There is, however, enough proof to eliminate at least three of them. Of the two years given by Sidney Geist 1908 seems to be too early. Aeroplanes were on display that year, but not in a separate exhibition but rather as a part of the annual automobile salon. Moreover, we have no evidence that Duchamp knew either Brancusi or Léger at that time. The later year 1920, on the other hand, is clearly too late since the First World War, the only time limit we have, had ended several years earlier. The third unreliable timing is the 1910 suggested by Barbu Breazianu alone. His motive for choosing this particular year seems to be a patriotic one. Brezianu believes that the three artists went to see "the flight of the world's first jetplane by the Rumanian inventor Henri Coanda." Such a plane was indeed constructed, but, contrary to Brezianu's claim, it never flew – and certainly not during an indoor exhibition. The story only proves how tempting the "legends of early aviation" may sometimes appear; it would have been of course a great delight for the people of Rumania to know that the father of modern sculpture witnessed the first jet flight, performed by another Rumanian. However, Coanda deserves to be mentioned here as he too was one of those pioneering aviators who had earlier studied art, namely sculpture. (On Coanda, see Munson 1969, p. 113–114.) According to Harry G. Stine, Coanda told him that he tried his luck alone with his plane near Paris in December 1910, resulting in a fire which destroyed the machine. (Stine 1989, pp. 90–92.) It had been on display in the second *Salon Aéronautique*, so in theory the artists could have seen it. I do not believe this was the case. Should they have secretly witnessed the acclaimed flight attempt and the disaster, there would still remain a question about the propeller: Coanda's "jet-plane" simply did not have such a piece of equipment.

Thus we are left with 1912 as the only remaining year. Most of today's commentators seem to believe that this is the closest guess as they print it in their books. Basically everything we know supports the year 1912: there was an aviation show that autumn and its timing qualifies for "avant la guerre de 14." The only problem, in my opinion, is that this "everything" is very little. What strikes me also is that no-one, to my knowledge, has seriously suggested the years 1911 and 1913 as alternatives (both years witnessed an aviation show) or even thought of the highly successful *Première Exposition Internationale de Locomotion Aérienne* of 1909 as a possibility. In the chapter *Paris 1909* it has already been mentioned that this exhibition was held at the *Grand Palais* in October 1909, that is, in the same place and at the same time as the seventh *Salon d'Automne*. It has also been noted that Brancusi, Duchamp, and Léger all took part in the Salon this year. Duchamp showed three paintings: *Sur le Falaise*, *Veules (Eglise)*, and *Etude du Nu*. (*Marcel Duchamp* 1993, 1 October, 1909.) Léger also showed three paintings, of which at least one, *Le Jardin de ma mére* (1905), is known to exist. (*Fernand Léger, Catalogue raisonné 1903– 1919*. Paris: Maeght Editeur 1990, pp. 18–19.) Brancusi participated with one work. According to Hans Billinger's biographical notes in (Giedion-Welcker 1958, p. 222.) the exhibit was *Tête d'enfant*. (Brancusi's participation is mentioned also in Hulten, Dumitresco & Istrati 1988, p. 323.)

What I have not yet said is that this particular *Salon d'Automne* was the only one where all three were exhibiting at the same time. Would it be illogical to assume that October 1909 was an excellent opportunity for them to meet and visit the aviation show that everybody was talking about? We have no photographs showing these three men standing in front of a propeller, but we have pictures of the aeronautical exhibition of 1909. In these images we can see the decorations admired by the English journalist, we can see the aeroplanes and the engines, the shiny Chauvière propellers and the beautiful balloons. And we can, if we want, on reasonable grounds sense the feeling of excitement and surprise as these three artists stood at the Gnome stand or passed by the Montgolfier in October 1909. But did the visit influence them? Although Brancusi spoke about the search for the essence of flight and Léger wrote about the beautiful shapes and colours of the aeroplanes, it seems that neither of them really made works directly inspired by any visit to an early aviation show. It is rather surprisingly Duchamp whose two works could be read as recollections of the actual exhibits. Both these works, the *Rotary Glass Plates* and the *Montgolfière* from the Rotorelief-series, are meant to be seen spinning around. Is it significant? Did Duchamp suffer in high places, did the idea of flying bring him to the verge of vertigo? I do not know.

■ Bibliography

NEWSPAPERS AND MAGAZINES

Aamulehti *(Tampere)*
Flight *(London)*
Helsingin Sanomat *(Helsinki)*
Hufvudstadsbladet (Helsingfors)
Kansan Lehti (Tampere)
Kerberos (Helsingfors)
Krasnaya Niva (Moskva)
Ogonek (St Petersburg)
Sisä-Suomi (Jyväskylä)
Sovremennaia Arkhitektura (Moskva)
Suomen Siivet (Helsinki)
Tammerfors Nyheter (Tammerfors)
The Aëronautical Journal (London)
Uusi Suometar (Helsinki)

Aalto, Alvar. "Min vän Kapten af Looping," *Kerberos*, 2/1921, pp. 10–11.
Abate, Rosario; Alegi, Gregory; Apostolo, Giorgio. *Aeroplani Caproni. Gianni Caproni and His Aircraft, 1910–1983.* Trento: Museo Caproni 1992.
Adaridi, B. *Moottorittomat lentokoneet ja heikkomoottorilentokoneet.* Helsinki: Otava 1925.
Aeronautical Sciences and Aviation in the Soviet Union. A Bibliography. Washington, D.C.: The Library of Congress 1955.
Ahonius, Rainer. *Suomen moottorilennon uranuurtaja. Adolf Aarno ja hänen Demoisellensa.* Tampere: Tampere-seura 1961.
Allwood, John. *The Great Exhibitions.* London: Studio Vista 1977.
Andersen, Troels. "Notes on Tatlin" in *Vladimir Tatlin.* Exhibition catalogue. Stockholm: Moderna Museet 1968, pp. 6–11.
Apollinaire, Guillaume. *Oeuvres complètes de Guillaume Apollinaire.* Vol. 3 and Vol. 4. Paris: André Balland et Jacques Lecat 1966.
Apollonio, Umbro (ed.). *Futurist Manifestos.* London: Thames and Hudson 1973.
Art of the Soviets. Painting, sculpture and architecture in a one-party state, 1917–1992. Ed. by M. C. Bown and B. Taylor. Manchester – New York: Manchester University Press 1993.
Asendorf, Christoph. "The Propeller and Avant-garde: Léger, Duchamp, Brancusi" in *Fernand Léger 1911–1924. Rhythm of Modern Life.* Munich: Prestel 1994.
Asendorf, Christoph. *Super Constellation – Flugzeug und Raumrevolution.* Wien – New York: Springer 1997.
Auerbach, Jeffrey A. *The Great Exhibition of 1851. A Nation on display.* New Haven – London: Yale University Press 1999.

Aviation. The Early Years. The Hulton Getty Picture Collection, with a text by Peter Almond. Köln: Könemann 1997.
Bach, Friedrich Teja. *Constantin Brancusi – Metamorphosen plasticher Form.* Köln: Dumont 1987.
Bach, Friedrich Teja; Rowell, Margit; Temkin, Ann. *Constantin Brancusi 1876–1957.* Cambridge, Mass. – London: Philadelphia Museum of Art / MIT Press 1995.
Bailes, Kendall E. *Technology and Society under Lenin and Stalin.* Princeton, N. J.: Princeton University Press 1978.
Banham, Reyner. *Theory and Design in the First Machine Age.* London: The Architectural Press 1967 (1960).
Banham, Reyner. "The Machine Aesthetic" in *Design by Choice.* New York: Rizzoli 1981
Barr, Alfred H. *Defining Modern Art. Selected Writings of Alfred H. Barr, Jr.* Edited by Irving Sandler and Amy Newman. New York: Harry N. Abrams, Inc. 1986.
Baxandall, Michael. *Patterns of Intention. On the Historical Explanation of Pictures.* New Haven – London: Yale University Press 1988.
Beaver, Patrick. *The Crystal Palace 1851–1936. A Portrait of Victorian Enterprise.* London: Hugh Evelyn 1977 (1970).
Begicheva, Hanna. "Komisar narkomosu," *Vitchizna.* 2/1968, pp. 159–170.
Behringer, Wolfgang. Ott-Koptschalijski, Constance. *Der Traum vom Fliegen. Zwischen Mythos und Technik.* Frankfurt-am-Main: S. Fischer 1991.
Benevolo, Leonardo. *History of Modern Architecture. Volume One.* London: Routledge & Kegan Paul 1971.
Bergman, Pär. *"Modernolatria" et "Simultaneità". Reserches sur deux tendances dans l'avantgarde litteraire en Italie et en France à la veille de la première guerre mondiale.* Studia Litterarum Upsalensia 2. Stockholm: Svenska Bokförlaget / Bonniers 1962.
Bogdanov, Alexander. *Red Star.* Bloomington: Indiana University Press 1984.
Borelli, Giovanni A. *The Flight of Birds.* London: The Aëronautical Society of Great Britain 1911 (*De motu animalium* 1680–1681).
Borhan, Pierre; D'Astier, Martine. *Les Envols de Jacques Lartique et les débuts de l'aviation.* Paris: Association des amis de Jacques-Henri Lartique/Philippe Sers Éditeur 1989.
Brezianu, Barbu. *Brancusi in Romania.* Bucuresti: Editura Academiei 1976.

Briggs, Asa. *Victorian Cities*. London: Penguin Books 1990 (1963).

Briggs, Asa. *Victorian People*. London: Penguin Books 1977 (1954).

Briggs, Asa. *Victorian Things*. London: B. T. Batsford 1988.

Bytschkow, Wladimir. "Nikolai Je. Shukowski und Otto Lilienthal" in *Die Schule Lilienthals. Der einfluss Otto Lilienthals auf die entwicklung der Flugtechnik in der Welt*. Herausgegeben von Werner Schipps. Berlin: MVT 1992.

Camfield, William. "Duchamp's Fountain: Aesthetic Object, Icon, or Anti-Art?" in *The Definitively Unfinished Marcel Duchamp*. Cambridge, Mass. – London: MIT Press 1991.

Canetti, Elias. *Crowds and Power*. Harmondsworth: Penguin Books 1981 (1960).

Carlier, Claude. *L'Affaire Clément Ader. La vérité rétablie*. Paris: Perrin 1990.

Carter, William C. *The Proustian Quest*. New York – London: New York University Press 1992.

Cassou, Jean; Leymarie, Jean. *Fernand Léger – Drawings and Guaches*. London: Thames and Hudson 1973.

Chadwick, George F. *The Works of Sir Joseph Paxton*. London: The Architectural Press 1961.

Chan-Magomedow, Selim O. *Pionere der sowjetischen Architektur*. Dresden: VEB Verlag der Kunst 1983.

Chave, Anna C. *Constantin Brancusi – Shifting the Bases of Art*. New Haven – London: Yale University Press 1993.

Chen, Kenneth; Wilson, Anthony. *Victorian Science and Engineering portrayed in The Illustrated London News*. London: Science Museum / Alan Sutton 1993.

Chernyshevsky, Nikolai. *What is To Be Done? Tales About New People*. London: Virago 1982.

Choe, Wolhee. *Toward an Aesthetic Criticism of Technology*. New York – Bern – Frankfurt am Main – Paris: Peter Lang 1989.

Cohen, Jean-Louis. *Le Corbusier and the Mystique of the USSR. Theories and Projects for Moscow, 1928–1936*. Princeton, N. J.: Priceton University Press 1992.

Corn, Joseph J. *The Winged Gospel. America's Romance with Aviation 1900–1950*. New York: Oxford University Press 1983.

Cooke, Catherine. "Professional diversity and its origins" in *The Avant-Garde. Russian Architecture in the Twenties*. Architectural Design Profile No 93. London: Academy Editions 1991.

Cultural Revolution in Russia, 1928–1931. Ed. by Sheila Fitzpatrick. Bloomington – London: Indiana University Press 1978.

Curtis, William J. R. *Le Corbusier: Ideas and Forms*. Oxford: Phaidon 1986.

Danin, Daniil. *Izbrannoe*. Moskva: Sovetskii Pisatel 1984.

Dollfus, Charles; Bouché, Henri. *Histoire de l'Aéronautique*. Paris: L'Illustration 1938.

Durant, Stuart. *Palais des Machines. Architect: Ferdinand Dutert*. London: Phaidon 1994.

Durgnat, Raymond. "From box-kite to Concorde," *Studio International*, October 1972, pp. 130–136.

Edwards, Folke. *Den barbariska modernismen. Futurismen och 1900-talet*. Malmö: Liber 1987.

Eliade, Mircea. "Brancusi and Mythology" in *Ordeal by Labyrinth*. Chicago: University of Chicago Press 1982.

Farman, Dick and Henry. *The Aviator's Companion*. London: Mills & Boon 1910.

Fernand Léger. Paris: Centre George Pompidou 1997.

Fonvielle, W. de. *Histoire de la navigation aérienne*. Paris: Hachette 1907.

Francia, Peter de. *Fernand Léger*. New Haven – London: Yale University Press 1983.

Friemert, Chup. *Die Gläserne Arche. Kristallpalast London 1851 und 1854*. München: Prestel 1984.

Frosterus, Sigurd. "Aeroplanet," *Argus* No 13 (1.7.1908), pp. 1–5.

Geist, Sidney. *Brancusi. The Sculpture and Drawings*. New York: Harry N. Abrams 1975.

Geist, Sidney. *Constantin Brancusi 1876–1957. A Retrospective Exhibition*. New York: The Solomon R. Guggenheim Foundation 1969.

Gervais, André. "Reflections: Of Art and Arrhe" in *The Definitively Unfinished Marcel Duchamp*. Cambridge, Mass. – London: MIT Press 1991.

Gibbs-Smith, Charles H. *Aviation. An Historical Survey from its Origins to the end of World War II*. Second edition. London: HMSO, 1985.

Gibbs-Smith, Charles H. *Clément Ader. His Flight Claims and his Place in History*. London: HMSO 1968.

Gibbs-Smith, Charles H. *The Great Exhibition of 1851*. Second edition. London: HMSO 1981.

Gibbs-Smith, Charles H. *The Rebirth of European Aviation 1902–1908*. London: HMSO 1974.

Giedion, Sigfried. *Space, Time and Architecture*. Cambridge, Mass.: Harvard University Press 1947 (1941).

Giedion-Welcker, Carola. *Constantin Brancusi 1876–1957*. Neuchâtel: Editions du Griffon 1958.

Goldstein, Laurence. *The Flying Machine and Modern Literature*. London: Macmillan 1986.

Gollin, Alfred. *No Longer an Island. Britain and the Wright Brothers 1902–1909*. London: Heinemann 1984.

Gozak, Andrei; Leonidov, Andrei. *Ivan Leonidov. The Complete Works*. London: Academy Editions 1988.

Green, Christopher. *Léger and the Avant-garde*. New Haven – London: Yale University Press 1976.

Groys, Boris. "Das Kunstwerk als nicht-funktionelle Maschine" in *Vladimir Tatlin – Leben, Werk, Wirkung*. Köln: DuMont 1993.

Guston, Bill. *Aircraft of the Soviet Union. The encyclopedia of Soviet aircraft since 1917*. London: Osprey 1983.

Guston, Bill. *The Osprey Encyclopedia of Russian Aircraft*. Oxford: Osprey Publishing 2000.

Harper, Harry. *Twenty-five Years of Flying*. London: Hutchinson & Co. 1929.

Hart, Clive. *The Prehistory of Flight*. Berkeley – Los Angeles – London: University of California Press, 1985.

Hindle, Brooke; Lubar, Steven. *Engines of Change. The American Industrial Revolution 1790–1860*. Washington, D.C. – London: Smithsonian Institution Press 1986.

Hulten, Pontus; Dumitresco, Natalia; Istrati, Alexandre. *Brancusi*. London – Boston: Faber and Faber 1988 (1986).

In Context. History and the History of Technology. Essays in Honor of Melvin Kranzberg, ed. by Stephen H. Cutliffe and Robert C. Post. London – Toronto: Associated University Presses 1989.

Ingold, F. P. "Ikarus Novus. Zum Selbstverständnis des Autors in der Moderne" in H. Segeberg (ed.), *Technik in der Literatur*. Frankfurt am Main: Suhrkamp 1987.

Janarmo, K. W. *Varhaisilmailumme 1753–1919*. Helsinki: Otava 1963.

Keay, Carolyn. *Henri Rousseau, Le Douanier*. London: Academy Editions 1976.

Kennedy, Ludovic (ed.). *A Book of Air Journeys*. London: Collins 1982.

Khlebnikov, Velimir. *Collected Works, Vol. I* (Letters and Theoretical Writings). Cambridge, Mass. – London: Harvard University Press 1987.

Klee, Paul. *The Diaries of Paul Klee 1898–1918*. Berkeley – Los Angeles – London: University of California Press 1964.

Klingender, Francis D. *Art and the Industrial Revolution*. Edited and revised by Arthur Elton. St. Albans: Paladin 1972.

Kollman, Franz. *Schönheit der Technik*. München: Albert Langen 1928.

Kopp, Anatole. *Town and Revolution. Soviet Architecture and City Planning 1917–1935*. London: Thames and Hudson 1970 (1967).

Kovalev, Aleksander. "Letatlin: Poisk novogo mira," *Iskusstvo*. 6/1990, pp. 28–34.

Krawetz, Georg. *Fem år som sovjetflygare*. Helsingfors: Holger Schildts Förlag 1936.

Körner, Éva. "Tatlin. Outlines of a Career in the Context of Contemporary Russian Avantgarde Art as Related to Eastern and Western Tendencies," *Acta Historiae Artium Academiae Scientiarum Hungariae*, tom. XXXI, fasc. 1–4, 1985, pp. 71–89.

Laboratory of Dreams. The Russian Avant-garde and Cultural Experiment. Ed. by John E. Bowlt and Olga Matich. Stanford, Calif.: Stanford University Press 1996.

Lassalle, E. J. *Les 100 premièrs aviateurs brevetés au monde et la naissance de l'aviation*. Paris: Nauticaero 1962.

Laugier, Claude; Richet, Michèle. *Léger. Oeuvres de Fernand Léger (1881–1955)*. Paris: Collections du Musée National d'art moderne 1981.

Lavrentiev, Alexander. *Laboratoriia konstruktivizma*. Moskva: Grant 2000.

Le Corbusier. *Vers une architecture*. Paris: Flammarion 1995 (1923).

Le Corbusier. *Urbanisme*. Paris: Flammarion 1994 (1925).

Le Corbusier. *La Ville Radieuse*. Boulogne: Éditions de l'architecture d'aujourd'hui 1933.

Le Corbusier. *Aircraft*. New York: Universe Books 1988 (1935).

Le Corbusier. "The Crystal Palace. A Tribute," *The Architectural Review*. February 1937, p. 72.

Le Corbusier. *Sketchbooks. Volume 1, 1914–1948*. London: Thames & Hudson 1981.

Le Corbusier et Pierre Jeanneret. *Oeuvre complète 1910–1929*. Zurich: Les Éditions d'Architecture 1967.

Léger, Fernand. *Functions of Painting*. London: Thames and Hudson 1973.

Lilienthal, Otto. *Der Vogelflug als Grundlage der Fliegekunst*. Berlin: R. Gaertner 1889.

Lissarague, Pierre. *Clément Ader. Inventeur d'Avions*. Toulouse: Bibliothèque historique Privat 1990.

Lista, Giovanni. "Apollinaire et la conquête de l'air," *La Revue des lettres modernes*. 1973, vol. 10, pp. 115–129.

Lloyd, Herbert F. "The Paris Aeronautical Exhibition," *The Aëronautical Journal*. October 1909, pp. 118–122.

Lodder, Christina. *Russian Constructivism*. New Haven – London: Yale University Press 1983.

Lyons, Eugene. *Assignment in Utopia*. London: George G. Harrap & Co. 1938.

Machine Art. Sixtieth-Anniversary Edition. New York: The Museum of Modern Art 1994 (1934).

Mandell, Richard D. *Paris 1900. The Great World's Fair*. Toronto: University of Toronto Press 1967.

Marcel Duchamp. (On occasion of the exhibition at Palazzo Grassi, Venice 1993) London: Thames and Hudson 1993.

Marey, E. J. *La machine animale. Locomotion terrestre et aérienne*. Paris: Germer Baillière 1873.

Martin, Marianne W. *Futurist Art and Theory 1909–1915*. London: Clarendon Press 1968.

Marx, Leo. *The Machine in the Garden*. New York: Oxford University Press 1964.

Mayakovsky, Vladimir. *Selected Works*, Vol. 3. Moscow: Raduga Publishers 1987.

McAllister, James W. *Beauty and Revolution in Science*. Ithaca – London: Cornell University Press 1996.

McKean, John. *Crystal Palace. Architects: John Paxton and Charles Fox*. London: Phaidon 1994.

Melnikov. The Muscles of Invention. Ed. by Arthur Wortmann. Rotterdam: Van Hezik-Fonds 90 1990.

Miller, Sanda. *Constantin Brancusi – A survey of his work*. Oxford: Clarendon Press 1995.

Milner, John. *Vladimir Tatlin and the Russian Avant-garde*. New Haven – London: Yale University Press 1983.

Mondrian, Piet. *Natural Reality and Abstract Reality. An Essay in Trialogue Form*. New York: George Braziller 1995.

Moedebeck, Hermann W. L. *Pocket-Book of Aeronautics*. London: Whittaker & Co. 1907.

Mumford, Lewis. *Technics and Civilization*. New York – Burlingame: Harcourt, Brace & World, Inc. 1963 (1934).

Munson, Kenneth. *Pioneer Aircraft 1903–1914*. London: Blandford Press 1969.

Nahum, Andrew. "The Imitation of Nature? Flapping flight and animal forms as models for human flight," *History and Technology*. 1995, vol. 12, pp. 225–260.

Nadar. *The Right to Fly*. London: Cassell, Petter, and Galpin 1866.

Nathan, Jacques. *La littérature du métal, de la vitesse et du chèque de 1880 à 1930*. Paris: Didier 1971.

Nemecek, Vaclav. *The History of Soviet Aircraft from 1918*. London: Willow Books 1986.

Nicolaou, Stéphane. *Santos-Dumont. Dandy et Génie de l'Aeronautique*. Boulogne – Le Bourget: E.T.A.I. & Musée de l'Air et de l'Espace 1997.

O'Connor, Timothy Edward. *The Politics of Soviet Culture. Anatoli Lunacharskii*. Ann Arbor, Mich.: UMI Research Press 1983.

Oy Nikolajeff Ab 50. Helsinki 1956.

Ozenfant, Amédée. *Foundations of Modern Art*. New York: Dover 1952 (1928).

Penrose, Harald. *An Ancient Air*. Shrewsbury: Airlife 1988.

Pettigrew, J. Bell. *Animal Locomotion or Walking, Swimming, and Flying, with a dissertation on Aëronautics*. New York: D. Appleton & Company 1874 (1873).

Pevsner, Nikolaus. *High Victorian Design. A Study of the Exhibits of 1851*. London: The Architectural Press 1951.

Pevsner, Nikolaus. *Pioneers of Modern Design*. New York: The Museum of Modern Art 1949.

Peyrey, François. *Les Oiseaux Artificiels*. Paris: H. Dunod & E. Pinat 1909.

Pound, Ezra. *Machine Art and Other Writings. The Lost Thought of the Italian Years*. Durham, N.C. – London: Duke University Press 1996.

Prendergast, Curtis. *The First Aviators*. Alexandria, Va.: Time-Life Books 1981.

Punin, Nikolay. *The Diaries of Nikolay Punin, 1904–1953*. Austin: University of Texas Press 1999.

Rakhtanov, I. A. *Na shirotah vremeni. Rassazi i ocherki*. Moskva: Sovetskii Pisatel 1980.

Reay, D. A. *The History of Man-powered Flight*. Oxford: Pergamon Press 1977.

Riverain, Jean. *Dictionnaire des aéronautes célèbres*. Paris: Larousse 1970.

Rodnykh, Aleksandr. *Plitsekrylye maschiny. Ornitoptery i ortoptery, ikh opisanie, istoriia i primenenie v zhizni*. (Populiarnaia biblioteka zhurnala "Nauka i tekhnika" vyp. 86) Leningrad: Izd. "Krasnoi gazety" 1929.

Sahel, Jacques. *Henry Farman et l'Aviation*. Paris: Éditions Bernard Grasset 1936.

Salmi, Hannu. *"Atoomipommilla kuuhun!" Tekniikan mentaalihistoriaa*. Helsinki: Edita 1996.

Sarje, Kimmo. *Sigurd Frosteruksen modernin käsite. Maailmankatsomus ja arkkitehtuuri*. Helsinki: Valtion taidemuseo 2000.

Schildt, Göran. *Alvar Aalto. The Early Years*. New York: Rizzoli 1984.

Schildt, Göran. *Alvar Aalto. The Decisive Years*. Helsinki: Otava 1986.

Schildt, Göran. *Alvar Aalto. The Mature Years*. New York: Rizzoli 1991.

Schroeder-Gudehus, Birgitte; Rasmussen, Anne. *Les Fastes du Progrés. Le guide des Expositions universelles 1851–1992*. Paris: Flammarion 1992.

Schwarz, Arturo. *The Complete Works of Marcel Duchamp*. London: Thames and Hudson 1969.

Seifert, Karl-Dieter; Wassermann, Michael. *Otto Lilienthal, Leben und Werk. Eine Biografie*. Hamburg: Urban Verlag 1992.

Seigel, Jerrold. *The Private Worlds of Marcel Duchamp*. Berkeley – Los Angeles – London: University of California Press 1995.

Shavrov, V. *Istoriia konstruktsii samoletov v SSSR do 1938 g*. Moskva: Mashinostroenie 1994.

Silberer, V. "The Art of Flying," *The Aëronautical Journal*. July 1908, pp. 50–52.

Siukonen, Jyrki. "Lentämisen kauneus," *TAIDE* 4/1991, pp. 33–40.

Siukonen, Jyrki. "Höyrykäyttöisen jättiläislepakon tapaus" in *Lentämisen kauneus*. Kuopio: Kuopion taidemuseo 1994, pp. 14–15.

Smith, Cyril Stanley. *A Search for Structure. Selected Essays on Science, Art, and History*. Cambridge, Mass. – London: MIT Press 1981.

Sobolew, Dmitri. "Der Einfluss Lilienthals auf

die Arbeiten russischer Luftfartpioniere" in *Die Schule Lilienthals. Der einfluss Otto Lilienthals auf die entwicklung der Flugtechnik in der Welt*. Herausgegeben von Werner Schipps. Berlin: MVT 1992.

Sochor, Eugene. "Aviation and art have evolved together in this century," *ICAO Bulletin*, July/August 1982, pp. 79–86.

Soldan-Brofeldt, Venny. *Kuinka on opittu lentämään?* Porvoo: WSOY 1910.

Souriau, Paul. *L'Esthétique du mouvement*. Paris: Félix Alcan 1889.

Spear, Athena T. *Brancusi's Birds*. New York: New York University Press 1969.

Starr, S. Frederick. *Melnikov. Solo Architect in a Mass Society*. Princeton, N.J.: Princeton University Press 1978.

Starr, S. Frederick. "Visionary Town Planning during the Cultural Revolution" in *Cultural Revolution in Russia, 1928–1931*. 1978, pp. 207–240.

Stern, Radu. "Letatlin: Natur versus Technik" in *Vladimir Tatlin – Leben, Werk, Wirkung*. Köln: DuMont 1993.

Stine, Harry G. "The Rises and Falls of Henri-Marie Coanda," *Air & Space*. August/September 1989, pp. 90–95.

Stites, Richard. *Revolutionary Dreams. Utopian Vision and Experimental Life in the Russian Revolution*. New York – Oxford: Oxford University Press 1989.

Stites, Richard. *Soviet Popular Culture: Entertainment and Society since 1900*. Cambridge: Cambridge University Press 1992.

Stoff, Joshua. *Picture History of Early Aviation, 1903–1913*. New York: Dover 1996.

Strigalev, Anatoli. "Konstantin Melnikov as a writer and theorist" in *Melnikov. The Muscles of Invention*. 1990, pp. 107–123.

Stubelius, Svante. *Airship, Aeroplane, Aircraft. Studies in the History of Terms for Aircraft in English*. Gothenburg Studies in English VII, Göteborg 1958.

Stubelius, Svante. *Balloon, Flying-machine, Helicopter*. Acta Universitatis Gothoburgensis, Göteborg Universitets Årsskrift vol. LXVI, Göteborg 1960.

Suomalainen, Kaarlo. *Ilman valloitus*. Helge Holstin mukaan sovitellen ja lisäellen suomentanut Kaarlo Suomalainen. Helsinki: Otava 1910.

Sussman, Herbert L. *Victorians and the Machine. The Literary Response to Technology*. Cambridge, Mass.: Harvard University Press 1968.

Sutton, Antony C. *Western Technology and Soviet Economic Development 1917 to 1930*. Hoover Institution Publication. Stanford: Stanford University 1968.

Tarkovsky, Andrey. *Sculpting in Time*. London: The Bodley Head 1986.

Teague, Walter Dorwin. *Design This Day. Technique of Order in the Machine Age*. London: Studio 1946 (1940).

Thorne, Robert. "Paxton and Prefabrication," *Architectural Design*. Vol 57, No 11/12 1987, pp. 22–28.

Tikhonravov, M. K. *Polet ptits i mashiny s mashushchimi kryljami. Vtoroe dopolnennoe izdanie*. Moskva: Oborongiz 1949.

Toporkov, A. "Technological and Artistic Form" in *Tradition of Constructivism*. Ed. by Stephen Bann. London: Thames and Hudson 1974, pp. 26–32.

Tsiolkovsky, Konstantin. *Beyond the Planet Earth*. Oxford: Pergamon Press 1960 (1920).

Vallier, Dora. *L'interieur de l'art. Entretiens avec Braque, Léger, Villon, Miró, Brancusi*. Paris: Éditions de Seuil 1982.

Varia, Radu. *Brancusi*. New York: Rizzoli 1986.

Verne, Jules. *Les Cinq Cents millions de la Bégum*. Paris: Librarie Hachette 1966 (1879).

Vladimir Tatlin. Exhibition catalogue. Stockholm: Moderna Museet 1968.

Vladimir Tatlin – Retrospektive. Köln: DuMont 1993.

Voisin, Gabriel. *Men, Women and 10,000 Kites*. London: Putnam 1963.

Wajcman, Judy. *Feminism Confronts Technology*. Cambridge: Polity Press 1991.

Wallace, Graham. *Flying Witness. Harry Harper and the Golden Age of Aviation*. London: Putnam 1958.

Wells, H. G. *A Modern Utopia*. London: J.M. Dent, 1994 (1905).

Wells, H. G. *The War in the Air*. Leipzig: Bernhard Tauchnitz 1909 (1908).

Wengenroth, Ulrich. "Was ist Technikgeschichte?" 1998. Published on the Internet: www.lrz-muenchen.de/~Ulrich_Wengenroth/Laufende Arbeiten/Was ist Technikgeschichte?

Wennberg, Kåa. *Flygbaronen Carl Cederström*. Lund 1999.

Wijk, Margareth. *Guillaume Apollinaire et l'esprit nouveau*. Études romanes de Lund 36. Lund: CWK Gleerup 1987.

Wohl, Robert. *A Passion for Wings. Aviation and the Western Imagination, 1908–1918*. New Haven – London: Yale University Press 1994.

The Wright Flyer. An Engineering Perspective. Ed. by Howard S. Wolko. Washington D.C.: National Air and Space Museum 1987.

Wykeham, Peter. *Santos-Dumont. A Study in Obsession*. London: Putnam 1962.

Zhadova, Larissa Alekseevna (ed.). *Tatlin*. New York: Rizzoli 1988 (1984).

■ Index of names (people, flying machines, buildings)

Following the name of a pioneer aviator appears the number of his pilot licence given by *l'Aéro-Club de France*. The first certificates (1 to 15) were written on 7 January 1909, in an alphabetical order.